THE NOTORIOUS TEXAS SWINDLER

The Mastermind Behind the Grayson County Five

PEPPER ANNE

Cover by TDW Fine Art

Check his work out at: https://www.tdwfineart.com

Editing by John T. Davis

You can find him here: https://johntonline.com

Assisting and Formatting by Laura Martinez, Owner of The Indie Author's Advocate

You can find her here: https://theindieauthorsadvocate.com

DEDICATION

When I first started researching the story about Bob's life, I had no idea what I was getting into, nor did I realize what I was going to uncover. The life of Bob Harold Leach is filled with crooks who are involved in a criminal empire and who are falsely idolized by many. As I questioned everything and everyone, including those involved in the crimes alongside Bob, I realized I was uncovering a crime ring too big not to write about with individuals who did and do not want to be called out. Nonetheless, I refused to back down and demanded answers until I got them. Had it not been for the fact that I was writing about a family member, I would have walked away from this project a long time ago.

Because I refused to back down, my family became targets to these individuals claiming they did not want anyone to know their affiliation with Bob. For this reason, I am protecting my loved ones as best I can by not mentioning their names in this section or any other part of the book, but without them, none of this would have been possible.

This book is dedicated to my family, for all the sacrifices that have been made while I was searching for a story to tell, one that you believed I was supposed to write. I am forever indebted to you for your endless support, for encouraging and believing in me, when others didn't and for your infinite love. I am so fortunate to be related to and surrounded by such amazing and caring people who refused to let me give up on a dream.

CONTENTS

Chapter One

IT'S FANNIN COUNTY TIME, BOYS

On May 1, 2006, the Texas Department of Criminal Justice's largest prison prepared to transfer one of its most high-profile offenders for a three-hour trip from the unit in Tennessee Colony to the Fannin County courthouse in Bonham, then back to the unit, all in one day, for a bench warrant to appear before a judge.

It's a common judicial procedure; one performed hundreds if not thousands of times every day throughout the sprawling Texas criminal justice system. Often, the process involves routine bureaucratic house cleaning; Richard Glaser, the Fannin Co. District Attorney, was just trying to close some old cases when the prisoner in question's file came up.

But Bob Harold Leach, the man summoned before the Honorable Jim Lovett on that drizzly, uncommonly warm spring day, was anything but a common inmate. He was perhaps the most notorious Texas outlaw since the heyday of Clyde Barrow.

When offenders are admitted into the Texas Department of Corrections (TDC), they go through an intake process that can take up to a month, to ensure the offender is properly entered into the system. During that time, a file, commonly called a "jacket" is created, comprised of the offender's personal information, including medical records, names of immediate family members and crimes that the offender has been convicted of, along with possible release dates. The outside of Bob's jacket bore markings in bold black ink, some heavily imprinted with a marker, flagging him as a security risk, with notations that in the event he was to ever be transferred from one facility to another, law enforcement along the route must be notified, and extra precautions taken.

The ominous warnings were justified. Five years earlier, Leach had set into motion one of the most infamous jailbreaks in modern Texas criminal history.

Before the affair was over, regional and national newspapers trumpeted the story accompanied by headlines in bold print. The "Grayson County Five" escaped Grayson County Jail, in the north Texas town of Sherman, in the late hours of Oct. 11, 2001 by digging their way to freedom through the underground air duct system of the old structure. A massive manhunt to end the trail of terror brought on by the fugitives was extended over a 180-mile radius, leading authorities through the north Texas region on a wild goose chase, the likes of which was seldom seen in modern times.

Bob, along with four other inmates, were not discovered missing until the early morning hours of Oct. 12. The Grayson County sheriff's department received a call from Bob's wife at the time, claiming she had been in touch with her fugitive husband throughout the night. [1]

The news spread rapidly. There's nothing like a jailbreak to sell papers and boost TV ratings. The public was warned that the fugitives were armed and dangerous and should not be approached. Instead, law enforcement should be contacted immediately.

Reported and contradictory sightings of the fugitives

swamped the airwaves at local police and sheriff's offices, as witnesses claimed to have seen the escapees, or a vehicle matching the description of the fugitives' getaway car. Law enforcement checked every possible lead, no matter how insubstantial the account.

Meanwhile, as daylight rose on the morning of Oct. 12, the FBI, the Texas Rangers, and U.S. Marshals joined local and state police, as well as sheriffs from surrounding counties, in what soon became a statewide manhunt. Fully aware of the imminent danger to the public—desperados were, by definition; desperate, authorities searched non-stop, day and night, all the while exhausted from lack of sleep. Steven Spielberg and Sam Peckinpah had made crowd-pleasing movies about Texas jailbreaks; the real thing wasn't nearly as entertaining. Nor was a happy ending automatically assured.

Jerry Riley and Jeremy Jon Reynolds, two of Bob Leach's fellow fugitives, were captured on Oct.12 in Collin County, approximately 48 miles south of Grayson County, and the county jail in Sherman, while Bryan Riley was apprehended on Oct.13 in Fannin County, approximately 30 miles east. Meanwhile, the last of the two escapees, Gerald Lynn Gantt and Leach himself, remained at large.

While on the run, both Leach and Gantt crossed state lines, into Oklahoma and Louisiana, thus enhancing their charges from the state to the federal level. But in the end, charges of interstate flight were the least of their worries.

They were soon captured, but not without resistance. And not without subjecting an innocent couple to a prolonged and terrible ordeal.

Before taking a husband and his wife captive in their home in Montague County, northwest of Fort Worth, the pair kidnapped a woman in Bonham, a hundred miles to the east. [2]

As the fugitives fled to the tiny town of St. Jo in

Montague County, they drove every back road imaginable, swiftly veering off one road and turning down another.

The woman that they had taken captive was able to escape when the fugitives, for reasons unbeknownst, got out of the vehicle and turned their heads for just a moment, and she was able to escape her captors, somewhere between the Cooke and Montague County lines. Seizing the very tiny window of opportunity, she tore out of the backseat as quickly as she could, running barefoot through pastures filled knee-deep with briar stickers, trying to put as much distance between her and the fugitives as possible. She finally made her way to a nearby home, pleading for help as they contacted authorities. [3]

Meanwhile, the fugitives were forced into precipitous flight when a peace officer spotted their stolen vehicle.

A high-speed chase quickly ensued between the lawman and the fugitives, with speeds reaching as high as 75 mph, too fast for a little windy two-lane back road. With nowhere to go, and desperately seeking a quick getaway, the fugitives sharply turned their vehicle onto a gravel road, throwing dust and rocks all around them, heading in the direction of a ranch-style house located a quarter-mile away.

Gantt charged through the back door of the house, maliciously taking a husband and wife, the homeowners, captive. (I. Forrester, personal communication, April 13,2011) Leach, meanwhile, stood outside, firing bullets from a stolen 30-06 deer rifle, warning the peace officer to stay back. [4]

The ensuing confrontation and shootout involved a host of law enforcement agencies including but not limited to the FBI, the Texas Rangers and officers from four county sheriff's offices, as well as local authorities.

What followed was a terrifying ordeal for the hostages. Inside the house, the couple, Vincent and Irma Forrester, were forced to sit on the floor with their hands tied behind their backs. The rope that bound their wrists together was tied so tightly that it started cutting the circulation off in Vincent's hands. Neither was able to move, both paralyzed with fear for what might happen next. (I. Forrester, personal communication, April 13, 2011), (V. Forrester, personal communication, April 13, 2011)

In the middle of all the chaos, a hostage negotiator managed to get Leach on the phone and convinced him to release the hostages. Realizing they were surrounded, with no way of escaping, Leach knew the cards were stacked against them.

Leach began to do his best to improve his position; He quickly showed remorse towards the couple and law enforcement, for putting them in harm's way. It worked, at least to some extent. Some later believed that his decision to take the couple hostage was done in haste, while others viewed him as a hardened criminal looking for a quick way out of a bad situation.

The phone that Leach used to communicate with the outside was hanging in the hallway in the center of the house. When he was not talking to the negotiator, Leach would leave the receiver to dangle off the hook, so everyone on the other end of the line was able to hear everything that was going on inside the house. Then, Leach would return to the call, every so often, surreptitiously, so as not to be noticed by his violent compadre, who maliciously taunted the couple, insisting that he would harm them the first chance he got.

It was during that interlude, when the phone was left off the hook, and Gantt was out of earshot, away from Leach and the hostages, either outside shooting his gun or taunting law enforcement, when the negotiator and other family members could overhear conversations between Leach and the couple.

They sounded like old acquaintances sitting around a table, having a cup of coffee, discussing cattle, and realizing they knew some of the same people from the local auction barns, instead of hostages that were being held against their will by two fugitives on the lam. Against all odds, Leach appeared to have ingratiated himself with the couple.

Meanwhile, Gantt incessantly ran in and out of the house like a madman, waving his gun in midair, shooting at anything he saw. He was a pistol-packing prick with a vengeance, looking to put a bullet in anyone that was trying to take him down.

The standoff was turning into quite a show. Law enforcement had a helicopter brought in to fly overhead to get a better layout of the area. Gantt happened to be standing in the front yard at the same time that the helicopter flew over the house. As the aircraft hovered overhead, Gantt raised his gun, firing at the helicopter. The aircraft was hit, and the pilot had no other choice but to land several miles down the road. (Interviews with confidential sources, personal communication, May 9, 2016)[5]

Authorities were at their wits' end. They were exhausted from lack of sleep, a consequence of trying to track down fugitives who had been on the run over half of Texas for days. The lawmen always seemed to be one step behind, and now that they finally had the last two escapees cornered, they had to figure out how to bring them in, once and for all. Hopefully without getting any more helicopters shot down.

Gantt went back inside the house and passed out drunk on the couch. He and Leach had stolen, among other things, a quantity of whiskey during the course of their flight.

There was now a window of opportunity for the couple to escape and they took it. Gantt awakened from his stupor and became enraged when he discovered Leach was trying to spirit the pair of captives to safety through a small bathroom window.

The pair scuffled, and Leach shot his hapless partner in

the abdomen. Gantt collapsed on a living room couch as lawmen converged on the house.

Eight hours after the fusillade of bullets began, the gun smoke settled. It was all over.

Leach surrendered peacefully. Gantt, the more violent of the pair, pleaded in hysterics for his life. Weakened by blood loss, he tried to make a plea deal with God ("I wasn't ready to go just yet.") and he sobbed, as first responders surrounded him. (Interviews with confidential sources, personal communication, June 2016)

The standoff between the pair of fugitives and authorities had ended. All five escapees were once again in custody. The press, the police and the public moved on to other concerns.

On Nov.25, 2005, D.A. Glaser told the Fannin County district clerk to put the case from Fannin County, involving Leach and Gantt, on the docket, so it, like many other older cases, could be closed out. (D.A. Richard Glaser, personal communication, Apr. 15, 2014)

However, during a pre-trial discovery, the defense attorney determined it would be best not to compel the victims of the crimes that were committed in Fannin County to replay the traumatic events in the course of a trial. Bob wasn't anxious to face a Fannin County jury, either. Therefore, a hearing was scheduled on May 1, 2006.

And so, a bench warrant was issued and Bob was readied for transport from the state prison facility in Tennessee Colony, en route to Bonham.

On the morning of the transfer, the administrators at the H.H. Coffield Unit carefully dotted every "I" and crossed every "T", while the warden and correctional officers coordinated with law enforcement officials on the route of the transport. Bob donned a standard orange jumpsuit. Ear muffs and a hood were placed over his head for the transport, which was how D.A. Glaser described seeing Bob for the first time.

Handcuffs were placed on his wrists, and a chain was wrapped around his waist that connected to the cuffs. Lastly, a plastic box was placed atop the cuffs, and manacles were fastened around his ankles, rendering him immobile.

Once outside, everyone, including Bob, paused long enough to take in the view. It was quite a party. Lined up on the opposite side of the formidable 15-foot chain link fence, topped with coiled razor wire, was a virtual caravan of law enforcement officials from state and federal levels. The elite troops consisted of deputies from the Sheriff's Department of Fannin County, DPS state troopers, U.S. Marshals and even a local SWAT team. A helicopter hovered overhead to shadow the caravan of cars during the transport.

Bob was handed over, and the caravan prepared to roll. Manacled inside the transport and locked down, with no way of seeing or hearing what was going on around him, Bob was in limbo, isolated from the outside world.

Because of the security risk that Bob represented, a diversion had been created by authorities to throw off busybodies, interlopers and nosy reporters. It was publicly understood that there was to be a hearing at the Fannin County Courthouse at 11:00 a.m. that morning.

However, upon arrival, instead of going to the courthouse, Bob was escorted to the jailhouse instead. The imposing Art Deco-style courthouse and other businesses around the courthouse square in Bonham had closed for the day because of the carefully-planned excursion. There were few cars, if any, on the square.

According to D.A. Glaser, snipers armed with long range rifles equipped with silencers were positioned strategically along the rooftops of buildings. The helicopter that had accompanied the transport remained in close range overhead, carefully watching, as the caravan of law officials transported Bob, nervously watching for the slightest sign that someone, anyone, might unexpectedly try to intervene and attempt to break him free.

Once inside the jailhouse, Bob was taken to a single isolated cell, where he was read his rights and, shortly thereafter a small hearing was conducted. It was a measure of Leach's notoriety that the formality was held inside his cell, rather than in open court.

He pled guilty to kidnapping and aggravated assault with a deadly weapon in Fannin County, where he received a 99-year sentence that ran consecutively with his other 13 life sentences. It was the capstone of a criminal career with few equals in the Lone Star State.

Chapter Two

SOUTHERN ROOTS

Bob's ancestors on the Leach side were Anglo-Saxon. They migrated to America in the 1700s from England and eventually settled in Tennessee before the Civil War began.

P.D. Thomas Leach, or Thomas, as he was known by his family, was Bob's great-great-great grandpa. He fought in the Civil War for the Confederacy and had six children--two daughters and four sons. After the Civil War ended, Thomas, like many other Southerners, migrated with his family to Texas in 1876. Many an abandoned log cabins had "GTT" − "Gone to Texas" − etched in the doorpost as their owners looked for fresh opportunities in the postwar aftermath. The family settled in Bastrop County, not far from the state capital, Austin.

Bob's ancestors spread out and worked for generations as farmers and cattlemen in the Lone Star State, and were prominently known and respected in their communities.

Bob's great-great grandfather, Anderson Norman Leach, Thomas' son, was born in Carroll County, Tennessee on November 26, 1865. In 1890, Anderson married and eventually had seven children, five girls and two boys. In 1900, they settled in Williamson County, on the edge of the Texas Hill Country, where Anderson worked as a corn and cotton farmer.

In the late nineteenth century, the Missouri-Kansas-Texas Railroad Company of Texas, also known as the "Katy", was the first railroad to travel from Denison, just north of Dallas, 350 miles south to San Antonio.

One of the stop-offs along the route was in the tiny town of Weir, located thirty miles north of Austin, where Anderson had his farm. Posters for a train called the, "Katy Flyer" hung outside the railway station, advertising roundtrip tickets to Austin for $1.00, with fine-dining amenities and a snack bar car along the route. Anderson always purchased his ticket at that very railway station to ride the Katy to the downtown train station at Third and Congress. From there, it was a short walk to the Driskill Hotel. Anderson didn't travel to Austin on farm business. He was there to gamble. And the Driskill hosted the hottest game in town.

The *Williamson County Sun,* in Georgetown, is the local paper of record. It has published numerous articles over the years about the Leach family, many of which described Bud Leach--Anderson's son, and Bob's great-grandfather--as being known for his friendly disposition and fine traits of character, as well as for being one of the most respected and successful cotton farmers and cattlemen in Williamson County. [1]

The stock market crash of October 1929 ushered in the Great Depression. While others were struggling to stay afloat during the hard times, Bud was doing very well in the farming and cattle industry. He was honored in 1937 and 1938 for bringing the first bale of cotton into Georgetown.[2]

WWII was in full swing and every young man that could sign up to join the war effort jumped at the chance to do so. A.D., Jr., Bob's paternal grandfather, enlisted in the Navy and served in the Pacific Theater, while his brother Riley enlisted in the Marine Corps. Numerous articles have been written about Riley, describing and labeling him as a much-decorated war hero who fought for the Second Marine Division in the Pacific campaign.[3]

Bud was one of many fathers in Williamson County who signed up for the war effort alongside both of his sons. He enlisted for the First World War, and again for the Second, but was not sent off to war.[4]

Back on the home front, Bud contributed to Red Cross blood drives and assisted in other patriotic wartime efforts.[5]

The widespread advent of radio brought the war into living rooms from coast to coast. On September 2, 1945, Japan signed the official instruments of surrender and the war was declared over.

Sometime shortly after the war ended, Bud wrote a letter to State Representative Lyndon B. Johnson, asking him to "Please send Riley back home." Johnson wholeheartedly approved Bud's request and on Monday, January 28, 1946, Bud received a telegram relaying the message that Riley would be landing in Seattle, on Friday, February 1, 1946. The Leach clan was finally reunited.[6]

All three of Bud's sons were raised around horses and cattle and they wanted to learn the business. Harold and Riley both enrolled in a Vocational Agriculture class and each one excelled in it. Riley eventually went into the construction business but Harold remained in the agriculture and cattle business and excelled in it. (F. Leach, personal communication, 2019)

Bob's dad, Marvin Dexter, was born in 1941, and he spent a lot of time around both of his uncles and his grandfather growing up, learning about cattle as he matured.

Marvin got married when he was young and by the time he was 22, he became a dad. On December 17, 1963, Bob Harold Leach was born in Marlin, thirty miles southeast of

Waco. Bob was named both for his great-uncle and a family friend, both well-respected cattlemen.

In 1892, the town of Marlin, on the banks of the Brazos River, gained an initial notoriety for its healing mineral water. Mineral wells and hot springs were in great demand in that era for their supposed healing powers. Resorts grew up around them. Marlin was no exception.

But the town's mineral water boom faded after the war, and the local economy returned to agriculture and ranching.

Bob's dad Marvin worked as a ranch manager during most of Bob's childhood, giving Bob complete access to cattle and horses on the ranch, therefore allowing him the opportunity to learn about cattle, just as his father and great-uncles before him did. It was also where he got to spend every free moment that he had with his little pony, Sugarfoot. (B. Davis, personal communication, Mar. 22, 2012)

Bob was seven when his parents divorced and Marvin was awarded sole custody of Bob. During the custody hearing, the judge requested that Bob be evaluated by a physician. The judge noted that when he talked to Bob, his responses were more vivid than a child's his age should have been. Bob's perception between reality and his imagination made it difficult for others to know when he was telling the truth and when he was not.

The physician that evaluated Bob recommended that he seek treatment for his overactive imagination. He furthermore stated that if Bob did not get the recommended treatment, then over time it would become worse, and he would go down a destructive path in life, possibly ending up in jail or prison.

It is not clear whether there were stipulations for Bob to continue treatment for his condition, or if they were written in the divorce decree, or if it was mandated by the judge, but nonetheless, neither parent took Bob to see a doctor for his condition, and as time went on, his 'imagination' worsened and his own sense of reality began to take precedence over the truth. Moreover, his sense of right and wrong began to erode.

Bob was in his late teens when he was first caught stealing cattle while working as a ranch hand at the same ranch that Marvin worked for. The ranch owner noticed several vials of cattle medicine had gone missing, and after doing his own investigation, he realized some of his workers were stealing from him. Marvin and a few other employees were stealing the medicine and reselling it to others at a cut-rate price. They were quickly let go from their positions, but the owner allowed Bob to stay on at the ranch and continue to work.

Not long after Marvin was let go, Bob was caught stealing cattle from the owner. Instead of pressing charges against Bob, the owner fired him and told him to leave the ranch immediately, never to return. (B. Davis, personal communication, Mar. 22, 2012)

Bob called his father the same day he was let go to explain what had happened, and he asked Marvin if he knew of a ranch where he could find work. Marvin had relocated to the town of DeLeon, in Central Texas, by that point. Bob followed him there, where Marvin introduced him to a renegade state trooper who eventually coaxed Bob into rustling more cattle. But that's getting ahead of ourselves.

Bob's criminal lifestyle began at an early age and he got caught up in so many different things that he couldn't get out of them, even if he wanted to. Bob's great-uncles, Riley and Harold, respected cattlemen both, were unaware of their grand-nephew's drift into lawlessness.

It's a classic question of "nature or nurture." Was Bob born with a reckless disregard for the truth, or did something in his seemingly-idyllic childhood make him that way?

Chapter Three

HELLO THERE, COMANCHE COUNTY

Comanche and DeLeon are neighboring towns in Comanche County in northwest Texas, linked by State Highway 16. Historically, the region was no stranger to violence.

In 1874, the infamous gunslinger John Wesley Hardin shot and killed former Texas Ranger and acting Deputy Sheriff of neighboring Brown County, Charlie Webb, outside the Jack Wright Saloon in Comanche. It was a high-profile killing, but by no means the only one.

During the nineteenth century, the closest railroad to Comanche was over a hundred miles away, making it almost impossible for regional law officials to get to local citizens promptly if they needed help. The citizens, oftentimes, were left to fend for themselves when problems arose, usually against hard-handed outlaws or Indian attacks. In the process, they sometimes took the law into their own hands.

During the post-Civil War era, cattle rustling was so rampant that citizens, bereft of official protection, formed their own vigilante mobs to enforce and uphold the law. The Hazel Dell, DeLeon and Sipe (pronounced "Seep") Springs mobs were created, and the citizens relied heavily on them for their own peace of mind and for a sense of security. Over time, however, the vigilante mobs became less concerned with upholding the law and more about settling individual scores. (Interview with confidential source, personal communication, Feb. 17, 2015)

No one knows for certain what year the incident happened, only that it occurred during the post-Civil War era, when one of the vigilante mobs--and it's not clear which one--apprehended a band of rough banditos that were believed to be breaking the law in some indeterminate fashion. The bandits were captured in Erath County, northeast of Comanche, and taken across the Comanche County line to be hanged without the courtesy of a trial.

Three of the outlaws were executed by the mob, while one, tied and bound on his way to the hanging, nevertheless managed to jump off his horse, narrowly escaping through the woods. The fifth and last man in the bunch had a noose tied around his neck while his horse was kicked out from underneath him. He managed to catch the rope between his teeth, while hanging in mid-air, and survived to testify against the vigilantes.

Due to that and similar incidents, state law enforcement agents made the journey to Comanche during the 1870s to investigate the vigilante mobs. For six months they spoke to citizens, urging them to come forward, and testify against the groups, but their attempts were unsuccessful. The townspeople did not want rustlers in their community, hence the reason the vigilante mobs were created in the first place. Nor did they want to inform on their neighbors; those citizens that were asked to testify were either related to someone in the mob or somehow otherwise connected to them. With no one willing to step forward and testify, law officials left Comanche in the same semi-lawless manner that they found it.

Nearly a century later, in 1976, law enforcement officials from various agencies and surrounding counties took interest in Comanche again. A local sheriff in the little town of Brownwood, approximately 30 miles northeast of Comanche, noticed multiple reports of high-end heavy equipment gone missing. An investigation, destined to uncover what was deemed as the largest theft ring in the state of Texas, began in Brown County, eventually extending to McCullough, Taylor and Bexar counties—a swath of crime hundreds of miles wide.[1]

The acting sheriff of Brown County, Danny Joe Neal, initiated the investigation. According to the *Brownwood Bulletin,* the initial investigation caught the attention of Texas Rangers Bob Faver of Brady, Sid Merchant of Abilene and Norman Autry of Brownwood. With the Texas Rangers in the picture, Sheriff Neal's inquiry accelerated and expanded.

According to Sheriff Neal, "One of the methods used to employ stealing the heavy equipment was to rent a large trailer, load a piece of equipment and pull it away. Equipment such as bulldozers, motor homes, boats, large diesel tractors, farm tractors, truck trailers, and other heavy items profiting hundreds of thousands of dollars were targeted by the organized theft ring."

Neal added, "Much of the stolen property was taken from local businesses and residents in the Comanche and Brownwood area. A majority of the equipment was unable to be recovered and was sold in Mexico and areas surrounding San Antonio. Law officials conducted surveillance by helicopters, and one source stated that law enforcement officers were also being investigated for their part in participating and devising the well-organized theft ring."

As the case progressed, residents wanted to know who was responsible for stealing the high-end heavy equipment; the more they talked, the more information came to light and it became too difficult for investigators to ignore. Some claimed certain individuals in law enforcement were solely responsible for the organization and participation of the theft ring. Others asserted that criminals, whose rap sheets ranged from petty thefts to more serious crimes, assisted the bad-apple cops with stealing the equipment.

They claimed these individuals would case local pastures, residences and local businesses, looking for equipment on which they could turn a quick buck. Once the equipment matching that criterion was found, it was then loaded onto a trailer and hauled off to sale.

Because no one initially expected law enforcement to be behind the crime spree, no one thought anything was out of the ordinary when law officials were seen patrolling the areas. In actuality, they were watching to make sure no one would come upon them while the equipment was being hijacked. Once the equipment was loaded and ready to haul off, a quick and clandestine message was relayed via handheld radio to let the patrolmen know that the job was done and everyone could leave the area.

To some who resided in the Brownwood area, the allegations against the individuals in law enforcement seemed not so far-fetched. The city's most famous—or infamous – citizen had once made headlines when she claimed to have been set up by local police.

Juanita Dale Slusher, far better known by her stage name of Candy Barr, was not only a renowned burlesque dancer, but also a close companion to Dallas nightclub owner Jack Ruby and mistress to the gangster Mickey Cohen. Candy claimed she was framed by local authorities in Brownwood for possession of marijuana.

According to an article in *Texas Monthly* magazine written by Gary Cartwright https://www.texasmonthly.com/articles/candy, in 1958, Candy was sentenced to 15 years in the joint for less than one ounce of grass. She claimed she was holding marijuana in an Alka-Seltzer bottle for a friend whose mother was coming to visit and the friend did not want to be caught with it. Meanwhile, the authorities set up surveillance to watch Candy's apartment and tapped her phone. Within hours of receiving the Alka-Seltzer bottle filled with marijuana, the authorities were at Candy's door to arrest her.[2]

Candy was paroled in 1963, and a few years after moving back to her hometown of Edna, she decided to pick up stakes and move to Brownwood. In 1969, a Brownwood cop entered her home while she was out of town at the time, and claimed to have found a stash of marijuana in a shoebox. The case was later dismissed due to lack of evidence and the fact that the officer illegally entered her home without a warrant. Because of this, some Brownwood residents were more inclined to believe the dancer over the police.

In the midst of the ongoing investigation of the theft ring, a presiding judge in Brown County, who initially helped oversee the case of the theft ring, was killed in a car accident before the case ever went to court. Rumors circulated throughout the Brownwood area, and some wondered if what happened to the judge was truly an accident. Some conspiracists theorized that the brake lines on the judge's car had been sabotaged. An investigation ruled that the accident was truly an accident, thus quashing—at least temporarily—the wild speculation. (Interview with confidential source, private communication, Mar. 11, 2015)

All the while, equipment continued to turn up missing, even as the investigation of the theft ring was still underway. Eventually, two individuals with reputations as hardened criminals were arrested. The trial was eventually held in January 1978 in Comanche County, where it was kept low key; both men were convicted in connection to the theft ring. Meanwhile, the investigation surrounding the possible involvement of corrupt law enforcement faded into the background.[3]

Less than a decade later, another trial, similar to the theft ring episode, played out once again, in a small courtroom in Comanche. On September 8, 1986, in the 220nd District Court, a trial was set in motion, *The State of Texas vs. Roy Kubiak*. Kubiak, a uniformed DPS state trooper, was accused of witness tampering, a felony. Kubiak was convicted.[4]

The acting District Attorney of Comanche County, Leslie Vance, stepped down from his position solely to represent Kubiak, while District Attorney Andy J. McMullen, from a neighboring county, stepped in to take charge of the prosecution during the trial. Presiding Judge James E. Morgan adjudicated the sentence to a misdemeanor, revoking Roy Kubiak's DPS license.

By then, Roy Kubiak would be playing a large and larcenous role in young Bob Leach's life.

Chapter Four

THE LAWMAN WANTS A FEW HEAD OF CATTLE

In the fall of 1980, Bob moved to nearby DeLeon. Bob was eighteen years old, a month or so shy of his nineteenth birthday. He had just accepted a job as a ranch hand on a local spread at Rocking M Ranch. It was there that his father introduced him to the local DPS state trooper, Roy Kubiak. Marvin, Bob's father, had known Kubiak and his family since Kubiak was a child, but it was Bob's first time ever meeting or hearing about the trooper.

Bob had been at the ranch for only a short time when he had his first encounter with the highway patrolman.

Kubiak responded to a call about a motorcyclist who had been involved in an accident not too far from the Rocking M Ranch. After the commotion from the wreck subsided, and the wreckage was cleared off the road, trooper Kubiak got into his patrol car, and drove to the nearby ranch.[1]

In addition to his DPS duties, Kubiak had some side action going—he wanted a cut-rate deal on some cattle from the ranch's owner, Joe Moore. And seeing as how he was in the neighborhood, he decided to pay a call.

Kubiak's dubious reputation as a lawman in the community oftentimes left others abuzz about his comings and goings. Most citizens in the area were already suspicious of him, especially since the rumors of the large-equipment theft ring in the 1970s was still fresh on everybody's minds; that and the fact that more than once Kubiak was seen associating with the criminals that were convicted for those crimes, and not in an exemplary manner, either. Because of this, some in the community were always wondering what he was up to.

Most felt that he was tied to the thieves from what they had seen or overheard firsthand. Some claim that Kubiak and the felons had been seen together on more than one occasion, offering equipment that was similar to what was reported missing or stolen by the victims of the crimes, at a fraction of the cost. Although the investigation surrounding law enforcement and its ties to the theft ring had been closed, many in the area wondered why Kubiak was not scrutinized more closely by the investigators overseeing the case. (Interview with confidential source, private communication, Feb. 17, 2015)

And he was not discreet about his dealings, law-abiding or not. For that very reason those that approached him did so with caution, for they never knew what to expect when dealing with him.

When Kubiak drove up to Rocking M Ranch, he saw Bob, with the rest of the cowboys, working the cattle in the cattle pens.

Bob was not hard to spot, because he was the youngest of them all, with thick, wavy blonde hair falling over the collar of his shirt. The boy had hazel eyes and dark-colored skin from working in the sun. Despite his youth, his stature was tall and lean, at six feet and 155 pounds.

Kubiak motioned to Bob to approach the patrol car. As Bob strolled over, Kubiak gazed around the lots at the different types of cattle that were being worked and branded.

He also noticed, off to the side, parked out by the barn, several pieces of farming equipment. They looked like they were in mint condition, barely even used. He certainly hadn't counted on there being more than just cattle to bargain with at the Rocking M.

As Kubiak's eyes glazed over at the possibilities of what he had just stumbled onto, he grinned to himself. He'd always been observant. Even as a child, he was always aware of what was going on around him. People in the Comanche area still talk about Kubiak and his siblings growing up piss poor; living in a rundown shack with dirt floors underneath their feet. There were some nights they didn't even get to eat. (Interview with confidential source, private communication, Feb. 17, 2015)

Bob approached Roy's car in some confusion, not sure why the trooper was out there in the first place, or why he even wanted to see him. Since Bob was new to the area, he had not heard the rumors about the trooper, so he assumed, like anyone else would, that the trooper was an upstanding lawman. Up until that moment he had not heard otherwise.

Kubiak towered over others standing over six feet tall and he tipped the scales at 200 lbs. His large frame was part of the reason why others would oftentimes feel intimidated by him. Under his uniform hat, he had dark hair fashioned in a buzz style cut. Sunglasses covered his beady eyes.

Kubiak extended his hand, and Bob removed his work gloves, firmly shaking Roy's hand, to acknowledge the friendly gesture by the trooper. Then Roy began to explain to Bob what he wanted.

According to a written statement given by Bob while he was at the Erath County Sheriff's Office, he explained how he and Kubiak first became acquainted.

"Listen, son, I know your dad really well. I've known him for years, since I was a kid, and he told me you're the best at working cattle that he knows, other than himself, and he's one hell of a cattleman. I know it, and so does everyone else, and for him to say that about you it's enough to get me out here, to want to talk to you. He assured me I could depend on you to help get me the cattle that I want, and that's why I'm here. It's been rumored you even covered for your dad when he stole several head of cattle from some of the ranchers that he worked for."

Kubiak put his hands in the air and with both index and middle fingers he motioned in a downward position, pumping his fingers up and down several times, as if to say his next statement belonged in quotation marks. "You tweaked the books and jimmied the numbers so no one would know about your dad stealing that cattle, didn't ya son? Hell, with guts like that, I figure we could make a little money together on our own by taking a few head of cattle and covering up the missing ones, like you did with your dad. What say you tweak a couple of numbers in the books for us?" Kubiak concluded, with a wry smile.

Bob didn't know what to say. This was a grownup, a law officer, to boot, and he was just a snot-nosed kid. He reckoned the best course of immediate action was to keep his mouth shut.

Kubiak looked around to see if anybody was in listening distance and continued. "I think I'm going to try my own hand at cattle this time, and I'm looking to buy a few head to start out with...for less than the market price. I'd bet my left nut it'd be a hell of a lot easier to get away with stealing cattle than it would any piece of farming equipment any ole day."

Kubiak squinted his eyes, looking out at the cattle that, at the moment, were being worked by the other hands. It was beginning to look like Moore had a pretty good setup, and certainly one that Kubiak didn't want to be left out of. Then he pointed to a few of the heifers, slowly drawing Bob's attention as he spoke.

"Looking around here, I see you got plenty of access to 'em, so let's see if we can make us a deal. What do you think? You want to work with the lawman, son, and get a little extra money on the side, just between us? I won't tell if you don't."

Kubiak nodded his head up and down as he waited for an answer from Bob, tapping his index finger on the hood of his patrol car, and grinning like a cat that had just caught an oversized and extremely delicious bird in his mouth.

Bob looked at Kubiak, surprised he was being propositioned by a state trooper, of all people, and completely thrown off his stride by what he had just heard. He said, "How do I know you're not trying to set me up? You're in law enforcement. Boys in law enforcement don't do that kind of thing. You catch the guys that do, and hang 'em."

"Son, I'm on your side of the law. This badge I got on, it lets me walk on both sides of the street. That means nobody questions my authority with it. Hell, this isn't my first go around with making a little extra 'money' on the side – it's just my first time messing with the cattle, and if I'm going to do this thing, you can bet your ass I'm gonna do it right. So, if I can help anybody out that I think might need a little extra money flowing in their direction while I'm pocketing some of my own, then I'm going to do what I can, to make sure we all get an even spread, providing it's all kept under wraps. Now, in the meantime, nothing says we can't make a little extra on the side, providing it's kept between us, and believe me, nobody, but us needs to know about this right here. With me calling all the shots, nobody'll question any of this, and I will be the one calling all the shots. Now, you want in on this little deal? You better jump while the coal's hot, son."

Bob looked him squarely in the eye and told him to keep talking. He wanted to hear what the man behind the badge had to say before he even considered agreeing to anything. Kubiak explained, in more detail, what it was he was looking for, as far as cattle were concerned, along with how much he wanted to pay per head.

Then Kubiak pulled out his ticket pad, and on the back of it, he wrote, "10 head at $110.00 per head for $1100.00." Then, without missing a beat, he looked directly at Bob, and told him all transactions would be paid in cash, never in the form of a check, and Bob could pocket any money that he received from Kubiak after the cattle were sold at auction. Half the market value of the cattle, Kubiak told him. Bob did the math; that could amount to a nice chunk of change. And all in untraceable cash. That was to ensure nobody but the two of them would know what was going on—no paper trail, no proof.[2]

After listening to Kubiak's proposition, Bob thought about it and figured, in his head, how much extra money that would give him, and he decided that he could do this. This highway patrolman would hide any proof of any of this ever happening. Could they actually get away with it, without anyone finding out that he was involved in it too? Damn right, they could.

Bob looked at Kubiak, shook his head and said, "I'm all in." The idea that he was in bed with a crooked cop bothered Bob not at all. Kubiak was right—no one looked beyond the badge.

Kubiak explained that he would pick the cattle up after dark because he did not want anyone seeing him loading them up on his trailer during hours when he was ostensibly on duty. He proposed to use the lights on the outside of the barn, and the headlights from his truck to pick out which ten cattle he wanted. Bob was to make sure that the cattle were confined next to the barn when Kubiak arrived so he could quickly pick them out, load them up and then haul them off. It was a simple, but bold, plan.[3]

The first rustling stint went off without a hitch. It went so well that Kubiak was pleasantly surprised by how easy it was to simply drive up to the ranch, pick out the stock he wanted, load them onto his trailer and haul them off, without raising any suspicion. The boy, Bob, was a natural.

They continued to make more deals, and the more cattle they stole, the more money they made. Kubiak paid Bob in hundred-dollar bills. Regardless of what the value of the cattle were at the time, he always paid Bob half the market price of what the cattle were selling for. Bob would easily get anywhere from $2,000 to $6,000 at one time. Bob was in high cotton for an eighteen-year old.

From the get go Kubiak was brazen with how he picked up and handled the cattle. On more than one occasion, he would load them up into Bob's trailer that was attached to the back of his work truck with the Rocking M Ranch logo on the side, and Kubiak would jump into the driver's seat and haul them off.[4]

Perhaps Kubiak was trying to throw others off into believing that any cattle seen leaving the ranch after hours could be viewed as Bob being the one moving them instead of Kubiak.

Kubiak often hauled the cattle to a wheat pasture located in Clifton, a cotton-farming community northwest of Waco. Other times, he would truck them off to a leased pasture located just outside of DeLeon. The pasture belonged to one of the town's more prominent citizens, who nonetheless was happy to help Kubiak unload his four-footed contraband for a cut of the action.[5]

All of a sudden, Bob became Moore's right-hand man; he was promoted from a ranch hand position to that of ranch manager, which allowed him even more access to the cattle at the ranch. He was called on to assist with buying cattle from the sale barns. Oftentimes, when the two were seen at sale barns together, Bob would not purchase any cattle until Moore nodded his head, giving a quick signal for Bob to bid on whatever cattle at the time were being sold.

Bob had had years of experience buying cattle while growing up, and the owner of the ranch quickly picked up on Bob's instinctive ability to guess the weight of a heifer or bull within ten to twenty pounds of its actual weight. It was a skill that most people can't command, and not many are able to do so with skill, especially during a fast-paced cattle auction.

His knowledge of cattle and horsemanship at a young age far exceeded what most people spent years trying to acquire. Because of Bob's upbringing, he learned these abilities by the time he was nineteen. As cattlemen measure such things, he was a near genius.

As Bob began to ease into his position as the ranch manager, Kubiak began to get more comfortable himself, coming and going more frequently than before. Kubiak started familiarizing himself with the layout of the ranch, and he was always there to see the cattle that were newly purchased from the sale barns. He knew every Brangus, Hereford, Charolais, Brindle, and Brahman that came across the cattle guard. As the cattle trailers drove in to drop them off, he was always there to watch them, like a bank robber casing a savings and loan.

His daily presence was noticed by all, especially the other hands. They began to get suspicious of Kubiak when they noticed him nosing around the cattle pens. And he was always underfoot, especially when the new cattle were being brought in, making him a downright nuisance. He would constantly pull the staff and ranch hands aside, indiscriminately taking them away from their job, to ask questions about the herd. Kubiak's behavior seemed obtrusive and unwarranted.

This bothered many, and they asked Bob why the trooper was always at the ranch. Bob was the ranch manager and if anybody would know what was going on, it would be him and if he didn't, he would be the one to get to the bottom of it. After all, he was the second in command to Moore.

It's not known if Moore was aware of Kubiak's constant presence at the ranch, but if he was, he might have believed that Bob would handle the situation at hand. If he had been aware of what either shyster was up to, surely, he would have forced both fellas off of his property and turned them in to the authorities.

Nonetheless, the ranch hands addressed their concerns with Bob about Kubiak. They wanted to know what his interest was in the cattle, and moreover, why he was always rummaging around the farming equipment.

Bob brushed their questions off as if it were no big deal, trying to hide the fact that he was involved with the trooper.

Bob began to realize that Kubiak was drawing a lot of attention to himself. The trooper was becoming a real problem. With all the questions people were asking Bob about him, things were beginning to get a little messy.

The more time that Kubiak spent at Rocking M, the more people began to talk about him. And not just the staff, but others in the area who occasionally stopped by, for one reason or another, noticed him carousing around like one of the hired hands.

Kubiak's ubiquitous presence created a rumor mill for the naysayers who still believed he was connected to the old heavy equipment theft ring.

The more money the pair pulled in from the stolen cattle, the more Bob wanted to spend his ill-gotten gains, and spend he did. Kubiak's presence at Rocking M might have brought a lot of attention on him, but Bob was drawing quite a bit of attention on himself by all the frivolous spending he was doing.

Bob's greed clouded his judgment, so much so, that he became careless to a fault. He was spending their earnings from the stolen cattle just as quickly as he was getting it. Bob bought a car and a truck, both in the same month, from the local dealership in town. He put a hefty amount of cash toward his down payment on both vehicles, and that's when people started asking where he got this money to buy two brand-new cars.

They questioned how it was possible for a nineteen-year-old kid on a ranch manager's salary to be able to make such exorbitant purchases. He was doing okay, by most standards he was doing well, but not well enough to pay for what he was buying on what was supposedly just a ranch manager's salary.

People surmised that he would have to have one or more side jobs to be able to pull in the amount of money that he was spending. And for somebody in his position, that was impossible to do. There just weren't enough hours in the day for him to work another job. He was at the ranch from dawn till dusk and then some, so the idea of him moonlighting somewhere, well, it just wasn't feasible.

With cattle reported missing from several other ranchers in the area, Kubiak's constant presence at Rocking M, and Bob spending more money than anybody else his age had access to, people wanted to know what exactly was going on.

As rumors about the cattle thefts spread, people started piecing the puzzle together. Was it possible that this kid was somehow involved with all the missing cattle, and was Kubiak running the show, again? Everyone's questions surrounding the events were certainly justified, especially with Kubiak's questionable track record.

Both gossip and well-known facts about the crimes spread

throughout the area. Many of the stories implicated Kubiak. Unfortunately, nobody in law enforcement wanted to challenge the trooper for the simple reason that they were fearful of what he might have over them. Or, perhaps, they were buying contraband from the trooper themselves.

Kubiak continued to acquire more cattle, through Bob's complicity, from Rocking M. In turn, Kubiak was able to convince his banker at Farmers & Merchants Bank in DeLeon that he was buying horses with the checks that he was cashing. And the banker cashed every check Kubiak gave him, without giving it a second thought.[6]

The checks Roy used to convince his banker that he was buying horses with were the same checks he acquired from the sale of the stolen cattle at auctions and to individuals around the area. A majority of his dealings were quick flips, so, as long as the individuals who were looking to buy cattle had cash or check in hand, Kubiak was able to get rid of them. Some of the cattle were sold to individuals that he knew, and others were to random strangers, but who had heard by word of mouth that he had a great deal on some cattle that he wanted to unload.

Kubiak would sell his stock just as quickly as he gathered them up, so as not to get caught.

In the end, the pair ended up stealing over $150,000 worth of cattle, and a few pieces of farming equipment from Bob's employer Joe Moore. With success growing, the pair became even more brazen.

Instead of gathering the purloined cattle at night with Bob's help, Kubiak began gathering them himself during the daylight hours while Bob was occupied with his legitimate duties. Oftentimes he demanded that Bob stop what he was doing to help him load the cattle on his trailer so he could be on his way.

Of course, this raised many questions with the other

hands, which is why they brought up Kubiak's presence at the ranch with Bob in the first place, but Bob had a way of diverting their attention away from Kubiak, at least for the time being.

It did not matter to Roy that the cattle he was taking had already been marked with the ranch's brand, he wanted them nonetheless. He had buyers with cash money and no questions.

Kubiak also had Bob delivering the cattle for him, and in those instances Bob would use his own work truck and a twenty-foot gooseneck trailer owned by the ranch to haul the cattle for Roy. While Bob unloaded the trooper's stolen cattle, Kubiak would sit back with a bottle of whiskey in his hand, watching, and comment about how he was one lucky son-of-a-bitch who had it made.

Bob delivered the stolen cattle to pastures located around the Comanche County area that were either owned or leased by friends of Roy, so they could easily be isolated until Roy could decide what he wanted to do with them.

Other times, Roy had Bob drop the cattle off at his friends' or neighbors' cow lots. Roy also requested his stolen stock be dropped off at Buster Hinson's pens located on Desdemona Highway, as Texas 16 was known, and still others delivered to more prominent individuals in the area (who did and do deny any participation in the enterprise).[7]

It wasn't too long after Kubiak started pulling all this that his buddies started showing up to the party with him, and the ones that did assisted Kubiak with stealing the Rocking M's cattle, in one way or another.

In Bob's statement, he recalled several instances when he came upon Kubiak and a few of his buddies loading up cattle that belonged to the Rocking M Ranch. Bob had no prior knowledge of what Kubiak was doing or what he was up to, so it surprised and angered Bob when he saw it.

Kubiak would simply slide onto the property owned by Moore, pop the lock on the gate and drive in to where the cattle were located. He was able to do this without being seen, because the pens that had the cattle in them were located across the road from the ranch, so it was easy for him to slip in and out whenever he fancied.

When Bob realized what was going on, he became so nervous, for the simple fact that Kubiak had now brought in his friends to help him out, instead of going through Bob, like they originally planned. Bob began to fear that Kubiak and his crooked cronies might retaliate against him or his family if he tried to stop them from coming onto the property. Bob had the authority to stop them, because of his position at the ranch, but he lacked the manpower to enforce it.

In the beginning, when Kubiak first approached Bob about rustling the cattle, Bob was all in, but somewhere along the way, Kubiak shoved Bob aside to take over for himself and his cohorts, leaving Bob out of what was really going on. The dynamics of their deal was changing and Bob's buddy was biting him hard like a rattler.

It didn't stop Bob's criminal behavior, but it did open his eyes enough to know that Kubiak couldn't be trusted anymore.

The first time Bob encountered Kubiak's little stunt was when he drove up to Rocking M Ranch on one rainy day at the same time Kubiak and a buddy named Darrell Kimmell were working seventeen head of heifers along with their calves, and both men were loading them into Kimmell's trailer.[8]

Bob couldn't believe what he saw. Here these two men were, so desperate to get their hands on cattle that they were branding them in the pouring rain. It was nothing but asses and elbows sloshing through the mud. And just as quickly as one heifer or calf was branded, it was loaded up into the trailer to be hauled off.

Bob later remarked that he thought they would have done that somewhere else, instead of in the pouring rain. There was mud everywhere. It was as if Kimmell and Kubiak neither one had any sense about what they were doing, much less were worried about getting caught.

Because of the storms that day, nobody was out milling around to catch sight of what was going on, because if they had been, they certainly would have said something to Bob about it. Questions had already been circulating at the ranch about Kubiak. And if the hands had seen the brazen theft by the lawman and his buddy, they would have been out there raising all kinds of hell and whooping somebody's ass. But for now, everything seemed to be in the hands of the long and larcenous arm of the law.

It was obvious that Kubiak and Kimmell were not leaving Rocking M Ranch without the cattle. And rain or shine, they were going to make sure they were branded before hauling them off.

Per Bob's recollection of the events that day, Kubiak told Bob that he made a check out to Kimmell for the cost of the cattle that they took. Bob believed that Kimmell took the check to the bank to cash for Kubiak and then Kimmell turned around and handed the money back to the trooper, who then paid Bob for his part of the stolen cattle. Kubiak hemmed and hawed around with what he and Kimmell were up to that day when he was talking to Bob about the event. Bob was not impressed.

Bob was now caught up to the fact that Kubiak was going around him to get the cattle he wanted, and in the process leaving Bob completely out of the loop about what was really going on. But Kimmell was under no illusions, and that made him a potential threat.

Kubiak decided to inform the authorities that the cattle they had just stolen were hauled to Kimmell's house. Kubiak had conveniently leased a pasture from his buddy Kimmell that was located directly across from Kimmell's house for moments just like these. How was he supposed to know that Kimmell was hiding stolen cattle in his pasture?

Things really began to unravel when Bob noticed his head count at Rocking M was way off, and not by just a few head either. His only conclusion was that Kubiak (and Kimmell) were skimming off the top, and taking more cattle than he and Bob had agreed on.

Bob had been able to hide the numbers of the missing cattle that he and Kubiak had stolen together, but now that Robocop was grabbing them up by the handful like they were M&Ms in a candy jar, it was beginning to get a lot tougher to fudge those numbers like before. It was only a matter of time before their little secret came out.

A couple of Bob's friends from childhood wanted to go deer hunting out at the ranch, so Bob invited them to go out. They had no idea that Bob was involved in stealing cattle, or that he was even associated with a crooked cop. A thought like that never would have crossed their mind, because that was not the Bob they knew. It was certainly not the same boy they grew up with. Bob managed to keep the criminal side of his self hidden well. Besides, he liked having the extra money.[9]

Bob drove them out to a pasture on the Rocking M to show them where they could set up their deer stand. As Bob pulled up to the gate, he noticed something was amiss, because the gate was wide open, instead of being locked. Somebody had apparently made their way onto the property without permission, and that somebody was Kubiak.

Out by the pens, Bob saw Kubiak and another man named Milton Smith loading up 20 head of Rocking M cattle into Smith's trailer. Apparently, Kubiak had cut his former amigo Kimmell out of the picture, just like he had Bob. Smith was the new recruit.

Bob was livid when he saw them out there, because, just like before with Kimmell, Kubiak hadn't said a word to Bob about getting more cattle. Bob got out of the truck and approached Kubiak to find out what the hell was going on, and why he was in fact bringing another friend with him to load up the cattle. What happened to 'keeping this just between us,' as Kubiak first mentioned?[10]

Kubiak put his hand up in the air to stop Bob from going any further, and told him in an aggressive tone that he left a few head in the pens that were already branded, but the ones that they had loaded up in Smith's trailer were unbranded, as if that was going to make everything alright.

Bob was smoking hot, but what could he do? He couldn't tell his friends what he and the trooper were up to, much less what the trooper was pulling behind Bob's back. The ranch's owner and Bob's fellow working hands wouldn't understand any of this, nobody that he knew would. Much less the law.

Bob had no one he could tell about the trooper taking things too far, for the simple fact he was in on it himself. It was clear that this thing was getting way out of hand and Bob believed he didn't have any other choice but to keep going along with it. He certainly wasn't putting the brakes on anything to keep the thievery from happening if it meant he was going to the pen for rustling.

Bob got back in the truck and proceeded to drive his friends to the deer stand. They asked Bob what was going on and why those men were out there loading cattle into a trailer. Bob was able to convince them that Kubiak and Smith had cattle that were grazing on the property and in fact belonged to them instead of Rocking M.

Later, on the way back from retrieving his friends from

the deer stand, he drove back by the pens where Kubiak and Smith were still hard at it. They were loading more cattle into Smith's trailer. As Bob got closer he noticed Smith had a pistol. What reason could Smith have for toting a pistol? Was Smith that desperate to take another man's cattle that he was willing to kill for it?[11]

Bob got out of the truck once again to talk to Kubiak while his friends stayed in the truck. Meanwhile, Smith made his way over to the truck to talk to Bob's friends while Bob had a few choice words with Kubiak. The men in the truck had no inkling that things could go from good to bad in an instant had Smith decided to throw down on them. And with his actions that day and the way he and Kubiak were acting, anything was possible.

Bob was worried and mad because, through no fault of their own, his friends were put in this potentially violent situation and he wanted to get them out of it quick. They were there only to visit Bob and to go deer hunting, that's it. Bob didn't want them around any of this.

All of this was happening because a simple-minded son-of-a-bitch wanted some cattle, so he decided to steal them instead of working for them. It was obvious that Smith was trying to intimidate Bob by talking to his friends while holding tight to his pistol. But just how far they were willing to take this, Bob did not know.

Bob never received any form of payment from Kubiak for the cattle that he and Smith stole from the Rocking M Ranch that day. And if that wasn't bad enough, Smith made it clear that he was doing some planting and he wanted a buggy full of fertilizer all for himself. Bob could get it, at no cost to him of course.

Bob often placed orders for horse feed, wheat, oat and sudan grass (which cattle grazed on) for the ranch from D&S Farm Center. It was as simple as picking up the phone, placing an order and picking it up from the supplier. Kubiak caught wind of this and decided that he wanted in on this deal too, so he had Bob order extra horse feed, oats and sudan for him as well. D&S also sold fertilizer and since Smith was starting to plant his own acreage, he put an order in for Bob to get an additional 10,000 lbs of fertilizer, at the expense of Rocking M Ranch of course, and it was to be delivered to Smith.

In fact, it worked out so well that Smith just decided to order all his fertilizer through Bob, by way of Kubiak. The trooper insisted that every time Bob placed an order for supplies from D&S, that fertilizer for his old buddy Smith be included in all those orders.

Bob was feeling intimidated by the trooper and his rough crowd of gun-toting friends. He thought he had it under control until he started seeing all this, but it was beginning to look more like Bob was a puppet and Kubiak was the puppet master. The deal that Bob had originally made with the trooper had gone up in smoke, and Kubiak was beginning to look more menacing by the minute, though Bob himself was far from innocent. He was in too deep and there was absolutely no way he could get out now.

Roy's frequent presence at the ranch became so hindersome that visitors started asking why he was constantly on the scene. He was always looking around the barn, at the tractors and equipment, and brazenly commenting to others in passing that he'd like to get his hands on a few of those pieces, because he could certainly find use for them somewhere.

Eventually, the ranch's heavy equipment items, such as tractors and backhoes, began to go missing. Roy placed an order for the vehicles with Bob as though he were ordering a pizza.

The more Roy continued to steal from the ranch, the

more reckless he became. He was so aggressive that he even started stealing from a few of the ranch hands, demanding that people show him respect, because he was, in his mind, still a lawman, albeit one outside the law.

The ranch became Kubiak's personal candy store. Nothing was off limits. He stole cases of oil from the ranch, and several times he was seen walking off with expensive bridles and reins.

When Bob noticed the cases of oil missing from the barn, he accused one of the hands of stealing it. Bob hadn't realized that Kubiak was the one who walked off with it.

The hand replied to Bob, "I didn't take it. It was the policeman that got it, because he was out there going through everything. I saw him. What's he doing out here all the time anyway, Jefe?"

No one was exempt from the thievery. If it was shiny or had a dollar value to it, it would end up in Kubiak's possession by the close of the next business day. On several occasions, the ranch hands would notice Kubiak on horseback, the horse wearing the very saddles and tack he had stolen from their own outfit. But no one spoke up. Roy's aggressive nature intimidated his victims, and they feared retaliation from the renegade trooper.

At least working on the Rocking M meant that Bob was a legitimate cowboy most of the time. But he often found occasion to wonder when Kubiak found time to do actual police work.

Chapter Five

FLIPPING STOLEN CATTLE

When most people met Bob for the first time, they were instantly attracted to his charisma and good-ole-boy charm. He always has an answer for everything and his version would always outdo anyone else's, every time. Many have said that Bob reminded them of someone from the Old West era. They imagined him running with the hard-fisted cowboys, cheating someone in a mean game of cards all while throwing back shots of tequila and aged old whiskey in a dusty saloon. (Interview with confidential source, private communication, Feb. 17, 2015)

Kubiak wasn't the only crook that Bob had come in contact with. He wasn't even the first crook Bob had been around with on a regular basis. He was just one of many, but he was the first one to convince Bob that he could just about get away with anything, with or without Kubiak's help.

The pair had already made more money than Bob had ever seen in his young life. What the two had made together was enough to make Bob want to stay in the game, only this time, Bob wanted to venture out on his own, and he wanted to do it without Kubiak.

Bob started going to the sale barns more frequently to pick out cattle that he wanted. Then he'd go to the cashier's desk at the sale barn to pay for them, but he always used a personal check, rather than the revolving line of credit most stock buyers employed. And none of his checks were ever any good. He didn't have the money to cover the expenses that he was incurring, and he was spending a lot.

There was never enough in the account to cover the cost of the cattle that he bought. By the time the check hit the bank, and it was discovered that the funds were insufficient, Bob was nowhere to be found, and neither were the cattle.

After he wrote a check for the cattle, he had one week to figure out how he was going to cover the cost of the check along with all the fees that he accrued from it. The fact that he got away with this more than once was a testament to his inborn charm.

He was constantly flipping cattle somewhere for money, so he either paid for it with what he had got from Kubiak, or he sold the cattle outright to someone else at a higher price. The more he did this, the more cattle he acquired. It got to a point where he was even getting loans from bankers to buy more cattle with.

Bob never had the same cattle for very long and he was running them in and out so much that he didn't even know what he had. As soon as a given sum of cash would come in, it was inevitably gone the next day.

Bob propositioned several individuals, at different times. In September 1985, he convinced investors to put up their own money to buy steers that were to be leased to the National Cutting Horse Association, or NCHA, for a cutting horse "workday," or practice session.

The art of "cutting" a particular cow out of a herd was developed over many years, starting with the 19th century trail drives, and it demanded an almost telepathic rapport between horse and rider. The horse in particular had to have above-average "cow sense" and cat-like reflexes. In order to practice for competition, they need to practice with livestock.

The owners and NCHA executives, as individuals, were not suckers and they certainly weren't naïve. They were educated businessmen, simply looking for a better opportunity in life, a chance to be able to provide more for their families, and they knew the horse show business. It was Bob's charismatic charm and knowledge of cattle that drew them in and led them to make decisions they would come to regret.

After the competition season was over, the cattle would be placed on property that was leased by the NCHA, so they could gain weight for the regular cattle market. When the lease expired, the cattle would be sold, and all the money, along with the profits, would be returned to each investor.

When asked by the investors that Bob wanted to partner with about leasing the steers to the NCHA as to why he would want to go into a partnership on such a profitable deal, Bob explained that he had only been approved for half of the amount of the loan, and therefore he needed the other half to get the total number of steers that he was required to lease to the NCHA. In order for that to happen, Bob wanted to partner up with someone who could come up with the rest of the money in order to buy the balance of steers required. No one, other than Bob, knew that the cattle he was working with were either purchased with hot checks, or acquired from Kubiak or bought with the money that was loaned to him by the investors. Plainly put, the cattle were not his to begin with.

By gaining the trust of one particular investor, Bob had someone to vouch for him to the others, whom he could entice into future partnerships with access to more money down the road. That individual, in turn, was deceived, going into business dealings with Bob, not knowing that until after the last partnership deal was finalized, and by then it was too late. The other investors who were propositioned by Bob, were included in the last and final deal, but by then everyone else involved had already lost their money. Some of the money that was paid back went to the one person who could vouch for Bob, and it came from the money Bob acquired while stealing cattle for Roy Kubiak. It was a classic pyramid scheme with a Wild West twist.

Chapter Six

THE CATTLE CONTRACT

As Bob continued to siphon money from the investors by pulling a classic confidence game, he decided to lease some of his own cattle to the NCHA by using the same cattle that he acquired from loans that he got from the local bankers. The terms of the loans were long enough to cover the length of the contract to lease the stock to the NCHA, which was usually for ninety days. Then Bob could turn around and pay the bankers back for the loan of the cattle while putting a little extra money in his own pocket.

In November 1985, while Kubiak was selling his stolen stock locally, Bob was leasing the steers that he acquired from hot checks and loans by the bankers to the NCHA. He thought if he could send them to the Will Rogers Coliseum in Ft. Worth, a hundred miles away, then he could double his money while still working with Kubiak. To him, it was the ideal way of making a little extra cash on cattle that he purchased on his own, while still rustling with Kubiak in DeLeon.

The Cattle contracts typically lasted anywhere from sixty to ninety days, and during the term of the lease, the cattle remained at the Will Rogers Coliseum under the supervision of the NCHA until they competed in the Fort Worth Fat Stock Show and Rodeo. Then, when the lease was up, Bob would get a check from the NCHA and he could turn around and sell the cattle outright, in turn, doubling his money.

On November 13, a man named Pat Jacobs introduced a cattle inspector from the NCHA to Bob and another employee of the ranch, who also happened to be an acquaintance of Bob's named Roger Willey.[1]

There is little known about Jacobs, or who he was, whether he was an accomplice to Bob or someone who had leased his own cattle at one time or another to the NCHA. The only known fact about him was that he was the one that put the inspector in touch with Bob.

Jacobs told the inspector that Bob was the manager of a ranch located outside of DeLeon, and that the owner of the ranch had some cattle that he wanted to lease.

Both, the cattle inspector and Jacobs, drove to meet with Bob at his home, and talk to him about leasing the cattle. That Wednesday afternoon was an almost perfect fall day. The temperature was in the mid-seventies, a light breeze in the air and there wasn't a cloud in sight.

Bob's house was down the road a little ways from the ranch headquarters. When the two men arrived, Bob met and shook the inspector's hand then Bob introduced the inspector to ranch hand Roger Willey.

Bob told the cattle inspector that he had one hundred head of cattle in a lot that he could lease to the NCHA for cutting horse exhibitions. He explained that they belonged to Moore, the owner of the ranch, but being that Bob was the ranch manager that he would be the main point of contact. Bob nodded his head in the direction of where the lot was located, and then pointed the cattle out to the inspector. This would later become one of Bob's signature moves for more cons that he would pull on others.[2]

After glancing over the stock, the cattle inspector told Bob that they looked like they would do for the NCHA cutting competitions, but that he would need at least 150 head for his needs, more than Bob had on display.

As the responsible agent for the ranch owner, Bob told the cattle inspector that he did in fact have access to 150 head of cattle, and that he could furnish the rest of them, along with the trucking and labor, for $40 a head. The two agreed, and the inspector told Bob to drop the cattle off at the Will Rogers Coliseum in Fort Worth, where the competition was to be held as part of the annual rodeo.[3]

A week later, the cattle inspector met with Willey in Cresson, seventy miles north of DeLeon. Willey was to ride with the inspector to the Will Rogers Coliseum to see where the cattle that the NCHA would be leasing from Bob would be kept, and inspect the conditions under which they would be held.[4]

On the drive to Fort Worth, Willey informed the inspector that he himself was in the process of moving, but that Bob would know how to get a hold of him if the inspector needed to contact him. It was not clear to the cattle inspector who it was exactly for whom Willey worked--for Bob directly, or for the owner of the ranch--but Willey clearly stated to the inspector that he himself was the cattle manager.

The following day, Bob contacted the inspector to tell him that, unfortunately, Moore, the owner of the ranch had backed out of the deal. But not to worry, Bob himself had 125 cattle that he could lease.

Of course, Moore wasn't even aware that Bob and Willey were speaking to a cattle inspector about leasing his cattle to the NCHA. In fact, it was essential that he remain in the dark. It was a well-planned con from the get-go.

Bob and Willey, both, were trying to gain the inspector's trust, to see if they could get away with using the cattle that Bob had acquired. They thought that if they could gain the trust of the inspector by showing him cattle that were sourced from a reputable ranch, the inspector would believe that they were upstanding and forthright cattlemen.

But that's what happened. It was a great way to move the cattle Bob had acquired through hot checks and loans without raising any suspicion from locals in the area.

After the cattle inspector hung up the phone with Bob, he returned to Bob's house to meet with him and Willey, once again. Both men confirmed that, yes indeed, Moore had backed out of the deal, stating that he did not have the necessary quantity of cattle to lease, but they could and would make other arrangements to supply the NCHA's needs, which they did.

Just as they planned, the cattle that Bob and Willey showed the inspector were from the same stock that were on loan to the bankers and others were ones that Bob acquired with the hot checks that he had written.

After inspecting the stock on offer, the inspector told Bob and Willey that some of the cattle needed to weigh more to meet competition standards. No problem; Bob and Willey simply got heavier stock by swapping out the skinnies for other, bigger cattle.

On November 22, the inspector drove back to Bob's house to inspect the cattle, once again, and approved them to be leased to the NCHA. The cattle were to be delivered no later than Sunday, November 24, by 6:00 p.m. to the Will Rogers Coliseum.[5]

Four days before Thanksgiving, while everybody was preparing for their holiday feast, Bob and Willey were busy loading 155 head into what the cattle inspector himself called a tractor-trailer to take them to Fort Worth.

That Sunday morning, when the inspector arrived once again at Bob's house, he saw a trailer loaded down with cattle, attached to the back of an extended-cab dually truck and a big smile on each man's face.

Bob and Willey drove two loads to the Will Rogers Coliseum to deliver the cattle, using the same truck and trailer.

Bob and Willey leased the "new" stock out to the NCHA under the same terms as before. The NCHA used 150 head of cattle and they paid on the previously-agreed on terms.

In January 1986, an official from the NCHA asked the inspector to whom they were supposed to make the check out for the lease of the cattle. When the inspector asked Bob and Willey, Willey spoke up and said to make the check out to him and he would give Bob his half. A check was then written to Roger Willey in the sum of over $6,000 for the cattle.[6]

Meanwhile, the investors on whom Bob had pulled the original pyramid scheme on belatedly began to compare notes. Things didn't seem to add up, causing the investors to ask even more questions, eventually leading them to their local sheriff's office, where they filed a complaint against Bob. There were three thefts by deception complaints in all, one from each investor; one was over $750 and less than $20,000 and two were over $20,000 each.[7]

It had appeared that Bob had left town and was nowhere to be seen. As the investigating officer from the sheriff's department started digging around, he contacted the central office of the NCHA, located in Fort Worth.

He asked the NCHA supervisor about Bob, and learned that Bob's membership in the NCHA had been suspended for writing hot checks to pay his dues. The supervisor told the investigating officer that he would have the inspector from the NCHA, the same man who leased the cattle from Bob originally, return his call, to answer any questions he might have.

Meanwhile, a private investigator, who happened to be a friend of one of the original investors, did a little digging into Bob's background and was able to place Bob in the town of Gonzales, located in Brazoria County down near the Texas Gulf Coast, at a ranch where Bob's father worked. (Interview with confidential source, private communication, Apr. 9, 2015)

The investigator contacted Bob's father and told him that several witnesses claimed to have seen Bob in the area and that he wanted to speak to him. Bob's dad denied that his son was anywhere in the vicinity. Then, after the investigator said he would drive to Gonzales to confront him in person, Bob finally got on the phone.

The investigator told Bob that he had 24 hours to return to Brown County and turn himself in, and that after that deadline passed, the private investigator was coming for him to haul his ass back himself.

The investigator took a hard line, fearing that Bob, being fluent in Spanish, would run off to Mexico, Gonzales being relatively close to the border.

Bob assured the investigator that he would turn himself in promptly, and the following Monday, after visiting family members in Waco, he did just that. Rather than driving back to Brown County on his own, he walked into the McClennan County courthouse in Waco where he turned himself in.

While Bob languished in the McClennan County Jail, the NCHA inspector who dealt with Bob and Willey had returned the sheriff investigator's call. The inspector stated that the only dealing he had with Bob or Willey was when he leased the cattle from both men. The inspector had no idea that Bob was swindling others out of their money. Had he known, he said, he never would have dealt with him, and he would have turned Bob in to the authorities.[8]

The inspector said he considered Bob a likable fella, a very charismatic individual. He described Bob as somebody who was very knowledgeable about the trade, and appeared professional in all his dealings. In fact, the inspector would have gladly leased more cattle from Bob, had he not been arrested for larceny.

Once Bob was discovered to have surrendered, the Brown County sheriff's office in Brownwood sent a patrol unit to pick him up and transfer him to their jurisdiction. Bob Harold Leach, cattle thief and con man, was coming home.

Chapter Seven

THINGS COME TO A HEAD

A deputy from Brown County drove Bob to the station. When they arrived, Bob was processed into the jail, fingerprinted and had his mug shot taken. As he went through the booking process, the deputy escorted him through the jail, then removed his cuffs and placed him in a holding cell.

Bob gave a statement about the events of his time with Roy Kubiak, explaining in full detail that the highway patrolman and he were stealing cattle, equipment, tack, and more from Bob's employer.

Bob was only at the Brown County Sheriff's Department for a short time. Erath County's own Sheriff's Department, where charges were also pending, found out Bob was in custody, and they expressed an interest in filing separate charges on Bob in their jurisdiction before Brown County got a crack at him. Seems there just wasn't enough of Bob to go around.

Suiting actions to words, Erath County sent an investigating officer, Sheriff Coffee and Texas Ranger Dendy, to the Brown County Sheriff's office to pick Bob up and take him into custody.[1]

Once remanded to Erath County, Bob was once again booked and admitted. He refused to answer any questions, stating that he wanted to speak with his attorney first. Bob used a public defender to represent him, but not long after that he hired an attorney that was able to help him with his charges. After doing so, Bob then explained how he pulled a con on the individuals he had fleeced in connection with the NCHA cattle scam. And boy, did he have a story to tell.

Bob explained that, to begin with, there never were any cattle for the investors to lease to the NCHA. The cattle that Bob pointed out to the individuals were from the stolen stock that he and Kubiak had taken. They were flipping the stolen cattle as quickly as they were coming in.

Bob was able to convince the investors that the cattle they were putting money towards belonged to them and the investors believed that "their" cattle would be leased to the NCHA, thus giving them a chance to double their money.

As with any livestock business dealings, when an investor puts a substantial amount of money towards a payment for a future investment, the investor is going to want to see "his" cattle, and to check on them at random times.

The investors weren't the only ones who wanted to inspect the cattle. The bankers from whom the investors borrowed the money to cover their loans, also wanted to see the livestock. The bankers only needed to see the cattle one time, in person, so they could approve the loans. After being shown what the bankers believed were the cattle that were being used as collateral towards the loans to the investors, the bankers then approved the transactions.

When the investors wanted to check on their cattle and showed up at Bob's house and requested to see them, Bob would take them to the pasture where the stolen cattle were being held. Bob would wave his hand vaguely in the direction of the livestock and tell them, "That's them, right over there," all the while knowing full well the cattle that he was showing the investors would be gone in a day or two, only to be replaced with more stolen stock.

If the investors wanted to get closer to the cattle to inspect them, Bob would always have an excuse as to why they couldn't get too close. His excuses ranged anywhere from, "It's too dark to see them right now," to "We don't want to spook the calves," to "It's feeding time, and we don't want to disturb them right now." The investors, figuring that, as ranch manager, Bob must know his business, always complied.

He would then quickly rush the investor along, temporarily diverting their attention away from the stolen stock.

The reason Bob didn't want the investors to inspect the cattle too closely was because the particular cattle he was showing them were always rotated out with the new stock that he had either stolen or written hot checks for, so he never had the same stock on hand. One day he might have a pen full of Santa Gertrudis cattle, and the next day he might have a load of Aberdeen Angus. He didn't want the investors to get too attached to them, and be able to visibly recognize "their" cattle, or they might be able to figure out what he was up to, especially since there had been reports of cattle theft in the area. He just wasn't ready for that kind of scrutiny, not just yet.

When asked what he did with all the money that was given to him to purchase the cattle, he replied, "I gambled it and high-rolled it." Another way of saying, perhaps, that the money he gambled with he was hoping he wouldn't get caught. And he did like to gamble.

But he did get caught. Bob was charged with three counts of theft by deception in Erath County and was sent to court, where he received ten years' probation for his crimes, along with the condition that if he violated his probation, he would be sent to the Texas Department of Corrections to serve the balance of his sentence.

Bob had charges pending in Comanche County as well, involving the same individuals that he knowingly and willingly deceived in Erath County. Bob was becoming one of the most popular felons in Texas; everybody wanted a piece of him.

Chapter Eight

THAT'S ONE DANDY OF A CONVERSATION, YOUR HONOR

While Bob was bouncing between Brown and Erath Counties, Kubiak was dealing with some pretty hefty charges of his own in Comanche County. His problem was he just couldn't shit without falling back in it. Bob's dad had recorded a conversation between himself and Kubiak, and what the trooper had to say concerning Bob was pretty damning evidence.

Kubiak was afraid that his old buddy Bob had decided to turn on him, and if the right person listened to Bob long enough, then Trooper Kubiak just might get into some real trouble. And he did not want any of that. He was going to cover his ass any way he could.

He began making phone calls to Bob's dad, Marvin, from the courthouse. He'd shuffle around some papers to make it look like he was working, then when nobody was looking, Kubiak would pick up the phone and make those incriminating calls.

He made several calls to Marvin, between Dec. 1-18, 1985. Marvin recorded one of those conversations between himself and the trooper, and in the course of the conversation,

Kubiak had threatened Bob's life. This recorded conversation between them is what led to Kubiak being charged with witness tampering.

In the lead-up to State of Texas vs. Roy Kubiak, Bob was scheduled to testify against his old mentor.

The transcription of the Dec. 18th call was admitted into evidence in the court of Judge James E. Morgan, where Kubiak was being tried. Part of the transcript of the call is reproduced below:

Roy: "What are you doing? I didn't call collect. I'm at the office."

Marvin: "Whose office?"

Roy: "Just an office up at City Hall."

Marvin: "Hey, I gotta have some money."

Roy: "Okay."

Marvin: "Bob's coming unwound."

Roy: "Did you talk to him?"

Marvin: "Yes."

Roy: "Did you tell him about that?"

Marvin: "What?"

Roy: "That I didn't have nothing to do with it?"

Marvin: "Yes, he'll do that when he gets out."

Roy: "No, Marvin, I'm serious. I'll just take my chances. I'm not the one in

trouble. I'll do what I said."

Marvin: "You told me you had $4,000."

Roy: "I can get it. If he would say I didn't have nothing to do with it. If he would

say the accusations he said against me were false, and he did it to cover up. If he says that, I'll do it."

Marvin: "Well he's coming unwound. He's tired of taking the damn rap. That's all

I know."

Roy: "Well, let him come unraveled. If he'll say that, I'm serious."

Marvin: "Okay then."

Roy: "If he'll do that, then I'll give it to you."

Marvin: "Well, I've gotta get him out of jail before he does that."

Roy: "Why?"

Marvin: "Because I've gotta get him out."

Roy: "Why? He ain't gotta talk to anybody when he gets out?"

Marvin: "Well, what do you care then?"

Roy: "When he gets out, he's gonna go to Comanche. They're going to arraign him over there. They've got two little bitty things over there on him."

Marvin: "No, this lawyer down here's got him fixed up."

Roy: "If he's got him fixed up, then why can't he get out?"

Marvin: "He's gonna go up there and get him out. I got to have the money to get

him up there. We ain't got no damn money. His wife is sitting over there now in DeLeon, behind on the damn car payment and everything else."

Roy: "Well, hey, you get him to do that and I'm serious. Oh well, now Marvin,

he's lied to me so many damn times."

Marvin: "I've gotta have this now."

Roy: "I'll get it, but you tell him to make that statement."

Marvin: "Well, when he gets out, he will."

Roy: "Oh no, I know him better than that. I do know him better than that. What

difference does it make? If he says it before or after, now tell me that."

Marvin: "He's not gonna say nothing till he gets out."

Roy: "Well I just soon leave him in there. Let him talk. I've done been through hell. I ain't going through this shit five more times. My gut has shrunk."

Marvin: "Okay."

Roy: "The only thing he's gotta say, the accusations he made against me were

false. When did you talk to him?"

Marvin: "Yesterday."

Roy: "Well, I told the boy I didn't know what he was doing, but he better slow

down."

Marvin: "He told me, 'I know more than what I'm saying I know.'"

Roy: "So! I don't know nothing."

Marvin: "I don't either."

Roy: "But if he says that. Well, when are you gonna try to get him out?"

Marvin: "If I had the money, he's gonna try to get him out Friday."

Roy: "What lawyer?"

Marvin: "One I got down there in Angleton."

Roy: "How much does he need?"

Marvin: "His wife needs $2,000, now to wire it to me. Give it to her and tell her your buying that damn plow from Darrell. That's all she needs to know."

Roy: "Wire it?"

Marvin: "No, give it to her and she can wire it. See, he's got that plow up there

that Darrell's got."

Roy: "Tell you what I'll do, I'll send you $2,000, but before I send any more, I

want him to make that statement."

Marvin: "When he gets out, he will Roy. Why is he gonna talk shit? You know I

don't know what in the hell he knows, but he hasn't said

anything yet. Why in the hell is he gonna say anything? He thinks you owe him some money."

Roy: "I don't owe him anything."

Marvin: "Well, he thinks you do."

Roy: "Well, whatever, but seriously if he'll make that doggone statement. I talk to

about three or four different lawyers and he's gonna get probation on everything."

Marvin: "Well just give it to her and just tell her it's for the damn plow. He's got

that plow up there I'm trying to sell to Darrell and everybody up there, and just tell her you bought the damn plow."

Roy: "You personally guarantee he's gonna make that statement when he gets

out?"

Marvin: "When he gets out, yes."

Roy: "Okay, I'm going to hold you to it."

Marvin: "Alright, now what did I tell you? He ain't talked yet has he?"

Roy: "It don't make a shit. I'll go to the Sheriff. I don't have nothing to hide."

Marvin: "Roy, he's coming unglued."

Roy: "I have to get the money."

Marvin: "You told me you already had it."

Roy: "What? Well, no, I've got to go get it. It's not easy."

Marvin: "Well, I've gotta have it today."

Roy: "Today?"

Marvin: "Yes. I've got $3,000."

Roy: "Okay, but hey, you guarantee me he'll make that statement?"

Marvin: "Okay, but I've got to have the money. I'm gonna call her and tell her

you're gonna give her the money."

Roy: "No, don't you tell her nothing. Let me see if I can get the money first. I'm

gonna see if I can go down to the bank and wire it."

Marvin: "Your name's gotta be on it, if you do."

Roy: "Oh it does?"

Marvin: "Yeah."

Roy: "Oh shit."

Marvin: "Unless you get somebody else to. See if you wire it to me, I have to say

who I got it from, such and such. You can wire it to this lawyer down here."

Roy: "Naw, my name will be on it then. How do you wire it through the bank?"

Marvin: "No, you wire it through the Western Union office."

Roy: "Then what do they do?"

Marvin: "Then I go down there and pick it up."

Roy: "Well, who can wire it besides the bank?"

Marvin: "You go to a Western Union office and you say, 'I'm wiring this money

to so and so,' and they go down there and pick it up, and you fill out a deal and it's got to say, well, hell anybody can't just walk in there."

Roy: "Okay, but you guarantee me he'll make that statement?"

Marvin: "When he gets out, yeah."

Roy: "Okay, when he gets out. When he gets out of this mess?"

Marvin: "No, when he gets out of jail. He wants out of jail, now."

Roy: "Okay, I'll get it after dinner."

Marvin: "I need it before dinner."

Roy: "I can't get it before dinner. The guy's at work."

Marvin: "Alright, get it after dinner. I'm gonna tell her you're gonna give her the

money."

Roy: "Don't tell her nothing."

Marvin: "Alright."

Roy: "Today?"

Marvin: "I've got to have it today."

Roy: "Alright, but hey you guarantee he's gonna make that statement?"

Marvin: "When he gets out, I guarantee it."

Roy: "I guarantee you, I guarantee you if I have to, I'll hire a hitman. I ain't

shitting you now."

Marvin: "Okay, come on he's gotta get out of jail, he's coming unglued."

Roy: "Okay, I'll see ya."

Marvin: "I'm serious."

Roy: "Okay."

Marvin: "Goodbye."[1]

After hearing the recording, between Bob's father and Roy Kubiak, Judge Morgan, inexplicably, dismissed it and adjudicated Roy's sentence down to a misdemeanor and revoked his DPS license, allowing him to skate on the most serious charges.[2]

Proof of checks that Roy had written to keep everybody quiet were also admitted into court, but were also dismissed by the judge. Kubiak was like a calf looking at a new gate, desperate to find a way out of his serious charges, and Judge Morgan was the out that Kubiak needed. After all the witnesses' testimonies, and proof against Roy that had been produced, Judge Morgan allowed him to walk away a free man. No one in the courtroom could quite recall ever having seen anything quite like it.

After further research into the court records surrounding

Kubiak's trial of tampering with a witness, there is no real explanation as to why Judge Morgan allowed Kubiak to walk free. The charges against Kubiak were felonies and it makes no sense for a judge to reduce the charges to misdemeanors, unless there was an exchange of money from one hand to the other. Or could someone possibly be covering up for some hidden charges from the old 1970s-era heavy equipment theft ring that they never wanted to come back to light?

During the writing of this book, several requests were made to meet and speak with Judge Morgan to get a better understanding of this case and possibly his side of the story, but he refused to answer any phone calls regarding the case. On a side note, the court reporter who sat in on the trial for Kubiak stated he would get back to this author with information pertaining to the trial, but ultimately refused to provide any information regarding the case.

Judge Morgan is the only one that can answer why Kubiak was set free from these criminal charges, and today he is still a presiding judge in Comanche County.

Chapter Nine

YER' MINGLING WITH THE WRONG CROWD THERE, SON

After Kubiak's fiasco of a trial in Comanche ended, Bob left the area and went to work at another ranch alongside his dad down in Brazoria County. Bob was still on probation from his charges in Erath County, which meant he had to watch every step he took, or he would end up in the very place he was trying to avoid, which was prison. But it seemed he just couldn't help himself.

While working on the ranch, he began hanging around a new crowd of people, and they were not an ideal fit for someone who was on probation.

Bob came in contact with a convicted felon named Harvey Glenn Edwards. The details about how they met are unclear, but sometime in 1989 they became acquainted with one another. The same time Bob started associating with Edwards, he also met another shady character, equally as sketchy as Edwards, by the name of Richard Calvin Lee. Lee ran in the same circle of people as Edwards. And they all stemmed from a pretty rough crowd.

This new group that Bob fell into was worse than any group he had ever encountered before, including Kubiak and his mean-fisted cronies. Overnight, Bob went from stealing cattle and running cons on random individuals to being around more professionally career-minded criminals, predators who got pure satisfaction out of preying on the public. As he began to get comfortable in this new lifestyle, he started using dope on a regular basis.

Soon, Bob was so deep into the world of drugs around him that he started selling it and running drugs for his new friends on the side. People started calling him 'Cowboy Bob,' the good ole boy who knew how to get his hands on all kinds of dope. Many times, he could be found at a party, standing by a fire pit made from an old rusted-out metal barrel, offering dope to anyone willing to pay for it. Roping and doping were his new thing, and if he didn't have any drugs on him at a given moment, he certainly knew how to get his hands on some.

Edwards racked up a pretty hefty rap sheet within a two-year time period. His charges ranged from cattle theft to burglary of a habitation. He was convicted in March 1986 in Nacogdoches County, and again in November of the same year in Jasper County. A couple of years later in April 1988, he was convicted, again for burglary of habitation in Brazoria County. It's not clear how much time he served in the big house for the crimes he committed, but sometime after committing them, he fell in with Bob.[1]

By April 1989, Bob had moved on from his father's ranch in Brazoria County, and was managing a ranch that ran mostly heifers located close to the town of Bryan. A young woman named Sharon, who worked as a sales representative for a local feed store was asked to call on the ranch that Bob worked for. The first time she made a sales call to the ranch and met Bob, he was very friendly and outgoing towards her. Through their working relationship, they became fast friends.[2]

Over the next couple of months, she asked Bob if he would board one of her horses for her, because it was not getting any exercise and she wanted to keep the horse active. Bob agreed to do so, and she delivered the horse over to his trailer house, so he could ride it for her. On a few occasions, he asked if he could borrow the horse for his own use and she agreed that he could.[3]

Bob was told to leave the ranch that he was managing in Bryan because—shades of old times--his employer discovered that Bob was stealing cattle from him. The man did not press any charges against Bob, rather he told him to get his stuff and get off the property immediately. (B. Davis, personal communication, Apr. 13, 2013)

In turn, Bob went to work as a ranch hand at yet another ranch located just outside of Chilton, located twenty-six miles south of Waco for a man named Bob Davis. Bob stayed in a trailer house in Bruceville-Eddy located approximately thirteen miles west of the Chilton area.

Davis was a respected and well-liked cattleman and remains a dear friend to the Leach family to this day. He knew Bob since childhood, and oftentimes referred to him as "Son," a fond childhood name given to Bob during his younger days while growing up on the ranch, alongside his dad and the rest of the hands.

Every time Bob got into trouble and needed a place to work, Davis always hired and re-hired Bob to work on his ranch. Despite his criminal bent, Bob was a good worker, and Davis knew that, and hoped steady work might keep him out of mischief. He was able to keep Bob busy running cattle, vaccinating and branding them, so much so that Bob didn't have time to think about getting into any trouble. There was no doubt that Bob knew what he was doing when he was working on the ranch, but once he set foot off of the property, it was anybody's guess what he was up to.

Harvey Glenn Edwards, Bob's badass running buddy from Brazoria County, was also afforded employment at the ranch as a hired hand. But no one would know, until a few days later that Edwards' days were numbered by his own dirty doings.

The thugs that Bob started hanging out with started showing up at his work and demanding to see him, trying to pull him off his job. The problem was, they were not allowed on the property, so could only get as far as the front gate when they were told to leave. They did, but it didn't stop them from always making an appearance and letting it known that when he got off of work, they expected to see him. They might not have had access to Bob while he was working on the ranch during the daytime, but they always made their presence known the second he set foot off of it.

It wasn't too long after Bob had agreed to board Sharon's horse in Bryan that he asked her if she would loan him $3,000, and she willingly agreed. He was doing her a favor by exercising her horse for her, so she thought nothing of it when he asked if he could borrow some money. She thought since he was helping her out she would do the same for him, so she gave it to him.

Because Sharon was a sales rep for a local feed company, part of her job description was to travel to various ranches in an assigned area. When Bob moved back to work on the ranch at Chilton, Sharon was able to stay in touch with him, because she also called on the ranch where he was employed.

Sometime in early October, she met with Bob to get reimbursed and retrieve her horse. When she drove out to his trailer house, she was pulling her gooseneck trailer, because she intended on taking her horse back with her, but as it happened, the horse wasn't on the premises. Bob explained to her that he was keeping her horse at his cousin's house located somewhere in Coryell County.

Not only that, Bob didn't have the money he'd borrowed.

But he promised he would get it and pay her back soon. She decided to leave her trailer at Bob's, so she didn't have to keep loading it up and taking it with her each time she went to meet him.

Over the course of the next few weeks, they spoke several more times about settling their business. Bob told her that he would meet her at his house again to give her the money that he owed her, and she could follow him to his cousin's house to get her horse.

At about 10:30 p.m. on October 30, she went to Bob's trailer house located in Bruceville-Eddy to meet him. When she arrived, she backed her truck up to her gooseneck trailer and got out. She went inside the trailer to look for Bob, where she saw Edwards sleeping in a recliner and she woke him. She asked Edwards if Bob was there and he told her no. Confused as to why he wasn't, she asked Edwards if she could use the bathroom. When she came out of the bathroom, she saw the door to Bob's bedroom was closed. She thought it was strange that the door was closed, especially since Edwards had just informed her that Bob was not there. Rather than going back outside to wait for Bob, she opened the door to his bedroom and went inside. She walked over to where the bed was at and pulled the covers back where she discovered Bob was sleeping. She woke him and went back outside to hook up her gooseneck trailer to the back of her truck.[4]

After she finished, she went back inside the house to get Bob. As he got dressed, he told her that someone owed him $10,000, and when he went to get his money, it wasn't where it was supposed to be. He also told her that he didn't know if he was going to live or die. Then he told her about someone putting snakes in a car. He wasn't making any sense. Was he high?

As he continued to ramble on, not going into details

about what he meant, or who it was that he feared was after him, she was beginning to wonder just what in the hell was really going on. The more he spoke the less sense he made. She was there for one reason and one reason only, to get her horse and money. That was it.

She began to feel uncomfortable, especially after catching Bob and this Edwards guy in a lie, for whatever reason she didn't know. She tried to change the subject, so she asked Bob if they could leave to get her horse.

He told her to look in the living room to see if Glenn was asleep, so they could sneak past him to go outside. Realizing that Edwards was still asleep, Bob made his way into the kitchen to fix a drink, and then he and Sharon went outside.

Bob had told her that her horse was at his cousin's house in Coryell County, approximately 30 miles away.

In short, he did not have the cash that he owed her. He told her that since they were going to Gatesville to get her horse anyway, they could stop for him to get her money, since they were going to be in the area. She was starting to get pissed, but she agreed to make the journey.

Another lie, of course the horse was not in Coryell County as Bob had told her. (Bob had actually given her horse to his boss as a repayment for the man's cattle that he had stolen. Once it was discovered what had happened with her horse, the gentleman returned Sharon's horse back to her.)[5]

It was originally supposed to be only her and Bob that went to get her horse that night, along with the money that he promised her, but somehow Edwards wound up going along for the ride. Bob explained that he would have Edwards ride with him to Gatesville, and after Bob helped her get her horse and money, Edwards could drop Bob off at a family member's house in Gatesville to stay for a day or so. Then, Edwards would drive Bob's truck back to his trailer house located in Bruceville-Eddy, while Bob stayed with his family in Gatesville. It was the middle of the night, and things were getting really confusing real fast.

Not only that, she noticed when Edwards started milling around outside that he reeked of liquor. And not the expensive kind either. He wasn't drunk but he wasn't far from it, which explained why he was three sheets to the wind when she first showed up.

She got into her truck and Bob and Edwards got into theirs, and with her trailer hooked up to the back of her truck, she followed Bob and Edwards to Gatesville, in Coryell County, located approximately forty-one miles northwest of the tiny twin Central Texas towns of Bruceville-Eddy.

Things didn't seem quite right, because along the route, Edwards and Bob pulled over several times, claiming that they were lost and that they missed their turn-off, both acting as if they didn't recognize where they were going.

After pulling over on the side of the road yet again, everyone got out of their trucks and Edwards and Bob approached Sharon. She became acutely aware that she was alone with two strange men in the middle of nowhere.

Her fears were well-founded. Edwards put a gun to her head, and he and Bob repeatedly told her to shut up, calling her a stupid bitch. She claimed that at one time Bob even held the gun on her.

Everything was happening so fast, and she was in such a state of shock from their actions.

Edwards told her to get in the back of her horse trailer, telling her to sit down. She refused, saying she hauled cattle in the trailer and didn't want to sit in the animal waste. She heard the pair talking in low tones, as if they were devising what their next move would be. And with Edwards' gun still pointed at her, Bob tied her hands behind her back. Then one of them placed a piece of duct tape over her mouth. Edwards told Bob to put her in Bob's truck, and then he yelled at Bob to get in her truck.[6]

Bob took off, and a short time later, Edwards got into Bob's truck with Sharon and sped out onto the paved road. It seems everyone, including Bob, was headed in the same direction. As they approached the main intersection, Edwards and Bob pulled over by FM 215 and the loop to get out and talk, leaving Sharon crouched in the floorboard of the truck. Then a few minutes later, Edwards got back in the truck with Sharon and drove onto the loop off 84 heading towards Waco, and Bob drove in the opposite direction heading towards Gatesville.[7]

Somewhere along Hwy 84, Edwards pulled over on the side of the road and placed tape over Sharon's eyes, to prevent her from being able to see where they were going; threatening and taunting her the whole way.[8]

She was able to figure out where they were at by the turns in the road. When they came upon three sets of railroad tracks located just outside of Bruceville-Eddy, she realized they were headed in the same direction of Bob's trailer house.

Once back at Bob's trailer, Edwards held her hostage for four days, terrorizing and sexually assaulting her, while she remained blindfolded the whole time. It's not clear where Bob went after he and Edwards parted ways outside of Gatesville, but Sharon stated that when she and Edwards got back to Bob's trailer that first night, someone else showed up shortly after them to speak to Edwards. She could hear their muffled voices but was unable to make out what they were saying.[9]

At the time, she was unable to identify the second person because she was blindfolded; however, she was able to see some things when her blindfold would occasionally move.

Her hands were tied behind her back during the days-long

assault, which prevented her from moving. She was terrified to even *try* to move for fear of what Edwards would do to her.

Edwards continued to terrorize her the whole time he held her captive, probing her with questions about Bob, demanding to know his whereabouts. Then he asked her how well she knew him. And to make the twisted charade even more bizarre, Edwards threw in that Bob had better hustle to get money together if she was going to live.

The next morning, Edwards told her that he was going to be gone for the day, but not to worry because his friend would be there with her, in case she needed anything, like food or water. She was told by Edwards that his friend was not to talk to her and she was not to speak to them either, and he told her that his friend would not hurt her. She was not to ask them any questions or acknowledge them in any way, unless she needed something. In other words, no talking was allowed.[10]

As soon as Sharon heard Edwards' truck drive off, she sat up and leaned against the window. She had sensed that Edwards friend was there, that there was another person in the room with her and she stated that she felt it was Bob, but she wasn't able to see him clearly enough because of the blindfold Edwards had placed over her eyes.

Edwards' friend placed a pillowcase over Sharon's head and then taped it shut. She and Edwards' friend remained in the trailer with the television on in the background, giving Sharon an idea of what time a day it was by the programs that were playing. Meanwhile, the 'friend' was nervously pacing the floor waiting for Edwards to return.[11]

Edwards was going about his business as if nothing had happened. He showed up to work at the ranch on time and stayed until the work was done, which was usually around sundown. Then he would get back in his truck and make the thirteen mile trek back to Bob's trailer for more criminal mischief. Nobody at the ranch knew that Sharon had been abducted, or that she was being held against her will in Bob's trailer. It would be several days later before anyone would know the extent of torture that Sharon endured in Bob's tiny little trailer in Bruceville-Eddy. (B. Davis, personal communication, Apr. 13, 2013)

On the second day that she was held captive, Edwards and the other individual in the room moved the terrorized and violated young woman from Bob's trailer house in Bruceville-Eddy to an Econo Lodge Motel room located in Abilene, approximately 180 miles northwest. She remained in the motel room for two more days, while Edwards continued to sexually assault her.

Sharon awoke in the middle of the night to swelling and sharp pains in her arms and hands from the tape that had been placed on her wrists. She woke Edwards, who happened to be sleeping next to her, to ask him if he would un-tape her hands. He did and they fell back asleep.

It wasn't until the third day that Sharon was able to make out who the other individual was that was in the room with her and Edwards.

The next morning when she awoke, with her hands and legs free, she heard the individual get up and move around. She saw underneath her blindfold, the man who she had suspected all along, make his way into the bathroom to get dressed and leave the room. It was Bob. Edwards' partner in crime, the one she couldn't ask any questions to and had to remain silent around was Bob.[12]

Neither he nor Edwards knew that she was awake, or that she could see what was going on around her.

Bob seemed to come and go. He would randomly show up at different times per Edward's request, to get food and watch Sharon when Edwards wanted to step away for a break of some sort.

When Bob left the room, Edward's would make off-handed remarks about him to Sharon, telling her that she better hope that Bob was able to get her out of this mess and pay his debt, or she and Bob would both be killed. Then he would follow up with comments about the mob coming to kill her or Bob, if he wasn't able to make things right.[13]

At times, it seemed as if Edwards was talking gibberish, because none of what he said made any sense. Why was Edwards torturing her, and more importantly why was Bob allowing it to go on?

Later that afternoon, on the third day, Edwards told Sharon that he realized she was an innocent victim in all this, and he had decided to let her live.[14]

Everything out of Edwards' mouth was frightening. Not only had he abducted and assaulted her, now he was trying to scare her even more. And the more he spoke the more bizarre the story got.

Edwards told her that the mob that Bob was mixed up with wanted them to kill her. He told her that Bob had a friend who had a newspaper who would print her obituary on special paper, so that when they got back to Waco, he could show the paper to the real guys who wanted her dead as proof that he had carried out their wishes. Then Edwards told her that if she went to the law to turn them in, Edwards himself would know how to find her and get her in the back when she least expected it.

Later that night, Edwards removed the tape from her eyes and told her that he and his friend were going to talk to Bob's mother-in-law. They were going for one reason and one reason only; to convince her that Bob was in real trouble and to see if she could help with getting Bob's wife off his back.

Edwards left Sharon in the motel room chained to the bed while he and his buddy went to have a few words with Bob's mother-in-law.

Bob's mother-in-law was also being held against her will at the same Econo Lodge Motel, two doors down from where Sharon had been. Though the details about her abduction are not clear, there are some similarities between the two events. According to police records, Bob's mother-in-law was abducted on Nov. 2 and she too had also been abducted by Edwards and another individual. She did not, however, see the face of Edwards 'partner-in-crime, but claimed that there were things about the other person that were very familiar to her, just as they were to her fellow female victim. She was, however, able to identify Edwards in a lineup.

Bob's mother-in-law had known Bob well enough to recognize his mannerisms and she believed that it was Bob who was helping Edwards in her abduction. Though the details are limited on how and when exactly it was that she got away, she, like Sharon, also managed to escape on November 2 to report the incident to authorities.

According to Sharon's statement, on the fourth and final day, November 2, Edwards had decided to let her go and she was finally able to escape, though her statement does not go into detail about how that happened.

The plan was that Edwards and Sharon would drop Edwards' friend off to get their car, and Edwards and Sharon would drive back to Waco in her truck on their own. Once they got back to Waco, Edwards told her that when he got to his truck she was free to go.

Later that evening, Edwards told her there was a problem. Because Sharon had been missing for four days, her family was concerned, and rightfully so. Sharon's mother had contacted the authorities to report her daughter missing. They in turn put out an APB on Sharon that went from San Antonio all the way to San Angelo; law enforcement was looking for her over half of Texas.

Edwards began to panic because everything was beginning

to fall apart. And it looked like he wasn't going to get out of this without getting caught.

Sharon was able to convince him that they could still leave and he could let her go once they got back to Waco, but they needed a new plan. She told him that they could ditch her truck and trailer in a remote area and then she could rent a car for him to drive them back to Waco. It would keep them from being recognized by the cops and once they got back to Waco, she could take him to his truck and then he could let her go, like they originally planned. It's not clear why Sharon helped Edwards come up with a new plan though, especially since he had kidnapped and raped her, but according to her, that's what happened.

She was able to rent a car for Edwards at the airport and they both got into the car together, but that's where her statement ends. According to court records, Edwards released her in an unidentified safe area where she was unharmed.

On the same day that both women were able to escape, Bob was caught with a handgun. That put him in violation of his probation from Erath County.

Bob was charged with aggravated kidnapping and unauthorized use of a motor vehicle, in the case of Sharon's abduction.

The charges in Coryell County stuck. The ones in Callahan County were dropped, because Bob's mother-in-law could not positively identify him as a party in her abduction. On April 26, 1990, the *Cross Plains Review* paper, in Callahan County, had a short write up about his charges. Under the section titled "Courthouse News" the charges against Bob in Callahan County were dropped, due to insufficient evidence. [15]

Edwards was charged with aggravated sexual assault and kidnapping with a deadly weapon for the Coryell County abduction and rape of Sharon, and charged with aggravated kidnapping with a deadly weapon in Callahan County in the case of Bob's mother-in-law.

Both Edwards and Bob were taken into custody to see a judge in connection with violating their probation. Edwards was taken to Coryell County Jail in Gatesville for outstanding warrants, while Bob was taken to the Callahan County Jail in Baird to be booked and await his arraignment in front of a judge.

Chapter Ten

ESCAPED! THE CALLAHAN COUNTY JAILBREAK

Six months later, while awaiting his court date, in the early morning hours on a storm-tossed April 25, 1990, Bob brazenly escaped the old two-story redbrick jail by running out of the building down a set of metal stairs from the second floor leading to the backside of the jail.

Sometime previously, after the last headcount of the night, in the late hours of April 24, as all the other inmates were settling down to sleep, Bob began busying himself by plying a smuggled saw blade against his cell door. He managed to steadily grind through the rusted metal, something he had been working on for close to three weeks now. He broke the bars apart from one another and crept past the guards to get outside.

According to records from the Callahan County Jail, the blade that Bob used was smuggled in to him during a visit at the jail on April 5, 1990, twenty days prior to the jailbreak, by Richard Calvin Lee, a fellow criminal whom Bob had met before violating his probation. During one of Lee's visits, he provided Bob the saw blade, along with detailed instructions that he would be waiting in his truck outside the jail to rendezvous once Bob was able to break free.1

Nervously trying to balance stealth with speed, Bob made his way down the street to the red and white 1989 Ford pickup where Lee was waiting to spirit him away.[2]

Whatever hour of the day or night, Lee's appearance always remained the same, with an unkempt mustache spread across his upper lip, a protruding double chin, black scraggly windblown hair and wearing the same oversized dark sunglasses, even in the middle of the night. Even in the middle of a jailbreak, he still looked like an unmade bed.

Standing 5'6", weighing only 180 lbs. dripping wet, and his hair perpetually disheveled, he gave the impression that he didn't care what others thought about him. On any given day, it was anybody's guess whether he bothered to shower before going out to greet the day. But Bob hadn't fallen in with him for his hygiene or fashion sense.

After Bob spotted the red and white Ford parked less than a block away, on the opposite side of the street from the jail, he quickly ran over and climbed inside.

According to the National Weather Service, under *This Day in Weather History*, 1990, https://www.weather.gov/abr. This_Day_in_Weather_History_Apr_25, meteorologists were nervously tracking a massive system of spring storms traveling from Nebraska to Texas, a system that ultimately spawned fifteen tornadoes in its path. One of the tornadoes was spotted outside of Weatherford, just west of Fort Worth, and quickly exploded into an F4, which the Fujita Scale ranked as one of the most destructive tornadoes measurable. Other parts of Texas had golf ball-sized hail with wind gusts up to 112 mph and some areas had 18 inches of rain. People were urged to stay indoors and those that lived in low-lying areas were advised to seek higher ground. The damage from the catastrophic storms caused 65 million dollars in damage due to flooding. Even Texans hardened to the peril of spring-time tornados blanched at the destruction.[3]

In the middle of the night, with treacherous storms all around, it was a perfect setup for a jailbreak. As the thunder boomed overhead, Bob and Richard Lee drove down Hwy. 20 eastbound on a three-hour trip, eventually landing Bob in Dallas. Considering it was the middle of the night, the distraction of the storms and tornadoes had served Bob well.

(For anonymity reasons and fear of retaliation from Lee, the person who came forward to share with the author what they know about the morning that Bob broke out of the Callahan County Jail's name is being withheld.)

Lee stopped to make a phone call somewhere along the way. The conversation that he had with the individual on the other end of the line was short, but to the point. Lee instructed the individual to meet him at a Waffle House located in the Dallas area sometime around 4:00 a.m. (Interview with confidential source, private communication, Feb. 12, 1991)

Lee had been an accessory to a crime. He was the one who enabled Bob to break himself out of jail by providing him the very saw blade to do it with. He was the one who picked Bob up and drove off into the night, and now he was looking for a safe place to hide Bob. But it had to be somewhere that the authorities weren't smart enough to look. Where, oh where could he go?

Bob, on the other hand, had no idea who Lee was calling or what was said, but after the call was made, Lee got back in the truck and the two continued to drive towards Dallas.

Sometime around 4:00 a.m., Lee went inside a local Waffle House to speak to the very individual he called just hours before. Lee sat down in a booth and got right to the point. Lee said he wanted to find a safe place for Bob to stay until he could get back to pick him up.

In short, Lee was expecting this individual to open up their home for a fugitive on the run from the law.

The individual, a criminal himself, just might have been a little more inclined to help Lee out, had his buddy not been harboring a fugitive who just broke out of a county jail less than a hundred miles away. Thanks, but no thanks, said Mr. Waffle House.

Bob once again had no idea who it was that Lee was going to see and he never saw the individual that Lee met with inside the Waffle House. Bob remained in the truck waiting on Lee the whole time. A little while later, Lee came back out to the truck, looking like things weren't going the way he planned, and he and Bob took off.

Bob was almost 100 miles away from his jail cell before anyone noticed he was gone. Law enforcement started interrogating everybody that was connected to Bob – from his family and friends to his hardened foes, to try to pinpoint his whereabouts. Authorities were desperate to find him so they could haul his ass back to the county jail. It wasn't until they received a tip from one of Lee's old running buddies, and Bob's most recent sidekick, Harvey Glenn Edwards, about Lee's involvement in the jailbreak.

Suddenly, the tables were beginning to turn on Lee, and now his 'ol buddy Edwards was rambling at the mouth to the law.

According to notes taken by one of the lead investigators in the case, Edwards stated that Lee was the one who smuggled in a saw blade to Bob three weeks prior to the jailbreak during one of their visits. Lee gave Bob specific instructions to meet him outside the jail, where he would be waiting in his truck to carry Bob off.

According to Edwards, Lee wanted Bob out of jail, no ifs and or buts about it, because Lee had some unfinished business with Bob that needed to be settled. Edwards did not go into detail about what Lee had on his mind, or what kind of business he wanted to settle with Bob, but the message was clear: Nine out of ten when Lee wanted something, he got it and this was one of those times. That's how Lee rolled.

If it hadn't been for public court records and a few key pieces of anonymously-provided information about the night Bob broke out of the Callahan County Jail, no one would have ever known the extent Lee went to in breaking Bob out of jail, much less that he was even involved in the escape at all. More importantly, no one would have known that Edwards was telling the tale on Lee.

Once authorities realized Bob had escaped, a blue warrant was issued for his arrest, notifying law enforcement to be on the lookout for a red and white 1989 Ford pickup truck with a Texas license plate registered to a Richard Calvin Lee.[4]

Though it took authorities some time to locate Bob, they finally did so in the small town of China Springs, twelve miles northwest of Waco. They discovered Bob at a family member's house, fast asleep in one of the bedrooms. He awoke to the sight of a SWAT team surrounding the house and invading his bedroom. And they had their guns pointed directly at him. Law enforcement had come for him, and they weren't going anywhere without him.

Bob surrendered and was taken into custody in Coryell County for pending charges of aggravated kidnapping, unlawful use of a motor vehicle and escaping the Callahan County Jail.

In short order, a trial was scheduled, and he met with the judge. He was ultimately sentenced to ten years for unauthorized use of a motor vehicle and twelve years for kidnapping Sharon, his female victim in Coryell County, and ten years for escape in Callahan County. His sentences were to run concurrently. Bob was promptly packed off to TDC to serve out his sentence.[5]

The raggedy-assed accomplice who smuggled the blade in for Bob to use in his escape was charged with facilitating the escape. However, his charges were dismissed, leaving many questions unanswered as to why he was not convicted and carted off to the Big House for his part in the escape.

The same individual that Lee leaned on for a favor the morning that Bob escaped the Callahan County Jail stepped forward with more alarming information, so alarming in fact that it raised many questions surrounding the abduction of Sharon and Bob's mother-in-law.

According to the witness statement, seven months prior to the abduction of Sharon and Bob's mother-in-law, Lee contacted this individual, wanting the two of them to do a job that matched the very description of what Bob was accused of committing. (Interview with confidential source, private communication, Feb. 12, 1991)

The witness claimed that Lee's exact words were that he wanted to "take care of" Bob, his wife and their young child right away, and someone would be hurt in the process. The individual left out details about exactly what kind of job Lee wanted done and he quickly turned Lee down. In fact, the witness had not heard from Lee again until Lee called the individual for an early morning meeting at the Waffle House, but with a statement like that, and the type of work the individual had done for Lee in the past, it was evident to them that Lee had it out for Bob.

Though the details are limited about what it was that Lee was asking for when he reached out to this person about a job, the witness stated that they realized after seeing a picture of Bob on the news in November 1989, that Lee had found someone else to do the very job that he was asking this person to do instead.

It's not clear what the job was or just what exactly it entailed, or who the person was that was hired to do the job, possibly Harvey Glenn Edwards, but the witness clearly stated after seeing Bob's picture on the news, and from what Lee was asking this individual to do, they felt compelled to come forward with this information. Lee, surmising the witness, had found someone else to complete the job.

Was Lee trying to extort Bob into doing something for him, or did Lee have other intentions behind his threats? The individual called upon to help Lee fulfill the job adamantly refused to be a part of what Lee was asking and had not heard from Lee again until the morning Bob had escaped the Callahan County Jail.

Questions regarding Lee's involvement in the abduction of the two women who were kidnapped by Edwards and Bob still remain today. Who all besides Bob and Edwards was involved in the abductions, if anyone? Was there a connection between the two abductions of the women and Lee? And why was Lee reaching out to other individuals for help about a job that had to do with Bob and his family? More importantly, what unfinished business did Lee have with Bob that he believed Bob owed him for? These questions still remain today.

Nothing more came of it and no charges ever brought against Lee regarding the abductions, but his actions the night Bob escaped the Callahan County Jail, along with his threats to others raised a lot of eyebrows. (Interview with confidential source, private communication, Feb. 12, 1991; Interview with confidential source, private communication, July 10, 2015; Interview with confidential source, private communication, Oct. 8, 2015)

Information surrounding Lee's charges for facilitating the escape in Callahan County were later dismissed and most of the records have been destroyed, all but a few pieces of evidence that were later found in a file and turned over to the authorities, once again, for a second review during the research of this book.

Instead of serving time for his crimes, Lee managed to walk away a free man. Bob, for his part, was back where he started—behind bars and stacking time.

Chapter Eleven

BOB MEETS TAMI

Bob was serving out his sentence at the W.F. Ramsey unit in Rosharon, south of Houston. During the fall months, his days at the prison were spent working with the horses which were kept at the unit as he helped prepare for horse shows that were put on by prison staff at the unit. College students would attend the events to judge the horses.

Even given his experience with horses, Bob occasionally got bucked off while attempting to break the wild animals in order to make them rideable. In one instance, the horse that Bob was working with flipped him, throwing him up into the air, causing him to land on his backside. Fortunately, he walked away without any broken bones, but he was mightily sore the next day. "Never a horse that couldn't be rode, never a cowboy that couldn't be throwed," as the saying went.

One evening, after coming in from working with the horses, Bob was settling into his bunk, when another inmate named Kenneth approached him.

Kenneth was a rough character with a long rap sheet ranging from larceny and drug possession, to domestic abuse with bodily injury, and he was well known for making terror-istic threats against his family. He'd get pure-dee satisfaction out of beating the hell out of each and every one of them. He was meaner than a pit bull on crack. In addition, he'd managed to turn drinking into an art form by racking up numerous charges of drunkenness and DWIs. In his own mind, he was a pillar of his own community. To just about everyone else, he was one sick fuck. (Interview with confidential source, private communication, June 19, 2018)

Kenneth had a habit of living life on the edge, devoid of remorse. He was not someone to be messed with and was regarded as such. His reputation preceded him as a renowned thug, but he had so far managed to abate serious prison time, serving minimal hours in the county jail, all the while paying court appointed fines for the majority of his more heinous mischief. But it was only a matter of time before he ended up behind bars in the state prison system, and that's just where Bob met him, at the W.F. Ramsey unit in Rosharon.

He looked like the rough customer he was. His neck was as wide around as a hundred-year-old Texas oak tree and he was as stout as one too, at 6'1" and 240 lbs. The irises of his eyes were a lighter shade of green than most, his hair was short and choppy, with hints of strawberry blonde, and his skin was rougher than dried-out leather.

His drug-induced days of backroom brawling and nights of ass-whippings during his rough honky-tonking combined to make him look a lot older than he actually was.

Kenneth was several years older than Bob and it showed. He bore a scar above his upper right lip, undoubtedly from a fight, and another well-hidden one on his upper right arm, not to mention all the visible ones he had on his forearms.

Kenneth was tied to the rougher crowd of folks that Bob had been mixed up with before he landed in prison, so

Kenneth was very familiar with Richard Calvin Lee, Bob's old criminal crony. However, Bob did not know that Kenneth and Lee were buddies when he first came in contact with Kenneth. (Interview with confidential source, private communication, June 19, 2018)

Most of Lee's close compadres had a record, which meant they had all done a little time in the pen, everybody except for Lee that is.

Kenneth handed Bob a picture that was taken ten months earlier of a woman at a New Year's Eve party in 1990. Bob was intrigued. He hadn't touched a woman in months, so the picture got a reaction out of him. The woman's name was Tami Dawn Holland.[1]

As Kenneth held the picture out for Bob to look at, he told him, "This is somebody I think you ought to write to while you're waiting to get out. She's really heavy into the party scene, you can't fault a gal for liking something like that, and she might be a little faster pace than what you're used to, but I think she just might be the change you need. If you can keep up, that is. Weren't most of the women you were around before you ended up here the 'stay at home' kind of gals? They cook your dinner, mind their manners and have everything ready for you type of women? Maybe what you need is an exciting kind of gal, one that makes you cook your own damn meals, and who doesn't mind hanging from the rafters buck-ass naked when the lights go out while the party's still going on. You better give this one a chance before somebody else hops on her. She'll do more than just hang from the rafters and ding your bell if you know what I mean. I think you're going to like her." (Interview with confidential source, private communication, June 19, 2018)

Bob shook his head, "No, man, I'm not looking for any kind of a relationship right now. I got divorced while I was in here and that just about killed me. I'm still trying to get over that. Man, I don't want to go through that again. I'm just trying to keep my head down, so I can get out of here and get my life back together. I just want to start over."

"Hell, boy, I'm not telling you to propose to her! I'm just saying, write her a letter and ask her how she's doin'. Maybe what you need is a change from what you're used to being around. She's different from the other types of women you're used to. She's the real independent type and she's got her own job, a fancy little car with some badass shit under the hood, a little college degree, man she's got it all. She doesn't need a man, but she's obviously looking for one. Hell, boy, she's probably got a vibrator tucked away for nights just like this. A gal like that, looking for a guy in prison, she's just lookin' for something a little different than what she can get out there in the free world. Maybe what she's wanting is somebody to sweep her off her feet and make a little love connection! Yeah!" Kenneth roared. "Why not let that be you?"

"What the hell am I going to sweep her off her feet with? Look at where we're at. What the hell is she doin' sending her picture into a prison anyway? A gal like that sending a picture into a prison looking for somebody she doesn't know to write to, it sounds like she's up to something or looking for trouble, to me. How many other men in here have she banged that she's desperate to find another one to latch onto? I'm not interested in hearing from some jailhouse whore. And what is she looking for in here that she can't find out there, anyway? Do you even know who she is?" (Interview with confidential source, private communication, June 19, 2018)

"Well, hell yes, I know who she is. I got this picture from a friend. I can vouch for her, she's alright. And she's not a jailhouse whore, I don't think. Hell you have to be married to do that kind of stuff in here, otherwise they're not gonna let her in here, not without getting it approved first. She's been around the neighborhood a few times, but I always say you can't fault a honey badger no matter how mean they get for wanting more than what they've already got, and you shouldn't either. You can't tell me you don't think she's attractive. Look at all that blonde hair sticking out everywhere. She looks like she's having a good time, just look at her. Look, just write her a damn letter and ask her how she's doin'. If you don't like her response, then you don't have to write her back. Just take a chance and see what comes of it. Hell, boy, you never know."

Bob nodded his head and told Kenneth to give him a few days to think it over. Bob didn't know what to say to this woman. Besides, he was still dealing with things from his past and trying like hell to get away from them. He had to admit, though, that he was around a rougher crowd of people than he had ever been around before.

And his addiction to drugs didn't help matters either. He had to admit that he could snort and smoke dope with the best of them, maybe even better than anybody else he knew. He sure enjoyed it. But look at where it had gotten him.

He'd fallen prey to addiction right after he left Comanche County. If the truth be told, it might have been while he was trying to leave Comanche County. He could have been his own best customer if he had enough money to cover his costs. Nonetheless, he loved it anyway.

He didn't want to have to explain any of that to somebody new, especially while he was in prison. Plus, Lee continued to write to Bob while he was at the Ramsey unit. And he wasn't writing to see if Bob needed anything or if he was doing okay, either. There was nothing friendly about his letters.

Every letter Lee mailed to Bob was filled with threats, telling him that he and Sharon, the woman he had abducted, had better keep their mouths shut or somebody was going to get hurt. The details were sketchy, but Lee's letters conveyed unmistakable menace to Bob. (Interview with confidential source, private communication, June 19, 2018).[2]

Bob wasn't the only one who saw Lee's threatening letters. It wasn't uncommon for another offender to receive the wrong mail by mistake. And by the time the wrong recipient that received the mail got halfway through the first page of the letter, they'd look at the back of the envelope to see who was threatening them, because somebody somewhere was about to get more than a fist in the face. (Interview with confidential source, private communication, Aug. 11, 2018).

Then the offender would notice the letter was addressed to Bob Leach and hesitantly pass it over to him. One of the offenders, who happened to get one of the menacing letters by mistake, asked Bob if everything was okay. "Do you need a little help there, Bob?" the fellow inmate asked. "What's going on?" the man asked.

Bob just looked at him and shook his head, and walked away. What could he say? He tried to get help from people on the outside, help from those who should have been able to assist him with the threats, but for some reason or other, they either didn't want to get involved or it didn't seem important to them. And Bob was desperately in need of help. (Interview with confidential source, private communication, Aug. 11, 2018).

Bob told his attorney, Sandy Gately, what was going on. He even showed her the letters, but nothing seemed to come from that. He contacted the District Attorney of Coryell County, Phillip Zeigler to see if he could help, but to no avail. Then, he reached out to Zeigler's deputy, District Attorney Investigator, Joe Bard, but still nothing happened.[3]

No matter how many letters Bob received from Lee, it

was becoming clear that the man was scared that Bob and his lady friend might start to talk, and from the sounds of it, Lee did not want that at all. It was beginning to look a lot like Lee was going to great lengths to cover any and all of his tracks, even with the people he talked to about doing a "job" for him.

It was beginning to look like Lee's ass had fallen into a big crack and he was trying like hell to pull it out. Lee was a realist when it came to looking in the mirror. He was fully aware that he was a shady character, but it didn't stop him from being one. In fact, he thrived on it. Sometimes, it was believed he even got off on it. But the fact remained, he just didn't want those who didn't know him personally to find out about that aspect of his character from somebody else. He wanted to keep something like that under wraps. First impressions, to him, were always the most important.

Apparently, Bob wasn't the only one that was warned to keep his mouth shut. He was, however, the only one to receive the threats in writing. Lee delivered his other threats verbally. He wanted to be sure they were received loud and clear. (Interview with confidential source, private communication, June 19, 2018)

It was a measure of his desperation that Lee implicated himself in his own handwriting in those letters to Bob, by using his own words, and it appeared that he was not smart enough to figure that out.[4]

Bob was overwhelmed with threatening innuendos and haunting interludes from his past. Not only did he not know how to handle them, but he didn't know what his real-life outcome would be from one minute to the next. He was just trying to figure everything out, and he wasn't getting any help from the outside world.

Meanwhile, he certainly didn't know what to say in a letter to some gal who was passing her picture around inside a prison, apparently desperate to find a man to write to. (Interview with confidential source, private communication, June 19, 2018) He kept wondering why a woman like that would want to correspond with a complete stranger in jail. He wasn't going to tell any of this to this woman, of course. But the fact of the matter was, he didn't know what to say to her.

Bob was dealing with some dangerous people who were still contacting him, and they made it perfectly clear that they weren't going anywhere, not anytime soon. And that they weren't done with him, just yet, no matter how much he wanted to distance himself from them.

The evenings at the Ramsey unit were quiet though, so much so that during those times of solitude, as Bob sat on his bunk, he began to realize what he missed the most was female companionship. There was something about the emotional bond, the human connection with someone who was willing to get to know him on a personal level, and more importantly, someone that simply wanted to know about his day.

It would be nice to have something that simple and basic, or even just to receive letters from someone who was interested in him, somebody to think about building a future with, but Bob was honest enough with himself to know that you can't meet anybody like that while wearing a pair of handcuffs and sitting behind metal bars.

He didn't even know how to explain any of this stuff to anyone in person, let alone writing it in a letter, because who would believe any of it anyway, or much less want to be involved with someone like himself? In his mind, starting a new relationship with someone while he was in prison just wasn't possible. He couldn't even find anyone on the outside to help him with the threats he was receiving from Lee, so how was a relationship behind bars ever going to work? And a two-hour visit with thick glass between the two of you is no way to get to know somebody. It would be awkward, to say the least.

Bob was ready for a change, though. He wanted to get his life back on track and get as far away as possible from the rough characters that had defined his life up till now. Then there was the reality of starting a relationship after having two failed marriages—one of which he was only just now coming out of. He wanted companionship, but he didn't want to go through the heartbreak of another failed marriage, or a failed relationship of any kind.

Bob saw Tami Dawn Holland's picture in October 1990, and with a very determined Kenneth coaxing him along to write her a letter, Bob finally picked up a pen. Bob thought he would reach out to see if anything came of it, and if it did, then he would figure out what he would say to her to explain as best he could about his past, along with the threats he was receiving from Lee. He wasn't going to get into all that with someone that he had just met, but if he found the right woman, and he hoped someday he would, then he knew he'd have to explain that part of his life to her. How could he possibly keep it a secret?

Maybe, in some small way, writing to this woman would help him to escape the realities of what he was going through.

That letter he wrote to her was the first of many more to come. It was the start of a long and ongoing correspondence between them, and the beginning of a relationship.

The more letters they wrote to one another, the more they began to open up and share their feelings with each other. They wrote about their likes and dislikes on many topics, what their hopes and dreams were for the future and things happening in their daily lives.

He shared with her his memories about growing up around cattle, reminiscing about his childhood, and how he had learned the trade at such a young age. He told her how when he was eight years old he would help his dad and the other ranch hands move cattle into the cattle pens, and he even wrote to her about his first love, the pony named Sugarfoot. He told her how he hoped to someday have his own ranch. He shared with her things as basic and everyday as his favorite sports teams, and things as intimate as his own hopes and dreams. He began to open up to her in ways that he never had with anybody else before.

She shared with him private information about herself, about growing up and going to grade school in Tulsa, Oklahoma, then later moving to Shreveport, Louisiana, where she graduated from Southwood High in 1978.[5]

She had been accepted into college in the backwoods coonass country in Louisiana. Her alumnus was the University of Louisiana in Monroe, where she attended classes after high school and eventually earned her Bachelor of Arts Degree in General Studies in 1982. Louisiana was home to her, and she liked it. She told him about all the jobs she had after graduation that allowed her the opportunity to travel. She shared with him her excitement about water skiing, both during and after college.

She told him about how she enjoyed dancing with her friends in honky-tonks till the early morning hours, and confessed that she did enjoy partying, maybe a little too much. At the same time, she threw in that she'd been saved when she was little, so she knew Jesus and although she believed in going to church, she just didn't always go.

She wrote in great detail about her family. She mentioned her father working for General Motors' ACDelco division, and she talked about her family's ups and downs, divulging the most intimate details about her life and theirs, sharing things with him that she might not have been so inclined to share with others. In a paradoxical way, perhaps the fact that

Bob was behind bars and inaccessible made Tami feel safe to confide in him.

They sent pictures and stories of their families back and forth to one another, as they began to learn more about each other. The more letters they wrote, the more connected they began to feel. Bob's feelings for her grew stronger through each letter and for each one that he had written to her, she sent him two more, sometimes three, to match it. Suddenly, he was becoming inundated with mail by this random woman he had only seen in a picture. But he discovered he looked forward to the letters.

Though they had not yet met face to face, he was beginning to feel a very deep connection to her. He was so comfortable writing to her, that he found it very easy to tell her about anything, without worrying about her passing any judgment on him whatsoever. More and more, with each letter he wrote to her, he felt that he could truly be himself with her and he began to open up even more to her through them each one.

Finally, they made arrangements for her to come visit in person after the Christmas holiday.

Then Tami penned a letter to Bob on the back of a Texas map in mid-December 1990. She had flipped her car during a winter storm while she was traveling between Dallas and Houston. It landed upside down, all four wheels in the air. She managed to walk away from the scene of the accident without a scratch on her.[6]

Her father drove all the way down from Houston to pick her up after that accident, and take her back home with him, so she could spend the holidays with her parents. She assured Bob, nonetheless, that she would be at the unit to see him on December 29. And sure enough, that very morning, bright and early, she was one of the first visitors through the door, all bright smiles. He was nervous about her visit, seeing her for the first time. He was over the moon to be able to finally meet her in person.[7]

The first time Bob saw Tami face to face, he was taken aback. He was nervous and unsure of what he would say to her. As a con man in the cattle racket, the words had always flowed off his tongue, but at this most important encounter, his words threatened to fail him.

He was comfortable expressing his feelings to her through letters and he felt that he could be himself through those, but somehow, meeting her for the first time, he was so nervous that he had butterflies in his stomach. He was almost afraid to speak to her, like a teenager talking to his high school crush for the first time.

Bob wasn't sure what to expect from someone that he'd only become acquainted with through letters, and he didn't know what she expected from him either, but somehow, seeing her in the flesh for the very first time, brought his nerves to the surface in a way he never thought possible. And he wasn't comfortable with the thought of it. No one had ever made him feel the way she had before. All he knew about her was what she had written to him through letters, and the pictures that they shared with one another, nothing else. Who was this woman, really? And what would she make of the real Bob Leach in person?

Bob had no idea that he was meeting a woman that would prove to be more dangerous than anyone he had ever encountered before, and who could pull off more than anything he and Kubiak ever tried to do together, all while getting away with it in the end, just as Kubiak had. She was, in a nutshell, a female version of what Kubiak was; and according to interviews with individuals who witnessed this behavior firsthand and were afraid of being retaliated against by her, they stated she was a well put-together con artist from the get go. But by the time it was discovered who and what she was, it would be too late. (Interview with confidential source, private communication, June 19, 2018)

After she arrived at the prison on that first morning, a prison guard walked him out into the visiting room and placed him on the opposite side of a piece of thick bullet-proof plexi-glass that separated visitors from inmates. Per standard TDC rules, there was no one-on-one contact between them and they weren't able to touch one another or shake hands. But they could see one another and talk.

As Bob entered the small area directly across from her, he sat on a metal barstool that was welded to the bottom of the floor. Just in front of where Bob was sitting, approximately three feet off the ground, was a wooden bench that Bob could lean on or set food on to eat during a visit. She of course could buy him food to eat, but only with change that she brought into the prison that was placed in a baggie. He was unable to go to the vending machines to get the food himself, only she was allowed to do that. Tami sat in a plastic chair directly across from Bob, with an identical wooden bench.

She was a long-legged gal standing 5'10" and built lean. She had a pleasant smile about her and she acted happy to see him. Her hair was shoulder length, like in the picture that Kenneth had shown to him, and it was blonde. Her eyes were brown, just as Bob remembered seeing in the picture. She appeared, at first glance, to be a sweet-spoken individual, hanging on his every word as he spoke, and once he finally managed to start talking, he couldn't stop. At first, he was quiet and nervous about what to say to her because he didn't know what she expected from him, and he was baffled at why he was at such a loss for words. But once he started talking to her, he began to relax.

For the first time in a long time, he slowly began to open up to her, and he told her about things from his past, only bits and pieces though, he didn't want to share too much. But it was more than he had shared with anyone else in a long time.

He told her how he violated his probation by getting caught with a gun, and how he had been involved with the wrong crowd of people. He just didn't tell her they were still reaching out to *him*. He told her that he had been unable to get away from them, no matter how hard he tried, and he did try.

He said that he wanted to change his life, but he didn't know how. He explained to her that everything he had been involved in was what landed him behind bars, and he was not innocent, but he wanted to be able to get out and make a fresh start.

But he spoke in generalities, for the most part. Bob didn't go into great detail with her about everything, because he didn't want to scare her off. He didn't know her and he certainly wasn't going to share every detail about his life with her, but to the extent he did share with her, he opened up to her more than he had to anybody else in a long time. She had a way of making him feel comfortable.

At times, when he stopped and thought about it, it scared him to think about what he had been through, and with the people with whom he had surrounded himself. He didn't know what he could possibly offer this woman, especially given the mess he had got himself into. There were no dates to go on, no way to wine and dine her, or to be able to convince her that he was the one for her.

All he had was an all-too-brief two-hour visit sitting behind a piece of plexiglass to tell his side of things, and he couldn't even tell her the whole story, at least not in a first encounter. He did, however, want to be upfront with her about some of his past dealings, and he shared with her a few things he was comfortable with her knowing, hoping he wouldn't scare her off.

She hung on every word that he said, listening to him as he opened up about his life, and the more that he talked, the more she listened. When he finally stopped talking, she assured him, in a comforting way, that everyone at some point in their life makes mistakes. She told him it's not uncommon for someone to fall into the wrong crowd. She let him know, under no uncertain conditions, that if he really wanted to get away from the people he was trying to avoid, then she would do her best to help him try.

Tami appeared to show deep concern for Bob at that first visit, just as she had through her letters to him, and she acted just as interested in him as he was in her.

She told him that Kenneth, the convict who first showed Bob her picture, had explained to her a little bit about Bob's past, but all in all, he told her, Bob was a good guy. What he did tell her was enough to let her know that she at least wanted to meet and speak to Bob in person.[8]

What Tami failed to mention was how closely connected she was to the same crowd of people that Bob told her he wanted to get and stay away from. She was more than just the dirty little party girl that Kenneth described her to be - she was also one helluva manipulator in a pair of high heel shoes, looking for a man behind bars to cling on to. (Interview with confidential source, private communication, June 19, 2018).

It's not clear how she came in contact with the very crowd of individuals that Bob was trying to get away from, whether it was through her job at EDS from the many private and very exclusive parties they hosted for the most elite executives looking for a swinging good time, or if it was through a mutual acquaintance. But nonetheless, she knew them and she was indeed connected to them. The exact how-when-why is still a matter of speculation. (Interview with confidential source, private communication, June 19, 2018; Interview with confidential source, personal communication, Apr. 13, 2013).

She appeared self-confident and outgoing, certainly not someone who would just randomly give her picture to an ex-con like Kenneth, looking to fix her up.

Nonetheless, Kenneth was the one that encouraged Bob to write to her. She, in turn, gave the impression, though, that she trusted Kenneth fully. Otherwise why would she be sitting in a visiting room with an ex-con she'd never met before?

She allowed Kenneth to share her picture with others. And when she received a letter from Bob in the mail, she acted almost like she was expecting it, perhaps waiting for it to arrive. It's not clear if she was corresponding with other offenders while she was writing to Bob, or if he was the only one, but as quickly as she received his letters, she responded back to him that fast.

9) She told Bob that, yes Kenneth had said that Bob had gotten involved with the wrong crowd, but that was all in the past. She said she wanted to be the one to help Bob move forward with a clean slate, and she assured him she was the woman to do it.

Bob never thought he could feel for any woman the way he felt for Tami. After their first visit, he was so overwhelmed with the realization that he could connect with someone on the level the way that he did with her, let alone be attracted to her. His feelings for her were as unexpected as they were intense, and he had a hard time imagining something like Tami ever happening to him at this point in his life.

Bob truly believed that she had his whole heart, and he was utterly stunned at how close they had become in such a short time by virtue of their letters. Meeting her in person only redoubled Bob's intense fascination.

He never dreamed that someone would take him head over heels, but Tami had done so. He felt an intimacy that far outpaced the simple act of exchanging letters. Her letters were in fact intimate, as she would go on and on about things in her life, and he really enjoyed reading about her experiences. As he sat in his cell reading her letters over and over, he began to feel he was living vicariously through her. She gave him strength when he needed it, while at the same time giving him something to look forward to. Tami made him feel like he had a future again.

Like all good con artists, she had a gift for telling the mark what he wanted most to hear.

After meeting her and talking to her from that first visit, he became completely dumbstruck at the possibility she represented. They'd met through a random acquaintance, in prison of all places, but Bob believed he was truly falling in love with this woman, someone he had only come to know through letters.

Overwhelmed by his feelings, and at how quickly things were moving between him and Tami, Bob wanted somebody to confide in, so he requested to speak to the prison chaplain. He explained to the man how they met, and his concerns about how fast they were moving in their relationship. Bob said he had only known her through her letters, but after meeting her, he felt like he was falling deeply in love with her. He confided that he was even beginning to think about marriage, although he was incarcerated.

The clergyman's response was that Bob would be surprised at the number of offenders who got married while they were incarcerated. He said that it was not uncommon or unheard of for marriages to take place while offenders were incarcerated. In fact, they happened more often than people realized. The clergyman assured Bob that he talked to offenders more often about marriage than others realize.

In the meantime, while Bob was beginning to develop strong feelings for Tami, Lee had backed off of his own threatening notes. Bob had discussed with Tami, without going into specifics, about how much he wanted to stay away from the rough crowd he was surrounded with before. By coincidence, perhaps, Lee's contact with Bob all but ceased. Somehow, the letters just stopped and the only mail he was receiving, besides family, was from Tami. Without Bob's knowledge though, Lee stayed updated on what Bob was up to through his constant contact with Kenneth and Tami.

The topic of marriage had come up, though it's not clear who brought it up first, if it was Tami or Bob. There was no question that at first, he was reluctant to marry her while he was still incarcerated. Yet when the subject was brought up at one of their subsequent visits, she was visibly excited at the possibility. She acted just as head over heels about him as he felt about her, even though she told him she had been married in the past.[10]

Bob spoke to the prison chaplain several more times before making the decision to actually ask Tami to marry him.

He considered waiting until he got out of prison before making his proposal, but he was worried that someone would steal her away from him in the meantime. It wasn't a risk he was willing to take.

He was elated at the idea of starting over with her, so he decided to go for it and marry her. In his heart, he truly thought she was the one for him.

They began writing to one another sometime in mid-October, and by late November she began calling the parole board on Bob's behalf to see if she could help move things along. By the end of December, when she went to meet him for the first time, their relationship was already blooming. By the end of January, they were already talking to one another about their plans to get married at the courthouse by proxy sometime in February.

To outsiders and their families, it looked like their relationship was moving too fast, but it also appeared to them that she was going to be a good influence on him, so no one disputed their marriage plans.

For the first time in a long time, Bob seemed happy and hopeful for the future. In fact, blessings were offered all around for the two of them. And, the whole time, Tami was right there alongside Bob, every step of the way, encouraging the marriage to happen, as was he. To those on the outside looking in, she seemed elated at the thought of marrying Bob.

They discussed waiting on getting their wedding bands for one another after Bob got out of prison. She said she wanted to exchange their wedding vows at a later date, after Bob made parole, in a private ceremony with just their friends and family. He wholeheartedly agreed.[11]

Bob was looking forward to having physical contact, or conjugal, visits with her, as married inmates were allowed to do, instead of having a plexiglass between them, and by actually getting married, in his mind, it would bring them closer together, even if it was only during her visits. He wanted to be able to touch and embrace her. And since they were getting married, she would be considered his immediate family.

Bob had originally wanted the marriage date set for February 14, 1991. He thought it would be romantic to get married on Valentine's Day, and he hoped she would think the same as well. He even went as far as trying to send her a single rose with a Valentine's Day card delivered to her the day before their nuptials were read, to remind her how much he loved her. He had tried to consider her feelings, and what she might have wanted for their special day.[12]

But for whatever reason, Valentine's Day came and went, and they officially wed on February 27, 1991 at the Dallas County courthouse. Tami recited her vows with a stand-in for Bob in front of the Justice of the Peace.

At the very same time, Bob was out in the fields at the Ramsey unit picking spinach with his cold bare hands, shivering in the brief, though brutal, Texas winter.

It might not have been as memorable a wedding for either of them as it could have been. But there was spinach to be picked and time to be served, so celebration of their nuptials would just have to wait.

Chapter Twelve

GOING BACK TO COMANCHE ON A BENCH WARRANT

Bob was openly optimistic about making a fresh start with Tami, so he began planning for his chance at parole. Tami hired an attorney by the name of Linda Risinger to help with getting Bob's parole approved.

Risinger recommended that if Bob wanted a chance of getting approved for parole, then he needed to go back to court in Comanche County to face his pending charges. He needed to get them off the table before the parole board would even consider accepting his request for parole. So, on the advice of his new attorney, Bob moved forward with his pending charges in that county. He put a request in and before long he was on his way back to Comanche County.

His charges amounted to theft for the John Deere tractor that belonged to Joe Moore, the owner of the ranch on which Bob had once worked. Bob was not innocent of these charges, he just happened to be the only one who got stuck with them.

Bob also faced another theft charge for "theft by deception" from one of the investors from whom he swindled money.

Both charges were felonies and Bob was convicted on both counts.

He had long prepared for this day while sitting in prison and he was ready for the clock to start ticking, so he could get it over with and out of the way.

After the trial, Bob was sent back to TDC to serve the remainder of his sentence. He wanted to put Comanche County, along with the rest of his criminal history, behind him and prepare for a fresh start.

Chapter Thirteen

MR. LEACH, YOUR PAROLE HAS BEEN APPROVED

Tami was working as a trainer in her hometown of Plano, 19 miles northeast of Dallas, still at Electronic Data Systems (EDS), the multibillion-dollar company that was founded by the well-known Texas billionaire Henry Ross Perot.

Tami travelled back and forth between her home life and job in Plano to visit Bob at the various TDC units he rotated between while he was in prison just so she could see him. (Interview with confidential source, private communication, May 12, 2013).

Sometime in the early Nineties, after Bob and Tami got married, Bob was approved for parole. Tami rented a house in Bruceville-Eddy, where Bob had been living prior to going to prison, where she awaited him when he finally got his walking papers from TDC.

The stipulations for Bob's parole were straightforward. He was required to have a dependable and steady job with income and a permanent place of residence before the parole board would even consider approving him. And he had to have some type of support system from people who were willing to check on him on a regular basis, such as friends or family. For him, it was Tami.

Bob went back to work for Davis in Chilton, while Tami continued to work at EDS, making the 140-mile round-trip to her job each day. (B. Davis, personal communication, Apr. 13, 2013).

According to some of the ranch hands who worked alongside of Bob, as soon as he started working at the ranch again, Tami began to show a real interest in his work. She wanted to know everything he was doing, right down to the type of cattle that he was working with. They stated that she'd never been around cattle before, and didn't have a clue what went on at ranches. She seemed to have enough sense, though, to know that there was money to be made in the cattle industry and she wanted to learn everything she could about it. (Interview with confidential sources, private communication, May 12, 2013).

Meanwhile, she would get up every morning before the crack of dawn, and leave the house to drive to her job in Plano. It was a four-hour round trip when all was said and done. At the end of each long day, she would drive to the ranch where Bob was working so she could see what he was doing with the cattle. (B. Davis, personal communication, Apr. 13, 2013).

Tami became so engrossed at what all the cowhands were doing, and she acted so in awe of Bob, that others who had known Bob prior to meeting her and knew about his past troubles in Comanche County stated she was unwittingly beginning to act the same way Kubiak did when he was getting in the way of the other ranch hands in Comanche County.

Tami began engaging with the ranch hands, asking them questions about the cattle and showing interest in what was going on while they were working the cattle in the pens. She even began hopping in the cattle pens with the hands and acting like she was helping them move the cattle along. (Interview with confidential sources, private communication, May 12, 2013)

She did all this while she was still adorned in the high heel shoes, dress pants and blouses which she wore to work at EDS. The ranch hands would tell her to get out of the pens so she didn't mess her clothes up, but she didn't care, she just hopped in and ran with the rest of them. She told them, "They're just clothes."

By the time all the cattle had been moved from one pen to the other, for whatever reason, she was covered in dirt and her clothes were all a mess. She didn't care though, and almost every day went through the same routine.

As one of the ranch hands put it, she was a cute thing, but she really looked out of place in what she had on and she was always in the way. Nobody could understand why she was driving so far every day from home, to work and back, and then out to the ranch to be around all of them. She was becoming quite the little nuisance.

For a gal who wanted everybody to believe she had it all together, the ranch hand stated that she sure spent a lot of time running around in circles like a dog chasing its own tail. It made absolutely no sense whatsoever to the rest of the hands.

But according to interviews with several individuals, who feared retaliation from Tami for coming forward, Tami was not the kind of woman to do things without there being a reason – she had an ulterior motive. Tami wanted to learn as much about the cattle business as she possibly could, the ins and outs of how everything worked – right down to every little detail. What no one knew about Tami, at the time, was that she was looking forward to pulling a few cons of her own on some unsuspecting victims. And one of those cons just happened to be rustling cattle, with Bob's help of course. She just wasn't ready to tell him about it yet. (Interview with confidential source, private communication, May 12, 2013); (Interview with confidential source, private communication, June 16, 2013)

Bob had no idea what she was doing, or that she had an ulterior motive for her annoying daily visits to the ranch. And no one else did either. He had fallen in love with her from the start. He was so proud of what he thought she was that he was strutting her around like a show pony, but it wouldn't take long for him and everyone else to figure out that she was devious and calculating. (Interview with confidential source, private communication, May 12, 2013)

Bob thought she was interested in him and what he did. No one at the time was aware of how deceitful Tami could be when she wanted something. She, like Lee, wanted to keep that under wraps, at least for the time being.

What no one realized at the time was that Lee was still harboring hard feelings towards Bob for their prior criminal mischief.

It would not be discovered until much later that Tami and Lee had known one another quite well. And, in retrospect, many wondered if Tami was not helping Lee take revenge on Bob.

But, at the time, everyone close to Bob truly believed that Tami had only good intentions for him. That's what she had led him to believe during their two-hour visits at the prison, along with all her handwritten letters. To think this dutiful sweetheart of a girl had a hidden agenda, or that Bob would once again fall prey to another criminally minded individual and go right alongside her full force, at the time seemed almost impossible for anybody to comprehend.

The more time that Tami spent around the ranch hands, the more relaxed she became around them. She began to engage even more with the hands, wanting to know as much as she could find out about their personal lives. It wasn't personal on Tami's part; and according to one individual who witnessed this behavior on more than one occasion, they stated she wasn't above using her body to achieve her ends. (Interview with confidential source, private communication, June 16, 2013)

Tami began trying to set up extra-marital affairs on the side with the hands, hoping to squeeze a little extra money out of them in the process. But as Tami would soon learn, some cons work and some don't, and this one, for Tami, didn't pan out. (Interview with confidential source, private communication, June 16, 2013)

The ranch hands were not interested in her at all. One hand stated she acted like it didn't bother her one bit, though. She continued to pursue them regardless, whether they worked with Bob or not. This was a side of her that nobody, least of all Bob, had seen until now.

At first, Tami's advances were discreet. But over time, her suggestive manner became more overt, even if Bob was in the same room.

It's not clear what Bob thought of her behavior, or when exactly it was that he became aware of its magnitude. He never commented to any of his fellow cowboys about it or said anything to her in front of them, and nothing more has ever surfaced about the subject. But as aggressive as Tami was with the hired hands, it would be hard to believe that Bob didn't notice it, right away. The question is—why did he put up with it? Was love really *that* blind?

On one occasion, a few of the hands went to Bob's house to talk to him about a few things related to the ranch. When they got there, Tami answered the door wearing a robe. She invited them all in and directed them into the living room, where they all had a seat and were told to wait for Bob. Tami said that Bob was in the shower, but that he would be out soon. Then, she left the room and a few minutes later came back, stark naked, wearing absolutely nothing except a big smile. (B. Davis, personal communication, Apr. 13, 2013)

While she stood in the entryway to the living room, bare-ass naked in front of the dumbstruck cowboys, they looked at her in disbelief. Each man stood up to walk quickly to the front door, and as they exited the house, they told Tami to let Bob know that they would talk to him later.

Given her boldness and given how far she was willing to go with others, some individuals later stated that Tami was beginning to earn herself a little reputation as a Texas-sized hussy. True to Kenneth's original description of Tami in prison, Tami was proving to be quite the little party gal, and according to a few individual's statements who wanted to remain anonymous, she was evidently quite the little nymphomaniac, to boot. Was it ultimately just an act, a means to an end? No one knew, and Tami wasn't telling. (Interview with confidential source, private communication, May 12, 2013); (Interview with confidential source, private communication, June 16, 2013)

According to witnesses, Tami's behavior only got worse. She was constantly flirting with the ranch hands, although they told her they were happily married and they were not interested in her whatsoever. She continued her advances, nonetheless.

Her husband seemed—or at least acted—oblivious to the whole situation. Bob was back at a job that he knew really well and he was good at it. He had friends at the ranch, people he was familiar with and who genuinely cared about his well-being. But that life he had idealized behind bars was beginning to slip away.

Tami assured Bob while he was in prison that she would be there for him when he got out. And he had no reason not to believe her. He had fallen in love with her through her many letters and her open-ended promises of a better life once he was released. The hope that she gave him while he was sitting on his bunk at night dreaming of the minute when he would finally be able to get out and live life again was now dissipating. It was beginning to look more and more like life with Tami was nothing but a pack of lies, a façade, and Bob was beginning to fall back into some of his old habits once again.

Over time, Bob's behavior began to change and his moods became erratic. There were days when Bob wouldn't even show up for work at all. Sometimes he'd be gone for days at a time.

It was soon discovered by several of the hands that Bob had gotten back on dope, and it was beginning to affect his work. When he did show up to work, he was one of the best and hardest working hands that the ranch had, but when he was high, he was a completely different person, almost unrecognizable.

It had appeared Bob was once again gravitating to the same bunch of lowlifes that hung around Lee, the very same running buddies he consorted with before he went to prison.

It's not clear how Bob came in contact with them, whether it was Tami's doing, or if they reached out to Bob on their own, but nonetheless, they were back in the picture. What's more puzzling to those who knew Bob, was why Tami suddenly began acting a little too comfortable around the people that potentially wanted to harm Bob. To those outside observers, it was almost as if she had known them better than he had all along.

Bob only stayed on at Davis' ranch for a few months after making parole, when he and Tami decided to move to north Texas, close to the Dallas area. It's not clear why they left for north Texas instead of staying in Bruceville-Eddy when they did. Perhaps Tami wanted to be closer to her job and family, or maybe she learned all she could about ranch living and was ready to run her own cons, with Bob of course.

A short time later, Bob was sent back to prison on a parole violation. The details are grey, but the upshot was, he was sent back to TDC to serve out his remaining sentence. The days when Tami had seemed like a lifeline out of crime and the prison system seemed like a distant memory.

Chapter Fourteen

HOW IT ALL STARTED

Bob made parole in January 1999 after serving more than ten years total in TDC. He got a job working as a stable manager at the Jolabec Stables, located outside of Prosper, a small country town north of Dallas not far from Carrollton, where he and Tami had been living before he was sent back to prison on a parole violation. The pair picked up stakes in Bruceville-Eddy and moved to the Carrollton area.[1]

Either by chance or design, Bob had settled back into his old outlaw life. But now he had a willing partner. Tami had expressed a real interest to Bob about running cons, and the one which she focused her attention on was stealing cattle, with Bob's help of course.

According to one individual who wanted to remain anonymous, the time that Tami spent out at Davis' ranch prior to moving back to north Texas, along with all her daily trips back and forth from Chilton to Plano and back again were about to pay off for her in a big way. They claimed that was something she would definitely make sure of. (Interview with confidential source, private communication, June 16, 2013)

The first known con that the pair pulled off together was

when they decided to answer an ad that was posted in the *Livestock Weekly* newspaper for ranchers who were looking for a place to pasture and care for their cattle.

It's not clear which of the duo came up with the idea, because Tami was just as gung ho about pulling a con, if not more so, than he was. Larceny just naturally seemed to suit them both.

But according to those who knew the couple during their first years together, Bob was the one who came up with the idea that cattle needed a place to graze, and Tami was the one who ran with the idea and got the ball rolling. (B. Davis, personal communication, Apr. 13, 2013)

Tami knew all about Bob's crooked dealings with Kubiak and how the pair managed to steal over $150,000 worth of cattle from Bob's employer, not to mention countless other victims around the Comanche area. She knew that they were making money hand over fist but, unlike Kubiak, and it appeared to others that Tami wanted to be the one to control the illicit proceeds.

Some later claimed it was her way of guaranteeing there would be some leftover cash in the kitty in the not-so-distant future. She may not have been stealing cattle behind Bob's back like Kubiak had done in years past, but certain individuals stated that Tami was stashing away more than her share of what she and Bob had brought in together, with him being none the wiser.

It was clear to a few who knew the couple, and who spoke to the author that from the beginning Tami wanted things done a certain way, and that she wanted Bob to only handle the cattle side of the business. After all, hustling cattle was something he had done many times over. And he was good at it.

Once her and Bob's con was up and running, she was the one who made all the decisions when it came to the money and she kept track of the books. Any financial decision that was made by the pair did not happen unless Tami approved it first. (Interview with confidential source, private communication, Jan. 16, 2014)[2]

So far, her only knowledge of cattle had been what she learned while she was getting in the way at Davis' ranch, so it was obvious that Tami couldn't do any of this without Bob's help. She would simply depend on Bob to show her what she hadn't yet learned and she was smart enough to figure out the rest by herself.

In order for their con to be a successful one, Tami had to grasp the concept of how things worked at the sale barns and she had to be able to fully understand how to pasture leases for cattle, because she would be dealing with a lot of ranchers. (Interview with confidential source, private communication, Jan. 16, 2014)

It's common for ranchers to put their cattle on a pasture lease during the spring and summer months for the benefit of cost. Depending on where the pasture is located and the type of contract that is set up between the landowner and rancher, cattle pastures have been known to lease for as low as $20 an acre.

It's not as common for ranchers to pasture their cattle during the winter months, due to the prevailing harsh weather that prevented any type of growth in the stock and the fallow conditions of the fields themselves. During the winter months, ranchers depended on feed and hay to keep their stock fed, although a few continued to rent winter pasturage. But it can cut into the rancher's profit margin if they're paying for feed and a pasture lease both.

Based on the terms of the contract between the landowner and the rancher, the rancher can either hire their own cowboys to feed hay and feed cubes to the cattle and do a headcount every few days to ensure the cattle are all accounted for, or the landowner can do this for the length of the agreement, if both parties willingly agree. Every contract is different and is based on the needs of each individual.

In the Western tradition, most contracts are still done using the honor system and a handshake.

Bob and Tami scanned the paper looking for ranchers who were looking for places to pasture and care for their herd. (B. Davis, personal communication, Apr. 13, 2013) Ranchers were always looking to get rid of their steers and bulls, and any extra tack that they wanted to sell, and for Bob and Tami the stock report ads were the perfect place to start.

The two figured that not only could they get money to pasture and care for the stock, but there was a potential for additional income by selling them at auction. And those same ranchers who were having their cattle delivered to the leased pasture were also inadvertently providing them with live inventory that they could turn around and sell at the sale barns.

Bob knew all too well that a decent-size bull or steer could bring in a lot of money. Best of all, he and Tami didn't need to hustle and accumulate their own stock, because it would be provided for them up front.

And the more ads they answered, the more cattle they could get their hands on to sell.

When a rancher takes their cattle to the sale barns, the heifers and steers are unloaded and the cattle are penned, sometimes with as many as fifty in a pen at a time. Brand inspectors place tags on the ear of each steer and heifer that belong to the particular rancher, along with a brief description of face markings and colors so they're easy to identify. There are also numbers on each tag that coincide with the rancher's name. This makes it easier to inventory the cattle and keep track of who they belong to. Once the cattle are tagged and the list is created, a copy of the list is given to the rancher and another is given to the office at the sale barn.

Because the sale barn is providing a service to the ranchers, they collect fees from each rancher for the sale of their cattle. They include a yard fee, which covers the cost of hay and grain, a commission fee with a percentage that is taken out of the check that is received for the sale of the stock, and a fee for insurance deductions.

Each heifer and steer is sold to the highest bidder and each one sells for the market value of what the cattle are going for at the time. The only paperwork that changes hands from the seller to the sale barn is the application for the fees that is given to the rancher upfront. And once the cattle are sold, the sale barn gives the rancher a check for the sale of their cattle. Traditionally, it's a very straightforward business.

Just like pasture leases are done using the honor system and a handshake, a majority of business dealings that are done at the sale barns are also done in the same manner. When a rancher brings in their cattle for sale at a sale barn, no one questions whether or not the cattle belong to them, because a majority of the rancher's dealings are done with a large number of cattle. This is common. Simply put, the cattle are unloaded and prepared for auction.

Most of the individuals that sell and buy their stock at the sale barns are honest and hard-working individuals. Computers and contracts are eroding the handshake model, but for the most part, as far as the sale barns are concerned, a man's word is still considered his bond.

Bob knew all too well that the ranchers whom he and Tami conned would be able to identify their stock and, if they lived close enough to where Bob and Tami and the pastured cattle were located, they could easily pop in and check on them. And that was something that neither one of them wanted, especially since they wanted to flip the cattle as quickly as they got them.

For this very reason, they started out by answering ads from individuals who lived a great distance away. And right off the bat, there in black and white in *Livestock Weekly,* was an ad that particularly stuck out. It had been placed by an individual looking for a place that he could lease for his cattle. Nothing unusual there.

But what caught the pair's eye was the fact that the man lived out of state and would not have easy access to the cattle, so he would be none the wiser of what Bob and Tami were up to. His only way of knowing how the cattle were doing was by talking to Bob or Tami over the phone.

For Bob and Tami, it was an ideal way to pull a con on an unsuspecting rancher who was simply looking for a place to keep his cattle. They had devised a plan to get rich by using other peoples' cattle that they acquired from the ads in the *Livestock Weekly* for pasturing, using the cattle as collateral for loans, while selling the same cattle at auction barns. (B. Davis, personal communication, Apr. 13, 2013) It was a variation of the scam that Bob and Kubiak had pulled. The classics, as far as Bob was concerned, never went out of style.

Before answering their first ad, Tami found various pastures that they could lease in Texas and Oklahoma to keep their stolen cattle under wraps. The couple ended up with a total of six leases in all that nobody would find out about until after the con was over and the authorities began to investigate the pair. (B. Davis, personal communication, Apr. 13, 2013)

The three leases that they had in Texas were located in Lake Ray Roberts, nearby Pilot Point north of Denton and Poyner, in East Texas. The other three hideout pastures they had were in Oklahoma − at Ringling, Boswell and another that was located between Wetumpka and Henryetta.

They planned to fleece as many suckers as possible, and slip away with their ill-gotten gains to live happily somewhere far, far away. And according to Bob, they had a two-year plan to accomplish the goal.

As mentioned, the first victim that they contacted lived out of state and he was assured that he could send his cattle to be pastured and cared for by Bob and Tami, an upstanding couple in a small Texas town. Pillars of the community, as they presented themselves. The distant rancher was satisfied with the arrangement and prepared his stock for shipping.

Once the cattle had arrived, Bob ensured they were settled in and he began to plan on how he was going to swap them out. He started to pull the same schemes he had previously employed when he was in Comanche County. Only this time, he had a partner whom he believed that he could truly trust. Since Tami was willing to handle the business side of things, he would do what he knew best, which was hustling the cattle, while conning everyone else.

All the extra time that Tami had spent out on the ranch with Bob and the other ranch hands down in Bruceville-Eddy, was finally beginning to pay off, according to one individual who claims to have seen this firsthand. She was finally getting what she wanted, the individual claimed, a well thought-out con masterminded by no one but her, with Bob guiding her along the way. Bob thought he was running the show; but others claimed Tami knew otherwise. (Interview with confidential source, private communication, Jan. 16, 2014)

It wasn't hard for Tami to convince him to do anything, because she knew he loved her and he'd do anything she asked, so it didn't take much to persuade him. And being that he was a natural con-artist, he'd go along with just about anything she asked him to do. The fact that they could get such easy money while running their con, in his mind, made it all the better. Tami controlled the financial aspects of the scheme, and any and all money would go through her. In her mind, Bob was the perfect patsy to take the fall, just as he had been many times before, and, just like before, he didn't even see it coming. Like a lot of con men, he had a blind eye when he himself was being conned. Bob was Tami's mark. He just didn't know it yet.

Tami was very business-minded, and she had made it a point to learn all the financial ins and outs of the cattle business. Hence, the reason she was always around Bob and the rest of the ranch hands in Bruceville-Eddy. The reckless and overt flirtatious behavior she engaged in at the time was a cover that served its own purpose, at least by the opinions of others.

Bob was supposed to tag and mark the cattle that they received from the out-of-state rancher in order, ironically, to prevent anyone from being able to steal them. Which was something of a joke, since the cattle were effectively stolen the moment the pair got their hands on them. Of course, with the scheme Bob and Tami were running, neither one of them had the intention to tag or mark any cows, steers or bulls, but that wouldn't be discovered until much later.[3]

As the first load of cattle came in, Tami and Bob got to hustling, taking them to the various leases and placing them in the pens to get them ready for transport to take to the sale barns.

Meanwhile, the pair continued to answer more ads in the *Livestock Weekly*, gathering up still more cattle to sell at auction. And the more cattle they pulled in, the bigger the con grew, and the more money the two had in their bank account. The con had become a full-time job.

Chapter Fifteen

SETTLING INTO MARRIED LIFE

Nothing ever stayed simple for long. Tami decided she wanted to have an open marriage with Bob. This was something Bob had never experienced before in his previous relationships, and based on interviews with others who witnessed this and in their own words, Tami was once again proving just how low her values were by opening her marriage up to her husband's rendezvous with various types of women. She was encouraging Bob to have as many extra-marital affairs as possible, just so they could bring in more money. Blackmail, not sex, was the end game. Bob, of course, was elated with this idea. (Interviews with confidential sources, private communication, Feb. 23, 2015)

Those who had been around Tami when Bob was first released from prison were not surprised by her open marriage demand, or that she was the one to bring it up first.

It wasn't until much later, after Bob and Tami's marriage ended and she decided to go rogue that others finally understood why Tami had been pushing for an open marriage all along. According to witnesses, her ploy was to go after women with big bank accounts and eventually blackmail them and their spouses, so she could pocket their money, along with Bob's help of course. She would easily be able to convince Bob to con them into investing their money into cattle, in turn making her and Bob's cattle schemes grow even more. It was a great way to increase their financial gain and float them by until the real money from the original cattle scheme of answering even more ads started rolling in. It was a win for sure by simply enforcing the victims to invest in the cattle and then turning around to blackmail them all at the same time. (Interview with confidential source, private communication, Feb. 23, 2015)

Once she and Bob won the suckers' trust by convincing them that Bob was indeed available to all the women and that Tami and Bob knew their business when it came to cattle, Tami would turn around and blackmail each one of them for more money than anyone could have ever suspected she was capable of doing. On some level, she might have even surprised herself with how well she made out, all in a dishonest days' work. Bob of course was on board with everything that Tami wanted to do and he went right along with it.

What no one would know at the time was that Tami was doing all of this to set up her own little nest egg, so that she could leave Bob hanging. (Interview with confidential source, private communication, Feb. 23, 2015)

The women that Tami approved of were, of course, ones who had a lot of money. It's not clear how she found them, if they were random women who appeared at first glance to have money and did, or if she befriended them to win over their confidence enough to learn about their background, it's not known. After doing a little digging into each woman's background, she would point out the ones that she thought Bob should go after. And, of course he did. Tami even went as far as helping Bob to set up dates with these women that she picked out for him. In the words of a family member, "There wasn't nothing those two wouldn't do for a twenty." (Interview with confidential source, private communication, Feb. 17, 2015) (Interview with confidential source, private communication, Mar. 4, 2015)

She readily approved all of Bob's extra-marital affairs, and she made each woman believe that her and Bob's relationship was over. She told each one that Bob was a great guy and they should hook up with him before somebody else did. And, to take it one step further, she befriended each woman, allowing them to come and go as they pleased. Between the open marriage scam and conning innocent ranchers and stockmen out of their money, she was beginning to become very satisfied with married life. (Interview with confidential source, private communication, Feb. 17, 2015) (Interview with confidential source, private communication, Mar. 4, 2015)

It's not clear what others in the small town thought about Bob and Tami's new swinging lifestyle. It was a small town with conservative views, so they certainly would not have agreed with what was going on next door to them, but perhaps at the time they didn't know.

One neighbor in particular who later found out about the rustling hustle commented that, "Bob was a good neighbor, but he knew that son of a bitch was stealing cattle!"

Tami and Bob eventually made it known to everyone that their marriage was not in any way a typical or traditional one, far from it. No one other than Bob's close friends and family has ever shared their views on the subject with outsiders. But privately, they were highly disappointed and shocked that Tami would bring up the subject, let alone act upon it. Especially considering how much time Bob had spent contemplating whether or not to marry her in the first place.

Tami now seemed like the complete opposite of everything she was saying that she was not during those weekend visits to the prison, and she had come to represent everything he was trying to stay away from. Her family might have been proud of everything she was pulling, but his certainly wasn't. Her actions stunned the whole Leach family, even to this day.

If there were any outside objections to their open marriage, they didn't come from the women Bob was having the affairs with. Every single one of those gals was on board with it, wholeheartedly. At least they were, until Bob and Tami's scams and blackmail began to bleed them dry.

While Bob and Tami were both busying themselves with hustling the women and cattle, he still managed to hold down his job at Jolabec Stables and Tami remained a faithful employee at EDS. It wasn't hard for either one of them to make their lives seem picture perfect to everyone on the outside. It was the inside they couldn't contain.

While Bob was continuing to work at the Jolabec Stables, he met a married couple who were taking riding lessons from one of the trainers at the stables. Bob and the trainer were talking, and Bob found out that the couple had quite a bit of money, which only made the pair more attractive to Bob. He was beginning to get this down to an art. After sometime later, Bob began a longtime sexual affair with the wife.[1]

Her name was Christi Suzann Gale. She graduated from the University of Texas in Austin in 1988, and in 1989, she got her pharmacy license from the Texas Pharmacy Board. She and her husband lived with their two kids, a son and a daughter in McKinney where she worked at the local Tom Thumb supermarket's pharmacy, located 14 miles east of Prosper.[2]

Christi and Bob's sexual affair became like second nature to the two of them. And based on interviews with others, Tami, very much approved of the two of them being together. In fact, Tami was so elated that she happily gave each of them her blessing. And, true to form, she went as far as befriending Christi the whole time the affair took place.

According to Christi's later courtroom testimony, right off the bat, Bob was able to convince her to put up front money for the down payment on a house the couple was buying in Pilot Point, as well as making an investment in their cattle "business."[3]

Apparently, it didn't take much convincing for her to give the two the money they needed, because a short time later they were able to purchase the ideal home and acreage down the road from their home on Peel Street. They had been eyeing the ranch style home southeast of Pilot Point when it first came on the market and neither one wanted to miss out on the lease to purchase option they were given.

It turned out Bob and Tami were paying the mortgage on both places, a home on Peel Street and a ranch style house with acreage on Lights Ranch Road (which Bob styled the "Rockin' L Ranch"), and needed Christi's money to make the nut.

Once they got settled into their new place, Christi began spending a lot of her free time at the ranch with the two of them. According to Bob, many times Christi would ride with him to the various leases just to see the cattle that he and Tami had acquired.

It was easy for Christi to come and go any time she pleased, because, according to her testimony, her husband worked in Saudi Arabia. She also boarded her horses at their stables, which gave her another reason to visit the Rockin' L Ranch. It appeared she was becoming really comfortable around the two of them. She might not have lived with them, per se, but she spent an awful lot of time at the house on the Lights Ranch Road with them and many nights with Bob at the house in Wetumpka, OK.[4]

It didn't take long for Christi to become known to

everyone at the ranch as Bob's girlfriend. She didn't bat an eye when Tami was introduced to others as Bob's wife, though. Perhaps Christi figured Bob and Tami's marriage would fizzle out sooner or later, and she would be the one who wound up being married to Bob. After all, that's what Tami had been telling everyone, including the women, from day one. Nonetheless, Christi didn't seem bothered by the fact that she herself was "the other woman," and that is exactly how others viewed her, even if she did have Tami's approval. It would have made a hell of a country song.

But it was unsustainable, as all the parties involved must have known.

It's not clear when Christi and her husband separated and eventually divorced, but in a distant day when she testified on the stand about her relationship with Bob, she was a single woman. Before the affair was over, Christi claimed that she fronted Bob and Tami close to $180,000. And she would end up filing for bankruptcy, thanks to her good pal Tami and her lover Bob.[5]

Bob and Tami were proud of the house and land that became known as Rockin' L Ranch. It didn't cost them a wink of sleep that they were able to obtain it, by running a con on a simple-minded pharmacist who practically moved in with them and wound up ruined for her trouble.

Shortly after Bob approached Christi, he approached another individual in the same fashion while he was working at Jolabec Stables and inquired about that person going into the cattle business with him and Tami. Bob told this individual that he and Tami owned a ranch nearby, and that they needed an investor to help them buy cattle. They were looking for a reputable business partner to help them get their new outfit off the ground.[6]

It's not clear if this individual went into business with Bob and Tami, or if they invested his money into the already well-established bait-and-switch con they were already running, but one thing was clear: Bob and Tami were constantly reaching out to more people to try to gain more money. There were lots of pigeons ready for plucking. And she was just as aggressive about it as he was.

Shortly after they leased the ranch, Bob moved about 150 head of stolen yearling cattle onto the premises. He used those cattle as collateral to borrow somewhere in the neighborhood of $60-$66,000 from the First State Bank in Celina, another small town near Prosper. Bob began to get more and more friendly with the bank president at the First State Bank, in the process gaining his trust and confidence. He became the trusted familiar face who dealt with the president regarding all business matters for him and Tami at the Rockin' L Ranch.[7]

Chapter Sixteen

ROLLING THE DICE

As their ill-gotten gains accumulated, Bob and Tami began settling in to their new lifestyle quite nicely.

It's not clear when Bob stopped working at the Jolabec Stables, but from what limited details are available about his time there, he was fired from his job as the stable manager because he was caught stealing money from Joyce Silvus, the woman who was running the place. She was impressed with Bob's knowledge of horsemanship and hired him to work at the stables, even though he had a prior prison record.[1]

Joyce and her daughter noticed several thousands of dollars came up missing, and since Bob had access to their money, they figured out he was the culprit pocketing their earnings. It wasn't any concern to Bob though, because he and Tami were doing quite well on their own with the cons they were running on other people. It is not clear if Joyce filed on Bob for taking off with her money, or if she just gave him the boot, but nonetheless, he was told to leave and never return.[2]

Bob and Tami were both sporting new top-shelf pickup trucks, and each one was just as happy about their new lifestyle as the other was. Bob had a 2000 blue Ford F350 diesel four-door dually. He was seen driving it everywhere. And they also acquired a new white Dodge one-ton four-door dually with four-wheel drive. With the money they were bringing in, they were beginning to make some big purchases for themselves and becoming more and more conspicuous in their small community.[3]

Along with all their other equipment they had on the ranch, they also purchased a Kubota four-wheel drive tractor that was a 70-horsepower model, a John Deere tractor, a diesel John Deere six-wheel Gator ATV, and a welding machine and trailer. All the new toys any self-respecting cattleman could wish for.[4]

And, as if all that wasn't enough, they also had horse and livestock trailers spread all over the place. For a moment, Bob and Tami were bringing in more than anything *Dallas'* villainous J.R. Ewing could have done, but at least from the outside looking in, they didn't appear to have as many enemies as he did.

Tami was described by many as "wearing the pants" with respect to the business. She made all of the ranch and financial decisions. And Bob was said to have been having affairs with multiple women, "sidelining" as one witness put it, with different partners. (Interviews with confidential sources, private communication, Feb. 23, 2015)[5 & 6]

It was Tami who came up with the idea of how to launch a bank fraud. Sometime in September 2000, Bob and Tami, and another couple of acquaintances, were sitting around Bob and Tami's kitchen table discussing how they could come up with ways to generate more income for the ranch. Tami left the table, went into her home office and created an invoice on her home computer. The invoice was alleged to be from the L&L Cattle Company and used the Lights Ranch Road address.[7]

The invoice indicated that one of the individuals at the table had purchased 190 head of heavy bred, crossbred cows at $725.00 each for a total purchase price of $137,750.00. On the invoice Tami had handwritten, "Thanks," with a recipient's name for a check for the full amount. Needless to say, this individual had not purchased the referenced cattle, nor did the cattle exist.[8]

Because Bob had recently been released from prison for cattle theft, he would have been unable to qualify for proper bank loans. So, Tami used her computer to produce fake tax records to document Bob's income. Tami also signed the original loan papers at the bank for him, to ensure the loan would go through for the purchase of actual cattle, using the 190 head of imaginary "cattle" as collateral.[9]

In turn, all the cattle that were purchased and signed by Tami herself were worked and branded at the Rockin' L Ranch with the RLR brand on them.

With Tami's control of their finances, the couple was able to secure a loan at the First State Bank in Celina in the amount of $100,000. The loan was basically a credit line to be used for purchasing cattle, as well as other cattle-related expenses at the ranch. The two were setting up their credit lines via manufactured, nonexistent cattle deals with financial institutions, conning them and others along the way.

On November 15, 2000, Bob and Tami signed the original loan agreement. It marked an equal partnership for the couple.

The agreed-upon arrangement stipulated that when Bob and Tami wished to purchase cattle or equipment, they would furnish an invoice or purchase order to the banker describing what was to be purchased. The property then was to be used as collateral by the bank, and subject to inspection by the lenders themselves.

The duo came up with yet another con, and this time they

were able to convince Tami's sister-in-law to be a part of it. She didn't need much convincing, either. After she heard what they were up to, she jumped in with both feet, hoping to be a part of the action.

The plan this time around was that Tami would print a fake invoice from her home computer that showed Bob purchasing cattle that didn't even exist. The fake invoice would show that he purchased, for instance, a quantity of livestock in the amount of X-number of dollars from the sister-in-law. It was of course a fraud, and there were no cattle to purchase.[10]

Tami's sister-in-law from a previous marriage was also employed at EDS, which meant she too had an account at EDS Federal Credit Union. Because of this, she was the perfect individual to have the money from the sale of the imaginary cattle wired into her account from the First State Bank of Celina. And then, once the funds were transferred into her account a few days later, she could turn around and forward the money from her account into Tami's companion account at EDS Federal Credit Union. It was a money-laundering scam, plain and simple.

The sister-in-law (whose name was redacted in the Freedom of Information documents that form the basis of this chapter) didn't know anything about cattle, nor did any of Tami's family, but they knew how to launder money better than Maytag.

Tami went one step further to protect her sister-in-law. She thought it would be best to put a bogus address down on the invoice for her, and if anything ever came to light, she didn't want her own real address on anything that might wind up as evidence. The fake address that Tami put down for her sister-in-law on the invoice was in fact the address to one of the rural leases that she and Bob held. The only paperwork with her legitimate information on it was the original address that she provided with her bank account information at EDS Federal Credit Union. (Interview with confidential source, private communication, Mar. 4, 2015)

The sister-in-law had to be aware of what Tami was up to before being approached with this new fraudulent scheme. In fact, it would have been impossible for Bob and Tami to proceed with the swindle without her active and enthusiastic participation. Maybe she was in it as much for the thrill as for the loot.

Just as Tami promised she would do, she typed up and printed a fake invoice on her home computer showing that Bob purchased 15 crossbred cows in the amount of $11,400 from the sister-in-law on November 27, 2000. But Bob and Tami weren't just using the sister-in-law's account to launder money through. They began passing checks of their own through Tami's account at EDS. Bob, in turn, issued a check for that amount that was drawn on his and Tami's joint account at EDS to the sister-in-law at the First State Bank for the alleged purchase.[11]

The very next day, on November 28, 2000, Tami deposited that check into her account at EDS Federal Credit Union. Then, she faxed the fake invoice to the bank from her fax machine in her office at EDS.

The bank advanced Bob and Tami the amount on the fake invoice for $11,400 of the previous $100,000 loan for which they were approved on November 29, 2000.

The advance from the First State Bank of Celina was deposited into Bob and Tami's joint account. No one was the wiser.

On December 1, 2000, Tami's sister-in-law transferred money from her EDS account into the EDS account of Bob and Tami and then made yet again another transfer on December 4.

According to Bob, the transfer was done in two separate

amounts to avoid EDS creating a cash transaction report on an amount of over $10,000.

Just as he had done in Comanche County with Trooper Kubiak, Bob started going to the sale barns and picking out more cattle and swapping out the ones he had on his lease.

As they were getting loans at the bank, Bob started reselling the same cattle they were using as collateral to bring more money in. And the more cattle he sold, the more cattle he'd purchase to replace what he had just disposed of. It was quite a tightrope to walk.[12]

One witness observed lots of eighteen-wheeler traffic at the ranch. Others saw several loads of mixed cattle including Brangus and other crossbreeds loaded on eighteen-wheel tractor trailers. It was believed that most of the cattle that had been loaded onto the trailers went south because the drivers mentioned several times to others about having to drive through the Dallas traffic.[13]

Later, several witnesses have claimed that Tami, not Bob, was the one who controlled all the log sheets. That made her the one who controlled the money. She was in charge of all the ranch finances; she did the books, made out the invoices, controlled the checkbook, and was the one who generally ran the business. Bob was the one who handled the cattle, and that's it.

All the while, Tami continued to work at EDS. Because of her seniority, she could pretty much come and go as she pleased. This was perfect for her, because she was able to use her office at EDS to continue printing invoices for the RLR, and it was easily covered up. In all the cons they would end up pulling together, Tami would end up being the master-mind, just like Trooper Kubiak. Countless interviews by others claiming, that just like Bob's long-ago partner, Tami would end up walking away free of all of her charges before it was said and done.

Chapter Seventeen

WELCOME TO THE PARTY RANCH

Bob and Tami were not only in the cattle business at the RLR in Pilot Point, but now in addition they were boarding horses and running a dude ranch. Bob was running cattle on approximately 1,000 acres, which also had a house on it, and the couple had a new lease located near the town of Aubrey, between Pilot Point and Denton, north of Dallas.

Business was beginning to look real good. As one individual put it, "Tami had wanted to go bigger and bring in more money, hence the reason they started the dude ranch." (Interview with confidential source, private communication, Mar. 4, 2015)

They also stated that what she was really looking to do was to carry out the endgame of her final con, which was to blackmail the women and their spouses from whom Bob was taking money. While she was at it, she planned to extort their friends as well. It was a come-one-come-all type of deal. As long as they had money in their pockets to play with Tami was all in.

Tami told Bob that they needed to open their ranch up to the public and make it a weekend getaway retreat for couples who were looking to unwind. That meant putting the word out.-(Interview with confidential source, private communication, Mar. 4, 2015)

She explained to Bob that since they were just a short drive from Dallas, city folks would pay to come out to go horseback riding on the trails around the property. They could enjoy champagne with picnic lunches and watch the sunset. Bob didn't believe anyone would pay to do something like that because, growing up around ranches, he had never thought about them as a retreat or a getaway destination. To him, a ranch was just a place to work damned hard.

The individual that was interviewed by the author also stated that, "Tami was looking to increase her wealth one person at a time, and this was her way of making that happen. To her, it was an ideal way of discreetly collecting money, not only from the women, but also their spouses and friends, ideally for many years to come. The evenings spent at the party ranch with her target suckers usually ended with her rubbing her forefinger and thumb together, as if she'd already cashed in on the big prize."

She decided it was time to advertise their little ranch, and she even went as far as having fliers printed up to help advertise the Rockin' L. It's not clear which papers Tami placed ads in for the RLR, but during the research of this book, one ad in particular was found in the *Denton Record-Chronicle*. And it must have been enough to bring in a crowd, because it certainly did. That little ad, along with the increasing word of mouth, kept them busy for some time.[1]

With all the amenities in place for a great weekend retreat, it needed a staff to match. A woman named Anna Novak became the partner and vice-president of marketing. She quickly learned the ins and outs of how everything worked at the party ranch. That, paired with her other qualifications, was one of the reasons why Tami hired her in the first place. Finally, in bold print, the ad listed none other than Bob, as the owner and professional cowboy. He got a kick out of that.

Guests started calling and coming out to enjoy the advertised amenities, and Tami would take their information and process their credit card payments, and somehow, she even contrived to get a hold of personal information like their Social Security numbers.

While the guests were taking trail rides and picnics, others who were witnessing the goings on, claim that Tami was checking guest's credit in her home office to see if she could find out just how much money her guests had in their bank accounts. Those with exceptional credit were always welcomed back to the ranch. As long as they had money to spend, the witnesses claimed, she was willing to offer them anything they wanted, and she did. Soon enough, she was catering to some of Texas' most elite doctors, lawyers, and judges, as well as people who just had a lot of money to throw around. Most were people in positions of influence who didn't particularly want their personal life on display, and the isolated party ranch was suitably discreet. Individuals commented that she wasn't dealing with the middle class anymore – Tami was moving uptown. (Interview with confidential source, private communication, Mar. 4, 2015)

In the not-so-distant future, when Christi Gale, the pharmacist who was Bob and Tami's original mark, gave her testimony about the time she spent with Bob and Tami, she stated that she gave Bob one of her credit cards to use, but he had somehow gained access to more than one. She claimed she had receipts for purchases that weren't signed by her and she wasn't exactly sure how that happened. She appeared dumbfounded as to how her information could so easily have been hacked. As it was, she was just the first of many.[2]

As the dude ranch got busier, Tami moved boldly ahead

with her scheme. Champagne and horseback rides were only the tip of the iceberg, as far as she was concerned. During the research of writing this book several individuals have stepped forward to tell of the events that occurred at the party ranch. They claimed that while she was inviting guests to enjoy the luxuries of country living, she was also running prostitution and an extortion racket on the side. One individual stated that the "RLR Ranch would become known by the locals as the second-best little whorehouse in Texas." (Interview with confidential source, private communication, May 12, 2013); (Interview with confidential source, private communication, June 16, 2013); (Interview with confidential source, private communication, Mar. 4, 2015)

During the evenings, after everyone was settled in for the night, she told the guests to make themselves at home. The male clientele at the ranch soon found out what *that* entailed, as well as the ladies. There wasn't one of them in the bunch that wasn't enjoying the luxury of running around bare ass, drunk and horny. That is, until Monday morning rolled around and everybody went back to their normal lives. (Interview with confidential source, private communication, Mar. 4, 2015)

One individual told the author that, even though he was married at the time, he attended the ranch and enjoyed the fact that he was a middle-aged man who was able to run around with a girl who was no more than half his age. He stated she was just one of many to pick from. His wife, back at home, was none the wiser. At least for a while. According to him, his liaisons at the RLR were not what ended his marriage, but they certainly didn't help.

The problem was, the customers had no idea they were being photographed and filmed while they were in compromising positions. Based on an interview with the author, the next day, after everyone returned back to their "real" lives,

Tami would contact them and let them know that if they didn't pay up, then their dirty little secret weekend of fun would be exposed. (Interview with confidential source, private communication, Mar. 4, 2015)

While Bob was busy stealing cattle during the day, Tami was busy blackmailing guests from the dude ranch at night. The two were relentless, but no matter how much money they pulled in on their schemes, it never seemed to be enough.

Tami's operation was brazen in its scope. Hundreds of people wound up being blackmailed over a period of three years. In the course of the writing of this book, one of the witnesses came forward to give an accurate description of what a visit to the party ranch entailed, but asked not to be mentioned by name for fear of retaliation by Tami. To this day, her victims still fear her. Like Kubiak before her, Tami was adept at using intimidation as her main weapon, so she was able to get away with all of her crimes.

There were aspects of the racket that might have almost qualified as comedy, if money and reputations had not been at stake. Witnesses have stated that when they were out at the Rockin' L Ranch, they would see Tami running around with a dildo, laughing the whole time while carrying it in her hand, asking if anybody needed one. There were people stacked up on top of each other in the barn, in the ranch house and all over the property. The "party ranch" more than lived up to its reputation.

Chapter Eighteen

SOMEBODY CALL THE BANKER, WE NEED MORE MONEY

As the party ranch continued to thrive on its own, Tami and Bob continued to carry out their other schemes, endlessly chasing more money. On January 19, 2001, Bob and Tami signed a loan agreement in the amount of $70,000 with the First State Bank with yet another fraudulent invoice. And again, they presented the invoice to the banker, using non-existent cattle as collateral. This wasn't the first credulous banker they'd dealt with, and he wouldn't be the last.[1]

Four days later, Tami caused a cashier's check to be issued to Bob at a Community Credit Union account in the amount of $56,800. Tami forged Bob's signature on the check and deposited the entire amount. (Interview with confidential source, private communication, Mar. 4, 2015)

While Tami and Bob continued to defraud the bankers, they also instructed two accomplices to go to the Farmers and Merchants Bank in the small town of Krum and attempt to get a loan using the 190 head of cattle on yet another fake invoice. The details about the pair are limited, but it was evident that Tami had no problem reaching out to others when it came to defrauding the banks. The bank loan officer, unfortunately for the duo, was very familiar with the cattle business, and questioned them extensively about the provenance of the livestock they were offering as collateral. Apparently, not satisfied with the couple's knowledge of the cattle business, the loan was not approved.[2]

In mid-June of 2001, Bob and Tami decided to try to obtain one last fraudulent loan from First State Bank.[3]

By that time, Bob had been having affairs with several women, not just Christi, most of them at Tami's behest. According to investigators, one such woman agreed to be a willing participant in a scheme to defraud the First State Bank out of $73,000. She agreed to allow Bob and Tami to have the money wired to her account, whereupon she would wire the funds back into their account, just like Tami's sister-in-law had done in the past.

The loan was approved and Bob and Tami signed the note. The loan agreement indicated that the loan was to be secured by 50 head of Brangus pairs and 23 head of tiger stripe pairs of cattle.[4]

On June 18, Tami sat down at her home computer, just like she had many times before, to create another fake invoice, a skill she had honed to perfection. This time, the invoice showed that Bob bought 50 pairs of Brangus and 23 pairs of tiger stripe that same day.

About the same time all this was going on, another of the women Bob was having an affair with started raising hell about repayment for another fictitious cattle deal in the amount of $20,000. He was able to convince her to invest more money into cattle by having her write another check and leading her to believe she was doubling her money.[5]

The details of that particular plan are rather sketchy, but in long order, on June 27, $24,000 was wired from the Western Vista Federal Credit Union into Bob and Tami's joint account at EDS Employees Federal Credit Union showing that the woman purchased 20 heavy-bred cows from Bob and Tami. In the memo line of the check, Tami indicated that the check was written for "20 Brangus cows."

When the woman actually wanted to see the cows that she had purchased, she was shown some Brangus cows that had been stolen elsewhere and that were, in any event, on their way out the door to be sold at an auction.

At the end of the day, Bob's paramour-turned-victim never owned any cattle at all, and was out $24,000 to boot. As would later be revealed, she was just one more name on a very long list.

Chapter Nineteen

IT'S TIME TO COME CLEAN

Sometime in mid-July, Bob and Tami's cattle scheme began to fall apart. One of the men who sent his cattle to lease on a pasture that Bob and Tami owned started to agitate the pair about the whereabouts of his livestock. Bob and Tami had been able to convince him to pasture his 1100-head herd, including 577 pairs of Brangus cattle, on their ranch. Almost immediately after the stock arrived, the ranch hands began sorting the cattle and hauling them to various sale barns in north Texas and southern Oklahoma. The cattle were sold without the man's permission, and once again Bob and Tami kept the money from the sales.[1]

One of the pair's neighbors began to get suspicious that something wasn't right at the ranch when they noticed on many occasions cattle would show up, be kept in a holding pen and then disappear a day or two later. Bob would not discuss what happened to the cattle and the nosey neighbor could not find them on any of the leased land.

Another witness later stated that Bob would load up cattle onto a 36-foot C&M trailer that he had hitched to the back of his new Ford four-door dually pickup and disappear.

They didn't know where he was going, but it was obvious that the cattle he was loading up into the trailer hadn't been on the ranch for very long. As the cattle would come in, they were put in the cattle pens and within a day or two later they were loaded up and hauled out. Such rapid turnover was uncharacteristic of cattle operations, which mostly operated at a seasonal pace.[2]

The persistent individual that kept inquiring about his 1100 head of stock became aware of what the pair were doing, and he notified Bob and Tami both that he was going to come to Pilot Point to get either his cattle back or get a check for the sale of the herd. But when he arrived, Bob and Tami both went into hiding. They began to liquidate and hide ranch assets from the authorities and banks. The long con was finally winding down.

Others started having problems getting a hold of Bob and Tami about their own cattle. As word began to spread regarding what the couple had been up to, others realized that their cattle too had sold off without their knowledge. Authorities had confirmed that the couple had been selling cattle in Oklahoma since January 2001. One individual alone lost $580,000 worth of cattle. And he had lots of company.[3]

Before it was all over with, Christi Gale claimed to have lent Bob close to $180,000, throughout the course of their relationship. It looked like she was passing money out to him hand over fist. She stated that he claimed he needed the money to put lights up around an arena and pens at the ranch, and make other improvements around the Rockin' L. Each time he asked for money, she would open up her pocketbook and hand it over freely with a big 'ol wink and a little bitty smile. She claimed she cashed in her IRAs, maxed out her credit cards and applied for loans from a local credit union. She later stated that even though he and Tami were selling a lot of cattle, Bob had told her that he could not pay her back. When the calls from him stopped, she decided to start making some calls of her own.[4]

Christi had paid for a cell phone for her and Bob's use, and she surreptitiously went through the phone's call log to see if there was another woman in the picture. She was pissed that Bob had stopped returning any of her calls, and she was in a dead heat to track him down. It seemed her only initial concern was to find out if there was another woman in the picture, rather than the whereabouts of all the money she shelled out. She wouldn't shift gears to focus on her money until much later when she decided to pull a fast one on Bob in a cheap cabin that she rented for him out by the lake.[5]

As she tracked Bob's calls, she found the names and numbers of some ranchers with whom Bob had done business and that's when she started calling people to see if they had heard from Bob, or knew of his whereabouts.

Anytime Christi did an interview with the media she used the alias Carly, maybe to save herself from any public humiliation, no one really knows.

One of the individuals she happened to contact was a rancher in Corpus Christi whom Bob and Tami had fleeced out of his cattle. In an interview given to *GQ* magazine in 2005 he stated that he received a call from a woman by the name of "Carly" who was claiming that she was Bob's lover.[6]

She then told him that Bob had confided to her that he was running a cattle scheme and that the rancher's cattle was more than likely all sold. She also volunteered some other choice words about her thoughts and feelings about Bob. In the end, the rancher described Christi as a scorned woman. He himself had no idea of Bob's whereabouts.

In Christi's court testimony against Bob in a trial in Wood County, she claimed that Bob had filled her in on the cattle scheme.[7]

The fact that Christi didn't contact anyone sooner to

make them aware of what was going on perhaps meant that she had to have known what Bob and Tami were up to for a lot longer than she was letting on.

What's not clear was why she decided to finally spill the beans on Bob and Tami in a moment of haste to a man they swindled money out of, instead of the authorities in the first place. Was she really just trying to get even for all those unreturned phone calls?

Christi was so close to the couple that it's impossible to believe she wasn't privy to at least a few of the things that were going on around her, including the hustling of cattle. If the neighbors could catch on to what was happening just on the other side of the fence, then Christi had to have seen more than her share of cattle coming and going during her daily visits to the ranch. A few weeks seems too long to keep a big secret like that, especially when others' livelihoods are at stake.

It hardly makes her version of events seem plausible, nor does she fit the description of a scorned woman. The only "scorned" one in this whole scenario was her husband given all the money he lost from her shelling it out to fund Bob and Tami's project. That poor son-of-a-bitch was earning a living for his family while working out of the country while his wife was busy passing his hard-earned wages out to con artists.

Not only had Christi contacted the ranchers that Bob had dealt with, she also reached out to members of Bob's family, informing them of her plight. The calls were disconcerting to Bob's kin because they had no idea who she was or why she seemed to be demanding money. They had only known about Tami, not this other woman claiming to be Bob's girlfriend. They were aware of Tami encouraging Bob to open up their marriage. But up until now, no one had a clue who Christi was, nor did they care to find out.

The Corpus Christi man who told his tale to *GQ* had paid

Bob and Tami to provide pasture and care for his 750 cows. Bob was supposed to brand them and attach ear tags as was customary, but Bob didn't. He took out mortgages on the cattle that he claimed as his own and borrowed money against the stock before he turned around and sold them.

It's not clear who called the law first and got the ball rolling. Maybe it was an aggrieved rancher or a suspicious neighbor. In any event, someone put Bob and Tami on the authorities' radar.

As law enforcement began to dig around, they discovered that Bob and Tami had stolen somewhere in the ballpark of $1.8 million dollars' worth of illegal cattle sales since early November 2000, an astonishing figure for a couple of do-it-yourself hustlers. Many of the victims told authorities that none of their cattle were insured and they faced bankruptcy.[8]

In one typical 2001 instance, 317 head of cattle were located, rounded up and subsequently recovered at various locations in the Pilot Point area of North Texas.

The cattle all belonged to the Sweetwater Land and Cattle Company, an outfit headquartered in Weatherford, west of Fort Worth. The cattle had been hidden in various pastures around the Denton County area and were being prepared to be shipped to sale barns in North Texas by Bob and Tami, needless to say without the permission of the SLACC. All the recovered cattle were driven onto tractor trailer rigs and transported back to the Weatherford ranch by Texas Rangers and investigators from the Cattle Raisers Association. Multiply this scenario by the dozens and Bob and Tami go from mere grifters to major players in the cattle theft circles.[9]

As in the way of such things, once word got out, more witnesses began coming forward telling investigators that Bob and Tami were in the stolen cattle business at the RLR, in addition to boarding horses and conducting a dude ranch type of operation. All the secrets were beginning to come out about what the two were up to, and all those nosey neighbors who had stood back and watched from afar were now coming forward with what they knew or had at least long suspected.

As the powers-that-be began to close in on Bob and Tami, neither one could be found. It's not clear who tipped the authorities off to Bob and Tami, it could have been the phone call that Christi made to the Corpus Christi rancher. A judge issued a search warrant for the property and when the investigators went to the property, they quickly learned that the ranch gate was locked and it looked as though no one had been in or out of the property in some time. Investigators attempted to contact Tami at EDS and they were told that she hadn't been into work that day. In fact, she and Bob were both on the run.[10]

Several grand jury subpoenas were obtained for sale barns in the region, including Pilot Point Livestock Auction, the Decatur Livestock Market and the Gainesville Livestock Market, all requesting info on all cattle sold at those particular sale barns by Bob or Tami.[11]

Meanwhile, an individual from the First State Bank in Celina told an investigator that he heard they were looking for Bob. They stated he had a vested interest in the case, in as much as Bob had mortgaged cattle at the bank. According to the terms of the mortgage, the bank had the right to inspect the cattle in question at any time.[12]

Additionally, the First Victoria National Bank in Victoria faxed investigators at the local sheriff's office a commercial security agreement pertaining to the mortgage of cattle. In the agreement, First Victoria also reserved the right to examine, inspect and audit the collateral (cattle) wherever they might be located. The bank requested that investigators act as its agents in attempting to locate the cattle in question.[13]

Early in the afternoon of July 16, the investigators located eight purebred Angus bulls with a hairpin style brand on the left side located in a pasture. Those bulls were positively identified as cattle that had been shipped from Wyoming to Pilot Point. They were allegedly used as collateral by Bob for a loan from the First State Bank of Celina. The bulls were thereupon turned over to the bank.[14]

On July 19, a search and seizure warrant was issued for a dark blue 2001 Ford F-350 Crew Cab four-by-four dually pickup and a black 1999 six foot by 35- foot CM1 Livestock trailer. Both were seized at RLR and impounded at the Denton Police Department impound lot. It was a damn shame. Bob had really loved that truck.[15]

But by then, he had bigger worries.

A week later, state search warrants were obtained by a federal judge for the Rockin' L and Bob and Tami's home on Peel Street. Authorities recovered some documents, but not much else.

Because Bob and Tami both mortgaged the herds of cattle at banks around the region, their actions fell into the category of federal crimes, which made the cattle federally insured.

When Bob finally relented and called Christi, he was able to convince her to rent motel rooms for him in Plano and the surrounding areas, where he could hide out for several days, while investigators continued to look for him. This was all in the wake of confessing to the rancher in Corpus Christi about being Bob's lover and conveniently dropping the bomb about the man's missing cattle. Why she still acquiesced and went on to help Bob is known only to her.

From her actions, along with her testimony in court, it was becoming clear that Christi wasn't sure why she was making the choices she made, whether helping to hide Bob out, or working with law enforcement.

She must have needed more time to figure things out. She

might have spilled the beans to the rancher about his cattle being sold out from underneath him, all the while convincing him she believed Bob was a "no good piece of chicken shit son of a bitch," but when Bob finally contacted her, she shelled out more money to hide him in places where the law couldn't find him. Her part in the whole scenario was becoming quite ridiculous. One minute she wanted to hide him out and the next she wanted to turn him in.[16]

It's not clear where Tami was or what she was doing while all this was going on. Some suspect she was hiding out at her parents' home while trying to rat hole the equipment targeted for seizure. But no one knew for sure.

The ballgame had changed. Now it wasn't just the county sheriffs and local cops Bob had to dodge. The FBI was after him because the cattle he and Tami had stolen were carried across state lines. Not to mention the fact they were federally insured by the banks and the bankers were now looking for them. It was beginning to look like Bob had made the big time and not in a good way.

Chapter Twenty

SHE GOT BOOKED AND CHARGED, AND HE'S ON THE RUN

As for Tami, she turned herself into the Denton County Jail at 10:10 a.m. on Tuesday, July 17, 2001, and was charged with a third degree-felony-- theft of livestock. Her bond was set at $50,000 and according to the local papers she was looking at a maximum 20-year prison sentence. It's not known why she decided to turn herself in, but she did.[1]

She was released from the jail later that afternoon, and within hours of turning herself in, her family paid her bail. The media had a heyday with it: "A Pilot Point woman wanted for theft of livestock over $20,000 in a $1.8 million cattle rustling case surrendered Tuesday morning at the Denton County Jail." The idea of a female cattle rustler was irresistible news candy.[2]

Reports about Bob were also printed in the daily rags, some of them claiming that, according to reports, Bob would face 10 years to life imprisonment for his part in the crimes. Authorities claimed that there were several additional federal and state charges stemming against Bob and Tami, as well as others who were also involved in the crimes. And that these charges were just the first of many to come.

But by now Bob was nowhere to be found. All of Bob's girlfriends had been renting motel rooms for him to hide out in and around Plano and surrounding areas. It had appeared that Christi wasn't the only one who was aiding and abetting a fugitive on the lam. If the stakes hadn't been so high, it would have been farcical.

While law enforcement was searching for Bob, Tami hired herself an attorney who promptly told her to get Bob to sign a statement that she was never involved in any of the cattle operations.

While law enforcement quickly began investigating the cattle theft and bank fraud capers the pair had allegedly engaged in, they never got around to looking into the black-mailing racket that others claimed Tami was conducting at the party ranch. Maybe it was because the victims of her latest scheme were too afraid to come forward for fear their indiscretions and secrets would be disclosed.

The fact that law enforcement overlooked the prostitu-tion and extortion racket at the party ranch was a plus for Tami. Many today believe that if investigators had taken the case surrounding Tami seriously and looked into everything that was going on, then Tami and many others would have ended up in a cellblock alongside Bob.

According to Bob and other witnesses who have told the author of this book, Tami and her family removed property from the ranch and hid it, so that Tami alone would later have access to it.

Among the items that were reportedly taken from the ranch were two 32-foot flatbed trailers with tandem dual wheels and ramps that were valued at $7,000 to $8,000 each, one John Deere Diesel Gator that was valued at $7,000, one 16-foot flatbed trailer that was valued at $800-$900, just to name a few items.

Not only were Tami and her family moving equipment off

the ranch to set aside for her, she was also printing up fake bills of sales to show proof of ownership to the federal agents who were seizing items from the ranch. (Interviews with confidential sources, private communication, Mar. 4, 2015)

Together, the family managed to make off with horses, cattle, farming equipment and many more items that were gained from laundering money and hustling cattle. While Tami was loudly proclaiming innocence, she was looking law enforcement right in the eye and collecting on yet another con. Fear didn't strike her as she rubbed her forefinger and thumb together, grinning at them all.

Tami may have claimed innocence for her part in the crimes, but she could be justly described as the mastermind. She was, after all, sitting right alongside Bob at the banks signing contracts, she was the one forging checks in Bob's name, signing them and creating fake invoices for cattle that never existed, all from her personal computer at home, and from her job at EDS. She was the one, according to employees and bystanders, who made all the financial decisions for the pair. And she planned to leave Bob on the hook for all of it.

Chapter Twenty-One

HIDING OUT IN MOTEL ROOMS

While authorities were looking for Bob, Christi received a phone call asking her to meet him. And she did so on a Wednesday night, at a Red Roof Inn in Plano after she got off work. Here she was, a reputedly respectable woman, walking out the door to meet her lover, a wanted fugitive hiding out in a motel room she was paying for.[1]

Her role in all this was baffling to those who wanted to know what she was really up to. Did she have a plan or was she just a helpless creature of impulse? Or was she just a crazy woman who got off on the drama?

She drove to the Red Roof Inn where she met Bob in the parking lot. She later stated in sworn testimony that she went inside his motel room with him, and they talked for a little while, then they both got into his car to get something to eat. Christi couldn't help but notice Bob had a pistol tucked into his waistband.[2]

She stated that she in no way felt threatened, nor was she forced to go anywhere with Bob against her will, nor was she afraid that he had a gun. But then she stated that Bob had threatened her kids, and she feared for their lives. For whatever reason--and it's never been explained--she didn't feel inclined to report any of this to the authorities just yet. Yet even in the face of threats to her children, she opted to go to dinner instead of screaming for the cops.[3&4]

They went to Ivey's restaurant located a little over a mile from the motel. She stated that they picked a table by the front door of the restaurant. Considering that the table was in plain view of everyone in the restaurant, and knowing that Bob was a wanted fugitive, she chose to act as if she could care less if anyone in the restaurant recognized either one of them. And so they ate like they were any other citizens out for a bite.[5]

As they talked, he told her that he had to go to Oklahoma to get some money that was owed to him from a cattle deal, and somehow get some help with all the mess that he had gotten himself into. He wanted to get an attorney to help him and explained that there was someone in Oklahoma that he could talk to about doing just that. Lawyers cost money.[6]

She in turn stated that since he owed her money, and he was ostensibly going to get what he was owed from a cattle deal, then she would go with him to get her cut.

She was very adamant about getting that money back, which might explain why she was so determined to stay with him in the first place, gun or no gun.

Then they got back into the car and went back to Bob's motel room where they had consensual sex. She claimed that Bob was depressed. She wanted to stay with him, hoping that he would eventually turn himself in to the authorities.[7]

Christi stated that the next morning, after they got up to go to Oklahoma, Bob threatened her son once again. She said that she felt nervous and wasn't sure what to do, and since her car needed gas, she decided to fill up at the local Albertson's grocery store down the road from the motel and go from there. She couldn't remember if she paid at the pump or went inside (which at the time would have been a great opportunity for her to ask for help), but she gassed up her car and went to a local ATM to get more cash for Bob. She stated to the jury that she had to go to Oklahoma if she wanted to get her money back or save her son, or both, so she drove up Hwy. 76 bound for Oklahoma, with Bob sitting alongside her in the passenger seat.[8]

Somewhere along the way, plans changed. Christi rented a cabin at a tourist court for Bob to hide out in Pottsboro, a tiny village not far from the Oklahoma line. It went from the two of them driving to Oklahoma. Now, all of a sudden, four men were going to meet them at this cabin in the middle of nowhere to bring Christi her money and help Bob out with his legal problems.

When she went to rent the cabin in Pottsboro, she claimed later under oath, she didn't feel threatened or felt that she was in any kind of danger. She stated that she didn't feel that Bob was going to hurt her in any way. She thought the four men would come and bring her the money.[9]

But once they got settled in the cabin, she claimed, she went to lay down in one of the rooms while they waited for the men to show up. Lying on the bed, she got a nervous feeling and wanted to leave. Suddenly, all the money she thought she had coming wasn't so important to her anymore.

When she got up to tell Bob she wanted to leave he told her they weren't going anywhere. While she was resting, Bob had gone through her purse. He had noticed her day planner was packed full with business cards from Texas Rangers and FBI agents. In disbelief, he took her cell phone and purse away from her.[10]

Did the authorities know that she was there with him now? And that she had spent the night with him the night before, and they ended the evening with their usual rough sex in the motel room that she was renting for him? She claimed her reason for staying with him was only because he was depressed, but it was beginning to look like to him the only reason she was there was to get her money, and then lead the law to his door.

With the official business cards laid out in front of her, she realized she'd just gotten caught. The simple-minded pharmacist was trying to play the con artist, but things weren't working out the way she thought they would.

Bob flew into a rage at her betrayal and tied her hands and feet together with the sash from a robe in the cabin. She claimed all of a sudden the sex wasn't consensual anymore. Somehow the romance they experienced the night before had been nightmarishly transformed into rape and assault.

Not long after that, the local 911 service received a call from Christi claiming that Bob had kidnapped and sexually assaulted her, and stolen her car. The details about how she 'got away' are grey. Others later claimed she certainly didn't seem as nonchalant leaving the cabin to call 911 as she had been when she first arrived to reserve their cabin.

It's not known when Christi first admitted to authorities that she helped Bob elude the police, either before she rented the cabin or after, but she eventually came clean with them. Her explanation for doing so was that she was convinced that at the time she thought he was innocent. She later ended up working with the authorities and testifying in court against Bob. She did not however, want to testify or bring any charges against Tami, who she was either frightened of or still friends with, it's not clear which. Nothing about their relationship was straightforward.

During the writing of this book, Christi was contacted by the author to see if she wanted to give her side of the story. After first agreeing to meet, she decided against it and became despondent and unwilling to talk. The only information she volunteered during the initial conversation was a warning to stay away from Tami. It's not clear if she was protecting her friend or warning against her.

Considering that Christi was hobnobbing with Tami one minute, hopping in the sack with Bob the next and at the same time dining with at least one of the Texas Rangers overseeing the case, it's unclear what Christi's intentions were, or where her loyalties lay. She does, however, claim to be the victim of the whole sordid tale.

What does she know about the party ranch set-up that she was not willing to share? How long had she known about Bob and Tami's cattle scheme and why did she wait so long to come forward? Was she trying to get her money back before deciding to say anything? And why was she warning the author to stay away from Tami? Is she scared of her, as so many others have claimed to be, which is why Tami got away with her crimes? Just how involved was Christi, if she was at all?

Despite her allegations of rape, it's clear that Christi was in no way forced to meet Bob, she was not forced into his car in the parking lot at the Red Roof Inn and she was not forced to go inside the restaurant with him, or to set off for Oklahoma. She went on her own free will.

At a later date, after Bob had been sentenced for his crimes, Christi filed a lawsuit against the pair for the money she claimed they owed her. She may have wanted to be rid of them, but she was still clawing at the chance to get her money back. If she had been as worried about her money when she was passing it out to Bob as she was when she was trying to get it all back, she would never have lost it.

Chapter Twenty-Two

HIGH-SPEED CAR CHASE

On Wednesday, July 25, at 5:11 p.m., the Grayson County Sheriff's Office received a phone call from Christi telling them she was at the Tackle Box, a tourist court located north of Pottsboro. She told the dispatcher that she was calling to report a kidnapping and a sexual assault made against her by her boyfriend, a sought-after criminal named Bob Leach. She said Bob was on the run in her 2000 red Ford Expedition and was headed south of FM 120 towards Pottsboro.[1]

Shortly, after the call came in, a Pottsboro officer spotted the Ford Expedition in question heading south. The Pottsboro officer engaged in pursuit after realizing the other driver was not stopping. The chase lasted for an hour, until Bob lost control of his vehicle and wound up stuck in a bar ditch near the town of Tioga, not far from his old stomping ground of Pilot Point.

Soon, officers from the Sherman Police Department, and the sheriff's departments of Whitesboro, Tioga, Collinsville, Grayson County, Gunter and assorted DPS troopers were all on the scene. This was turning out to be the highlight of everyone's day. It was like Woodstock for North Texas law enforcement.

But for the moment it was a standoff. The officers could not entice Bob to get out of the car, and they knew Bob had a gun. A sergeant from Grayson County Sheriff's Office Special Response Unit tried using a loudspeaker to coax Bob out of the vehicle, but there was no response from Bob. The sun had gone down. The officers could not see clearly into the vehicle. Was he unconscious?

Bob, as far as they could tell, remained inside, unmoving.

Investigators weren't sure what they were going to find inside the vehicle, because they had received information about Bob being depressed. He might have committed suicide in the vehicle.

After having no luck forcing the car doors, the officers threw gas with flash bangs at the vehicle, hoping to provoke a response. Nothing.

They made their way to the vehicle and they saw, to their considerable surprise, that Bob was nowhere to be found. The Ford was empty. Somehow, he managed to escape the vehicle without even being noticed by the surrounding officers and he had taken off into a nearby wooded area to find shelter.

Once it was discovered that Bob had fled to the woods, the police brought tracking dogs in from the Buster Cole Prison Unit in Bonham. Officers on horseback were also brought in to help with the search.[2]

The authorities, who were embarrassed by the "standoff" with an empty car, were desperate to find Bob, and reached out to other agencies for help. They even went as far as to try to get an aircraft of some sort to help in finding him but were notified that the closest available plane was in Lubbock, 400 miles to the west. Bob had slipped away once more.

Bob had become one of the most sought-after fugitives in

Texas, and everybody wanted a piece of him. Not only did he have outstanding felony warrants out of Denton County from the rustling charges, he also had a State of Texas parole violation and he was considered a suspect in the kidnapping and sexual assault of Christi.

The Grayson County Sheriff's Department, Texas Department of Public Safety troopers, and even a Texas Ranger all hopped into the mix. As did the FBI, the Cattle Association Rangers, and guards from the Bonham Prison, who assisted in the manhunt on horseback.

As the search continued, new agents and deputies were brought in to help relieve the law enforcement officials who had been searching all night, to no avail. Prison officials from Bonham Prison even brought new sets of dogs in to help in the search. A roving search with a thermal imager had also been conducted.

Law enforcement worked tirelessly, doing everything they could think of to find Bob and bring him in, while the media was running a frenzy of reports about the search, and keeping the public updated as the events unfolded. Everybody in Grayson County and the surrounding areas were now on watch for Bob Harold Leach.

A phone call came into the Grayson County Sheriff's dispatch at 9:00 a.m. the next morning, from a man calling to report that when he went out to his horse barn he noticed in the center stall, underneath the feeder, someone's legs sticking out. It was just the tip that law officials needed to help them with Bob's whereabouts.[3]

When authorities arrived at the man's home, he walked outside to greet them, holding a rifle in one hand and a pistol in the other.

He had heard all the news reports so he knew, like everyone else in North Texas and Southern Oklahoma, about a convicted felon named Bob Leach who was on the run in the area. So, when he spotted a stranger's legs in his horse barn, he naturally called 911.

After getting his statement, the officers directed the homeowner to go back inside and put his weapons down. They would take it from there.

As the lawmen made their way into the barn, guns drawn, they spotted Bob, sitting on the edge of the feeder. He was wearing a pair of shorts with a T-shirt and a pair of tennis shoes, and he had a pistol pointed directly at his own chest.

Deputies surrounded Bob, unsure of what he would do. This was what they had trained for, hoping in spite of that it would never happen, but they were prepared for moments like this. One trooper had a shotgun aimed at Bob, while a Grayson County officer had his service revolver pointed at him. They told Bob to please put his gun down several times. They told him nothing was worth losing his life over.

Bob asked the officer that was talking to him what his name was, and the man replied to Bob that his name was Mike. Eventually, Mike and one of his fellow officers were finally able to coax Bob into surrendering his weapon.

Bob lowered the barrel of the 9mm pistol toward the ground and de-cocked it, making sure the barrel of the gun was pointed in the direction of the ground the whole time. Then, after he was done, he threw the 9mm away from him, so Mike could retrieve it. Bob laid on the ground as he was instructed to do, then was handcuffed and helped up to his feet where law officials escorted him to one of the deputy's cars which transported him to the Grayson County Jail.

Once Bob was in custody, he was charged with aggravated kidnapping and sexual assault, along with the outstanding Denton County warrant for his rustling charges and a State of Texas parole violation warrant.

Chapter Twenty-Three

ESCAPED! THE GRAYSON COUNTY JAILBREAK

Once Bob was in custody at the Grayson County Jail, he was escorted to cellblock D. There wasn't an inmate in the county jail that didn't know the name Bob Leach, and every single one of them believed he had a lot of money. And in fact he did, though he and Tami acquired it all illegally. But thanks to Tami and her family, who had worked feverishly moving equipment offsite and passing off fake bills of sales to the federal agents for property that didn't belong to them, she had been able to hide it all in hidden accounts and under her family members' names. She was convinced that no one—not the authorities and certainly not Bob, was smart enough to unwind her schemes. (Interviews with confidential sources, private communication, Mar. 4, 2015)

Bob was technically right, he *did* have money...but he didn't think Tami would be the one to wind up with it.

Once Bob got to Grayson County Jail, things seemed to quiet down, but only for a little while. Sometime in late July or early August, Bob started talking to other inmates, and the subject was a jailbreak.

Bob approached four inmates with a proposition that if they would get him out of jail, he would pay them $50,000. He had been such a media sensation, with his and Tami's cattle rustling scheme splashed all over the news, along with his most recent car chase involving several counties'-worth of law enforcement agencies − there was no reason for the inmates not to believe he was good for it...once he got out, that is.

They figured he had to have balls to keep everybody on their toes, and thanks to the local media, the idea that he and Tami had something substantial stashed away was on everybody's minds. Nobody thought to look primarily at Tami because they were too busy looking at Bob.

If conversation had been lagging before, it certainly wasn't now. Everyone in cellblock D was abuzz, especially with an offer of $50,000 to get him out of the county jail floating around.[1]

It was only a matter of time before every cell pod in cellblock D that had an inmate assigned to it knew that a jailbreak was about to go down. And the more—the rumor circulated the more interest it generated.

It seemed everybody on the wrong side of the law was pitching in to help Bob, in one way or another. Some inmates tied off bed sheets to use as a rope, another offered up a pair of forgotten fingernail clippers that one of the guards mindlessly left behind, and others just pitched in to help in any way they could, just for the hell of it.

They were interested in seeing if the five could actually pull it off, so everyone in the county jail banded together to see where it could lead. It was a distraction from the tedium, if nothing else. Each inmate was living through the fantasy of being free, and the fact that these five inmates were determined to try what most people only read about in books made it all that more interesting.

The first inmate Bob approached was a twenty-year-old kid named Gerald Lynn Gantt. He was the youngest of the group.

Gantt was known by the other inmates as Jay, or sometimes Jared. It's not clear if it was his actual name, or one he acquired during his short stints in the joint. Gantt had been problematic from the day he was born, always bouncing around from one juvenile hall to the next, eventually ending up at the state school for boys in Gainesville. He was right at home there alongside other members of his family. Gantt ended up in the Grayson County Jail for charges of assault with a deadly weapon and aggravated robbery. He wasn't yet old enough to drink, but his rap sheet was already as long as his young arm.

At first, Bob and Gantt spent a lot of time together trying to figure out the specifics of how they were going to escape. It wasn't until they heard workers directly above them in the ceiling crawling around and installing new air conditioning units that they realized how easy it would be for them to do the same thing. Once they figured out how to get up there, that is. They could do it without anyone knowing what they were up to if they were careful enough.

Sometime in early to mid-September, Bob approached two more inmates with the same proposition that he offered Gantt. Their names were Bryan Jeremy Riley and Jeremy Jon Reynolds.

Riley was from Sherman and twenty-seven when Bob first approached him to see if he wanted to join the criminal enterprise. His charges ranged from aggravated sexual assault to burglary, just to name a few.

Reynolds was from the tiny town of Gordonville and he was twenty-one when Bob first introduced himself. Reynolds was a genuine menace to society. His criminal jacket included attempted theft and assault on a public servant, capital murder and evading arrest. And unlike Gantt, he was able to legally suck down a bottle of whiskey, if the mood hit him just right. Compared to the others in the group, he appeared to be the roughest and by far meanest go-getter out of the bunch. Reynolds had become acquainted with Gantt while he was in jail and the two became fast friends.

It just so happened that one of the other inmates had a set of forbidden nail clippers that a guard had forgotten to retrieve, and another inmate found out about the clippers by word of mouth. They began clipping at the screws that were holding the lights in place in the ceiling. This went on for two months. Eventually, Reynolds and Gantt began clipping at the screws on the lights, too. It was maddening and incremental progress, but they didn't have anywhere else to be.

After the screws were clipped and they began working on the vent, Riley took the nail clippers and broke them, and disposed of the fragments. He didn't want the guards to catch even a whiff of chicanery.

Reynolds, Gantt and Riley tried to get into one of the vents, but quickly discovered that there were no welds in the section of vent they were working on. It was all one solid piece, next to impossible to break into. They had to come up with another plan.

Someone suggested using a broom to break the vent out, but they were afraid of the noise that it would make, so they asked a few of the other inmates to "beat" to rap music while they were beating on the vent. And it worked. It seemed everybody in cellblock D was pitching in to help, in one way or another, and no matter what type of music they preferred to listen to at the time, everybody in cellblock D was rapping to the beat of a jailbreak.

They ran into yet another small hiccup in their plan. They didn't think at the time that they would be able to get through one of the bars that blocked the vent. They would need a saw blade to accomplish that.

That's when Bob told Reynolds to call his wife Jennifer and bring her in on the plan. If there was any chance of getting the bar off the vent then they had to get their hands on a saw blade, and it had to come from someone on the outside. That's where Reynolds' wife came in, but she wasn't the only one called upon to help.

Jennifer was supposed to contact Tami's sixteen-year-old niece, Ashley Nicole Holland, to help smuggle the saw blades into the jail. Ashley was also the one who relayed specific details to her aunt Tami about the pending jailbreak - cluing her in on places that Bob talked about going once he got out, including details about the specifics of the escape itself. This would later work to Tami's advantage and, more importantly, explain why some individuals that Bob set out to see after he broke out of the Grayson County Jail chose to make themselves scarce, but that's getting a little ahead of ourselves.

But the plan required more outside accomplices than an inmate's wife and a teenager in order to succeed, so Bob reached out to one of the women that Tami had given him *carte blanche* to play around with. Her name was Haley Phillips and she was nineteen years old.

Haley traveled like a gypsy between her hometown of Cheyenne, Wyoming and Texas, bouncing around from one town to the next while living out of a small travel trailer. She'd leave her trailer parked in Denton at some off-the-road trailer park while she worked as a waitress at Raphael's Restaurant in Aubrey, a small town south of Pilot Point. That's when she and Bob first started messing around together.

But helping Bob bust out of the county jail wasn't the only thing Haley did. In a not-so-distant day, after the dust from the escape settled and everyone had had their day in court, Haley would be named in a lawsuit alongside Bob and Tami by one of the bankers the pair had fleeced, that all three, including Haley, had allegedly gotten loans for on the stolen cattle.

Based on the lawsuit that was filed by the aggrieved banker, it appears Haley wasn't just involved in the escape, but she also participated in the cattle scams.

For whatever reason, charges were never pressed against Haley for her part in those crimes.

Haley's nineteen-year old friend Kimberly Jean Neta Stallings, who also worked at Raphael's as a waitress, was also pulled into the mix.

According to a statement later given by Kim, she served as a sort of courier between Haley and Bob. She mailed numerous packages and letters for Haley to Bob using false names. She claimed to not have any idea what was in any of the packages that she was sending to the jail and each one was always pre-addressed. Kim trusted her friend Haley would have no reason to throw her under the bus, or so she claimed.[2]

It was a he-said-she-said situation regarding who was involved in the events leading up to the jailbreak and who wasn't. But, as in every story laced with lies, sex and betrayal, when the chips begin to fall and the authorities start to lean hard on suspected "persons of interest," some willing participants play the innocent act a lot better than others.

Before Kim sent the last and final package containing the saw blades via Fed-Ex, Haley high-tailed it to New Mexico leaving her friend Kim to hold the bag.[3]

Bob approached another inmate, Tracy Ledbetter to see if he could get *his* wife, Jennifer, to help. Bob wanted to make three-way calls to the women who were assisting with the escape to assure himself that things were going smoothly, which is where Ledbetter's wife came in.[4]

Bob added her to his visiting list as his legal counsel.

Because of the attorney-client privilege, when a client talks to their attorney, the conversation is kept confidential, so Bob was able to speak with her in privacy.

And that was how Bob Leach carefully orchestrated the Grayson County Jail escape.

Chapter Twenty-Four

FUCK BIN LADEN, CATCH ME IF YOU CAN

With Ledbetter's and Reynolds' wives making three-way calls for Bob, things were beginning to fall into place. Both women would relay information about the jailbreak to Ashley, who would in turn relay the information to Haley and, of course, her Aunt Tami.[1]

But Ashley wasn't just relaying information to her Aunt Tami about what was going on inside the jail. She was also relaying information to Bob about what her Aunt Tami was up to on the outside, and from the sounds of it she was keeping herself mightily busy.

During one of the visits that Ashley paid to the jailhouse, she informed Bob that his beloved wife had been spiriting away pieces of property that the feds would soon be looking for to Tami's Uncle Keith and Aunt Barbara Hocutt's home in Nocona.[2]

In the words of one of Bob's family members, 'this was just more proof of how conniving old hot pants Tami really was', and according to her niece, she was moving the equipment off the ranch as fast as she could. Tami wasn't just blackmailing folks at the party ranch and conning others out of their beef with him, but now she was turning the tables on Bob, her partner in crime. (Interviews with confidential sources, private communication, Feb. 23, 2015)

Bob knew how duplicitous Tami could be, because he had seen how she scammed others. What he didn't foresee, thanks to Ashley's disclosures, was how quickly she turned on him.

It was understood that any packages that were to be sent to Bob would be addressed to Reynolds, so they would seem less conspicuous, especially considering Bob had already broken out of another county jail using a pair of saw blades several years back. For the moment, he didn't want to draw any extra attention to himself, in the event things went south.

All of this effort and deceit was just to get a pair of saw blades into the county jail so they could whittle a bar in a vent to get into the ceiling and dig the rest of the way out of the Grayson County Jail, all so one man could get revenge on his wife and a few others for doing him wrong, while the others who participated in the crime could get paid for busting him out.

Up until this point, nobody had considered backing out. This was becoming more déjà vu by the minute, only this time Bob had some stragglers to contend with.

Ledbetter, for instance, was transferred out of the county lockup before the jailbreak was executed. His wife Jennifer, however, continued to help with the escape, hoping to profit from it in some way.[3]

While Bob was busy getting everything set up on the outside for the escape and assisting with plans on the inside, he kept busy with visitors who were constantly coming into the jail to see him, including Ashley and Haley. And then there was another fellow named Robert Conaway. The records indicate that Conaway visited Bob every Wednesday without fail.[4]

It's not clear when or how Bob came in contact with Conaway, whether it was while Bob and Tami were hustling cattle or while they were, as the individuals interviewed by the author put it, "hosting big sex orgies at the party ranch", no one really knows for sure. They stated that, "one day he just showed up like a little lost dog and just never would leave." (Interviews with confidential sources, private communication, Feb. 23, 2015)

The last and final inmate of the Grayson County Five, Jerry Riley, no relation to Bryan Riley, was approached by Reynolds approximately one week before the escape. Reynolds offered Jerry the same proposition that he, Gantt and Bryan were offered by Bob. Jerry was twenty-four years old and from Collinsville, and was in for aggravated sexual assault.

Jerry told the others that he could dislodge a brick out of the shower for them to use in their escape, and Bob, being the delegator of the situation, told him to do it.

Jerry started by using a spoon to dig at the mortar to loosen the brick, then he used the earpiece from his glasses to remove it. He was careful in doing this, because a few of the guards always checked the shower area and he didn't want them to notice that there was a brick out of place. After he was done, he put the brick back and scraped some of the putty from the walls to hide it until they were ready to use it.

Before the Fed-Ex package containing the saw blades that Kim sent to Reynolds ever arrived at the Grayson County Jail, the five inmates had already come up with another plan to get into the ceiling. They began using the brick that Jerry had whittled out of the wall to break open a grate. Each inmate, except for Bob, took a turn at swinging the brick at the grate, trying to break it free. While all this was going on,

Bob would flush the toilet repeatedly to help drown out the noise of the brick hitting the metal grate.

To prevent the guards from seeing what was going on, they used a towel as a curtain for privacy by hanging a rope up and tying it off on the bars in the cell.

Each time, after they hit the grate, they would stop to see if there were any guards on the block, then Bob would flush the toilet and they'd swing at it again, trying to loosen it. It was tedious and nerve-wracking, but slowly they began to see results.

The Friday before the jailbreak went down, they finally got one edge of the grate loose enough to where they could break it out. The next morning, it only took an hour and a half to pull the grate completely out by using ropes that they fashioned from plastic bags and torn sheets.

Gantt broke out one of the bars in the vent, and by Sunday, he and Reynolds were in the ceiling casing the joint. Gantt noticed that the workers who had installed the air-conditioning units had left behind a ladder, an electrical cord and work lights. He grabbed the extension cord and a light to help him find his way around. Soon, they managed to break the lock on a gate that led to the basement. Now they essentially had the run of the building.

Once they realized where they were, they began working in shifts trying to dig their way out. The first "shift" didn't start until after the 5:00 p.m. headcount, then they would return back to their cells in time for the 10:00 p.m. headcount.

Reynolds and Gantt took the first shift, then Reynolds and Bryan Riley took the second. They rotated, going back into the basement to dig in groups of two at a time. They worked out a schedule until they were digging three times a day, the goal being to dig a space big enough to squeeze through. They had their work cut out for them. They dug the hole with whatever pieces of metal they found underneath the building like shovels, along with bowls and cups.

While all this was going on, Bob was keeping the guards entertained with constant chatter, trying to deflect from the fact that there were two inmates crawling around in the ceiling trying to make their way into the basement to dig. It was a job well-suited for him, because he could blow smoke up anyone's ass better than anyone else. That was the one thing he and Tami were good at.

There was never a shortage of prisoners' uniforms because the guards didn't bother to count them, so it was easy to grab extras. After the guards would gather up all the uniforms from the other inmates, they would leave them in a heap in the catwalk area. When the guards were not looking, the inmates would fish them back into the block and that's how they got extra uniforms. The inmates would keep one to use in the day room and store two extras in the ceiling to dig with.

When they were done digging on their shift, they would shed their muddy uniforms, leaving them in the ceiling and then return to their cells. They would wash off the remaining mud in the toilet or sink in their cell, then make their way to the shower for a final rinse off.

Bryan Riley was having a case of second thoughts and wanted to back out of the escape, so he confronted Bob about it, telling him that he wanted out. The only reason he had agreed to go through with it in the first place was so that he could look down at the chicks from the ceiling. He was of course referring to all the female guards working in the jail.[5]

Besides that, Bryan wasn't looking at as much time as the others, and adding an escape to his list of charges wasn't something he was interested in doing. After he thought about it and realized how much extra time he could get from attempting to flee the jailhouse, it suddenly wasn't worth it to him. So he told Bob he wanted out.

There's a certain lingo when one convict tells another convict that they want to back out of their agreed deal, and however Bryan phrased it to Bob, it didn't go over as well as the younger man thought it would. To say the least.

When Bryan confronted Bob about backing out of the deal, Bob threatened him and told him he would kill him if he didn't follow through with their plans, and then Bob punched Bryan in the mouth.

Everyone had always said, Bob could be a mean son-of-a-bitch when he wanted to be, and this was one of those times. Bryan had no other choice but to go on, unless he wanted another confrontation with bad boy Bob. He swallowed his reservations and the digging continued.

Jerry had been a construction worker before his run-ins with the law, so he was familiar with parts of the building structure and where they could dig to make the most progress. Because of his knowledge in the construction field, things didn't really start moving along for the inmates until Jerry joined in - otherwise they might still be looking at the chicks and trying to figure out where to dig.

Before Jerry was moved to cellblock D, he had been housed in cellblock G close to where the old separation or divider was located. While he was underneath the building, he was able to figure out where to dig by using the sewer pipes as guidelines, while listening to the elevator and the slider by the front door. This of course made it easier for him to know where to dig and where not to.

On Monday, Jerry dug under the concrete wall and by Tuesday he found an electrical light socket that was closer to their excavation site. They scrounged up a fresh light bulb and presto!—light to dig by.

By the time Wednesday rolled around, they were digging heavily in shifts until they made their way outside.

According to the jailhouse records, Ashley showed up at the jail on Wednesday, October 10 at 12:52 p.m. to see Bob. Because all jailhouse visits are recorded, neither Bob nor Ashley spoke much for fear of being overheard planning the escape. Instead, they used hand gestures to communicate.

Bob let her know that the jailbreak was still on and that it would either happen later that night or the following night, Thursday. She would receive a call letting her know where to pick him up.

Before the visit was over, Ashley told Bob that she would be staying at her dad's house. Tim Holland, Tami's brother, lived in Plano.

The only details that are known about Tim Holland, other than the fact that he is Ashley's father, is that he was the first one to call and report Bob missing from the jail. He and Tami both would later play a vital role in intentionally creating mass confusion for the authorities regarding the whereabouts of Ashley, and who she was with the night Bob escaped the Grayson County Jail. This would later prove that Tim and Tami both knew a lot more about Bob's escape than either one wanted to let on.

Sometime in the late morning or early afternoon on Wednesday, a package had been dropped off by Fed-Ex and checked into the mailroom at the Grayson County Jail. It was addressed to Reynolds and the sender's name was "Monique."

As planned, Haley's package, using her false name, had finally arrived, but a guard who became suspicious of the package, refused to give it to Reynolds. The guard discarded the envelope because it looked suspicious and the saw blades concealed inside were never found.

Later that afternoon, Bob told everyone to tear up their mail before they left, so there was no evidence of anything left behind, so all five inmates ripped up their mail and flushed it down the toilet.

On the final day of the escape, Jerry was in the basement completing the rest of the hole.

According to a statement given by Gary Eugene Robison, Bob's cellmate, Robison tried to get the attention of one of the guards to let her know about the impending escape, but for whatever reason he wasn't able to communicate with her. It's not clear why Robison decided to rat out his cellmate or for that matter what he was thinking, but what is known is that after all five convicts jimmied their way out of the jail, Robison was one of the first ones to talk.

When it later came time for Robison to tell his side of the story, the only thing he admitted to was stuffing Bob's bed so it would look like someone was in it.

Apparently, the week prior to the jailbreak, everybody was testing out stuffing their bed sheets with newspapers to see if any of the guards noticed. Because it seemed to work, and none of the guards caught on to what was going on, they used that method to throw off the guards on duty the night of the escape.

As the evening wore on, everybody began to get antsy. Gantt and Bryan wanted to double check that the lights in the basement were still working, so they made one last run through the ceiling into the basement before the 10:00 p.m. headcount.

At approximately 9:30 p.m., a deputy was returning to the Sheriff's office adjacent to the jailhouse to fill out his end-of-shift paperwork. As he entered the parking lot, he noticed something that seemed a little off. The lights on the outside of the jail were not burning. He called in to dispatch to report it and then went inside to complete his report.[6]

At the same time the deputy noticed the lights on the outside of the jail were out, Gantt and Bryan were messing with the lighting in preparation for their escape. Frantically reconnecting the wiring to the lights, they rushed back to their pods just in time for the ten o'clock head count. The lights on the jail exterior were once again illuminated.[7]

About twenty minutes later, an inmate known only to others as "Blinky" made a cryptic phone call to Ashley. "Tonight's the night to meet the cowboys," he told her.

When the deputy who had first noticed the lights were out went back outside at 10 p.m. to leave for the night, he walked back over to the west side of the parking lot and noticed that the lights on the outside of the jail were on again, so he left for the night, thinking no more about it.[8]

At the time of the 10 p.m. headcount, there were fourteen inmates on D-block, and every inmate was accounted for. After the count was done, and the guard left, the five inmates began their getaway. Gantt stepped out of his cell pod first, then Bob, Bryan, Jerry, and Reynolds, each one following the next.[9]

Bob's cellmate and a few others left behind in cellblock D got to work stuffing the mattresses to make it look like the five missing inmates were all in their bunks. Then one of the other inmates replaced the broken grate in the ceiling as best he could.

The hole that they so laboriously dug was four feet long, two feet wide and approximately two feet deep. Inside the large hole was another smaller-sized hole that extended underneath the foundation wall and led up and out to the outside of the building.

Once outside, the five escapees ripped off their orange uniforms, wadded them up and threw them in the mud next to the hole. They removed their identification bracelets and hung them on a piece of metal that was sticking out from the concrete, so as not to be missed. The only message they were sending that night was, 'We're outta here!' They were wearing nothing but T-shirts, boxer shorts and socks.

Before crawling through the hole, one of them, and it's not clear who, wrote a handwritten message on the wall that read, "Fuck Bin Laden, Catch me if you Can," along with a mud sculpture of a hand with an extended middle finger.

So far, the Grayson County jailbreak was a roaring success.

Chapter Twenty-Five

"DID YOU JUST SEE THAT?"

When all five convicts popped out of the hole, they took off running down the street, yelling from the excitement of it all, each one wearing what they had on before they crawled through the hole to freedom - boxer shorts, T-shirts and socks. It was a sight to behold and certainly one that nobody at that time of night expected to see.

Gantt, Bob and Reynolds took off running down Elm Street in the direction of the Monterrey Oaks Apartments, where they planned to rendezvous. Jerry and Bryan took off running towards Liberty Bail Bonds, located directly across the street from the jail. Of all the times to lose their sense of direction, this was not it.

Their destination was of course the residence of Reynolds' father, Gary Reynolds who resided at Monterrey Oaks Apartments.

While all this was going on, a woman made a late visit to the bond company to fill out some paperwork to bail her son out of the nearby jail. She got to the bail bonds company at approximately 10:30. When she was done filling out the paperwork, the employee of the bond company asked her if she would mind waiting outside, while the employee went across the street to the jail to post bail for the young man.[1]

As the two women were walking down the sidewalk, the woman started looking in her purse for her keys, so she could wait in her car while the employee of the bail bonds company went over to the jail.

Suddenly, both women noticed something out of the corner of their eyes that startled them. They saw two muddy, half-naked figures running down the street in a southwesterly direction, away from the jail.

Everything that happened was unexpected and happened so fast that the two women weren't sure they were seeing what they thought they were witnessing, because it was definitely out of the ordinary. They were in complete and utter shock, not to mention disbelief. And each of them had a feeling that something wasn't right.

The woman quickly grabbed her keys from her purse and told the employee that she was going to wait in her car for her until she got back. As she hurriedly got off the street and into her car, she locked the car doors once she was inside.

The mud-stained figures they saw were, of course, Bryan Riley and Jerry, two of the five escapees that had just crawled out of the tunnel from the back of the jail. Momentarily disoriented, they were running in the opposite direction from their companions.

A few seconds after the women witnessed the men running down the street, a young man ran up to the employee of the bond company, who was standing on the sidewalk and asked her, "Did you just see that!?" he asked, in a high-pitched voice laced with fear. He was pointing southward down Elm Street as he was talking to her. She told him that she could barely see any people running, but that she was going to the jail and she would let them know what they saw. Or thought they saw.

All three individuals had a feeling that something wasn't quite right about what they had seen or heard, but none of them could put their finger on what it was, exactly, at the time that it happened. All they knew is that something seemed eerily out of place and amiss.

Jerry heard one of the other escapees whistling and hollering while they were running in the direction of the apartment, as if they were trying to get his and Bryan's attention to get them to turn around. That's when he and Bryan both turned to run towards the others.

The individual, who was doing the whistling and hollering, was of course Bob. He called out to Jerry and Bryan the same way he did when he was trying to corral cattle into the pens, and it worked.

Once again, everyone was back together and running in the same direction towards the Monterrey Oaks Apartments.

There was a lot going on downtown on the square in Sherman the night the escapees broke out of the jail. It was a big to-do in the tiny town of Sherman.

When the employee from Liberty Bail Bonds got to the jail, she told the female officer what had happened, and that she felt that they needed to know something about it wasn't right. The desk sergeant promised that she would look into it. She got the paperwork together for the woman's son and then she left the jail.

Reynolds' apartment was only a few blocks from the Grayson County Jail. It also happened to be on the first floor.[2]

The convicts got to the apartment at approximately 11:00 and went inside for a shower, a smoke and a change of clothes. They were giddy with excitement.

Reynolds had two cell phones. He gave his work phone to the fugitives, so they could communicate with others while they were on the outside, and he kept his personal cell phone for himself.[3]

After everyone finished showering, Bob called Ashley to let her know where to meet them. Then everyone piled into Reynolds' Chevy pickup and he drove them to meet Ashley.

Once they arrived at their destination, Bob called Ashley to let her know that they were at their agreed-upon meeting place. She had parked on the opposite side of the building where they were supposed to meet, so Bob had to call her two more times until they finally made contact.[4]

When they finally spotted Ashley's silver dually pickup truck in the parking lot, all five fugitives climbed inside. Ashley later testified that she said she was not aware that the other four convicts would be going with her and Bob in the wake of the escape. She later stated she was frightened and overwhelmed to see the other four escapees climbing into her truck.

Bob got into the driver's seat, forcing Ashley to move over and the other four scurried to get in the backseat.

By midnight, Jeremy Reynolds' father, Gary Reynolds had turned his truck around and drove back home to the Monterrey Oaks Apartments, leaving all five convicts in the care of a teenage girl.

Once the employee from Liberty Bail Bonds got back to her office, she called the jail again at midnight to see if they knew anything about the people she saw running down the street. The individual that she spoke with informed her that they were still looking into it. Astonishingly, no alarm had yet been raised.

Sometime around 12:30 a.m., Bob called Tami from Ashley's phone to let her know he was out of the Grayson County Jail and that he only had a five-hour window to get out of Dodge. After the morning head count at the jail, every cop in a hundred-mile radius would be looking for him.[5]

It's not clear what all was said between Bob and Tami on the phone that night, but by the end of the conversation, all five escapees and Ashley were headed to Tami's parents and Ashley's grandparents, an older couple named Harold Lloyd and Delphia Joyce Holland. Their house was located in McKinney. Tami had been staying with them since her and Bob's home had been seized by the authorities.

The one hiccup in their plans that night was that Tami wouldn't answer the door when they got there. As it turned out, a number of folks were laying low in the wake of Bob's escape. It turned out that Ashley had been keeping her Aunt Tami abreast of all of Bob's plans about wanting to get even with her and a few others who also had been involved in the cattle con, and who also knew about Tami videotaping clients at the party ranch. Whether real or imaginary, Bob felt like he had scores to settle. (Interviews with confidential sources, private communication, Feb. 23, 2015)[6]

According to Bob and others who witnessed the events that were going on at the party ranch, some of those same individuals who were caught running around bare ass on tape were the same ones who participated in all the illegal activities that were going on during the daylight hours, which might explain why they refused to step forward or have any problems letting Bob take the rap for everything. They were happy to let him take the fall while they stayed in the shadows.

If, as it turned out, Bob was going to go down for what he and others, primarily Tami, did together, he shouldn't have had to do it alone. But it was Bob who took the blame for everything.

Meanwhile, Tami was busy moving equipment around, amassing capital for future payoffs to anyone in the justice system that would help her to stay out of prison. To hell with

Bob, she was looking out for number one. (Interviews with confidential sources, private communication, Feb. 23, 2015)

Bob wasn't mad that he got caught and had to answer for his part in the crimes, because even he knew he would have to do so eventually. No, he was mad that the others who were involved in the crimes with him didn't have to face the same music.

Like Tami, Christi was in hiding as well. Bob, after all, had caught her with all the business cards of law officers in her day planner. She was playing both sides, which did not endear her to her outlaw boyfriend, to say the least. Her nerves were so rattled she didn't know whether to wind her ass or scratch her watch.

Tami knew that if Bob broke out of the Grayson County Jail and he was able to get to her, she would be dead before the event was over.

But in the end, in the words of one individual that was interviewed by the author, "Tami would somehow manage to come out looking like a painted rose, instead of the thorn that everyone saw her as. She used everyone, including her young niece." (Interviews with confidential sources, private communication, Feb. 23, 2015)

What sixteen-year old teenager would jump at the chance to make weekly visits to the jailhouse to visit their aunt's husband instead of hanging out with their like-minded friends, without somehow being coerced into it?

Chapter Twenty-Six

CELL BLOCK D IS IN DISARRAY

As they sped off into the night, each one more apprehensive than the next at the possibility of dying, they agreed going back to jail was not an option. There were other pertinent matters at hand and, most importantly, people that needed to be dealt with first.

While Bob was out for revenge on his co-conspirators, the other four were not-so-patiently waiting for their money. And then there was the simple-minded misfit teenager just along for the ride.

It was anybody's guess where the night would take them, but their first stop was to see Tami. She had been staying at her parent's house in McKinney since her and Bob's home had been seized by the authorities. The truth was she didn't have anywhere else to go.

Based on interviews conducted by the Grayson County Sheriff's Office with two of the fugitives, Tami knew Bob was coming to see her the night he broke out of the Grayson County Jail, because he had called her prior to stopping by.[1]

According to Bob, once they got to the house, he saw a

set of blinds in one of the rooms move as if someone was peering through them.

Bob and Ashley walked up to the front door so Bob could talk to Tami. He knew she had to be in the house. He told Ashley to call Tami from her phone to get her to come outside to talk. But Tami refused to step foot outside the door. And she wasn't about to let him in.

Instead, she remained in the house the whole time, yelling at Bob through the front door. Not exactly a loving husband-and-wife reunion.

Bob yelled back at her to open the door and she screamed, "No!" Then she screamed at Ashley to get away from Bob, but according to Bob, Ashley just stood there watching the whole thing play out.

While all this was going on, the other four escapees remained in the backseat of the truck, unaware of the domestic drama playing out at the house.

After Tami refused to open the door, Bob walked back to the truck with Ashley on his heels. They got back into the truck and left McKinney, ending up on Hwy 380 heading aimlessly in the direction of Princeton, a small town northeast of Dallas. At a loss as to where to go next, they pulled off on the side of the road at a Chevron gas station to figure out their next move. It was the only thing for miles that was open this time of night.

What's disconcerting about Tami's actions the night Bob escaped the Grayson County Jail was that she contacted her brother Tim first instead of calling the Grayson County Sheriff's Office. According to the timeline of events, it took them both one-hour to report Bob missing. And when the call was finally made to the Grayson County Sheriff's Office, it was Tim not Tami who reported it.[2]

Each one's multiple phone conversations with the dispatch operator didn't quite match up to what the escapees and Ashley later claimed happened in their written statements to police. It was beginning to look like Tami had left out two key pieces of information – the fact that Bob had indeed stopped by to see her and that her niece Ashley was with him.

It's not clear why Tami or Tim didn't notify the authorities about the jailbreak, especially considering the fact that Tami and Bob had just had a heated yelling match through the front door of Tami's parent's home. Perhaps Tami was hoping that nobody would tie her to the escape, since her niece was in the center of everything.

No one realized that Bob and the other four convicts were missing from the Grayson County Jail until a call came in to a dispatch operator in the jail from Tami's brother, Tim, at approximately 1:35 a.m. He identified himself and told the dispatcher that Bob had been using his sixteen-year old daughter Ashley's cell phone to make calls and that, specifically, Bob had been calling his sister Tami.[3]

Ten minutes after Tim hung up with the clerk in the jail, Tami called the Grayson County Sheriff's Office and spoke with the same officer. Tami asked the clerk if Bob was still in jail, knowing full well that he wasn't.

For the most part, Tami repeated the same story that Tim had just told. The only difference between hers and Tim's phone conversations with the officer is that Tami provided more detailed information than Tim did about his missing daughter.

Tami told the clerk the one thing Tim *was* sure about when he talked to Tami was that Ashley was in the house with him when he went to bed last night and he was certain that she was still there when he went to bed.

But when Tim went into Ashley's room around midnight to check to see if she was there, he saw that she was gone.

Tim looked outside to see if her truck was there, but it was gone, too.

Based on the statements given by the escapees and Ashley, they all admitted to going by the Hollands' house to see Tami that night. Not only does everyone's story coincide with one another, but the fact that Tami admitted to being at her parents' home when Bob and the escapees went by the house that night seemed to indicate she knew about the jailbreak long before she or her brother Tim ever reported it to the authorities. What's not clear is why Tami never would admit to the authorities or anyone else that they stopped by to see her.

Why did Tami wait so long to notify the authorities about Bob's escape? And why did Tami and her brother Tim withhold crucial information about Ashley being on the run with Bob?

According to Ashley's statement, which she later gave to authorities, her Aunt Tami knew that Bob was planning on breaking out of the Grayson County Jail but claimed that she didn't think he was serious about it. In Tami's case, that statement beggared belief.[4]

For anyone else to hear Tami's assertion, and believe it at the time, without knowing Bob's prior and extensive history of jimmying his way out of jail, it might be plausible. But Tami knew Bob and his track record, and she knew he had every intention of breaking out of that little jail in Sherman, Texas. He certainly had the expertise. And she still didn't say anything about it at all, at least not to anyone in law enforcement, not in time to prevent it. In her defense, though, she played it off by disingenuously saying she didn't *really* think he was going to do it.

Shortly after Ashley informed the detectives about Tami's knowledge of the escape, she also told them that one of the escapees had sexually assaulted her. The details about the assault are limited because Ashley was a minor at the time. But given Tami's demonstrated lack of concern for others, including the safety of her sixteen-year old niece, the news didn't seem to faze her one bit. If Tami was so concerned about her niece as she claimed to be the night Bob escaped, instead of yelling through the door at her to get away from Bob, why didn't she open the door to pull Ashley inside with her?[5]

The Corporal Officer who was on duty at the time that both calls came through told two officers to make sure that Bob was securely locked away in D-block. Each one confirmed that Bob had in fact been there when they did the ten p.m. headcount. The Corporal Officer then told two other officers on duty to go back to D-block and physically inspect Bob's face and his armband. A few minutes later, one of the officers sent to check on Bob called the Corporal and told her to come to the second floor.[6]

When the Corporal Officer arrived on D-block, she saw newspapers crammed in a mattress cover to resemble a human figure. All inmates were ordered to line up against the glass so another headcount could be done. This time, instead of there being fourteen inmates accounted for there were only nine. The Grayson County Jail was now on lockdown and the remaining nine inmates were escorted to holding where they were questioned about the other five inmates who had gone missing.

It was a chaotic scene inside the jail. There were sheets and clothes thrown all over the floor on cell block D, and mattress covers were lying all over the place. The brick that Jerry pried out of the top section of the shower was missing. There were pieces of rope made from the mattress covers and plastic trash bags. And on some of the ropes there were paperclips and what looked like staples that were tied to the ropes, holding them in place. There were extra toothbrushes, which the inmates used to help dig with, and the metal grate which the escapees had pulled off the wall to get into the ceiling was lying on the floor, because the inmate who was supposed to replace it after everyone left wasn't able to put it back in place properly.

But the mess on the floor couldn't compare to what the guard saw when he looked up at the ceiling. Up above him, where two bars should have been, there was only one in its place. The other bar had been removed, and in its place was a hole that measured 8 x 16 inches, where the inmates crawled through to get into the crawlspace in the ceiling.

As the remaining nine jailers sat in the holding cell, the Lieutenant Officer and Corporal Officer began questioning each of the prisoners, who of course knew about the escape all along to find out what had happened. It wasn't until the Corporal Officer spoke with Bob's cellmate, Gary Robison, when she and the other officers found out what the escapees had been planning and where they were going.[7]

According to Robison, Reynolds' father had an apartment located a couple of blocks south of where the jail was located, and that was where the escapees talked about going to in the immediate aftermath of the escape.[8]

The staff in the jail began pulling each inmate's visitation list to get addresses of friends and family. They were particularly interested in the address of Reynolds' father.

Meanwhile, Tim called back to the Grayson County Sheriff's Office to volunteer more information to the clerk. This time, Tim stated that he was concerned that his aunt and uncle, Barbara and Keith Holcutt who lived in Nocona, would be one of the stop-offs for Bob and the escapees. He said he was worried for their safety.[9]

It's not clear if Tim was worried that Bob might find out that the rumors about the equipment being liquidated by Tami were in fact true, or if Tim genuinely felt concern for the old couple. Nonetheless, he mentioned all of this to the clerk in dispatch.

Was Tim simply trying to point the finger in another direction, hoping to temporarily divert any questions directed towards him or Tami, (notably that his sister was hiding the fact that she had seen Ashley with Bob prior to them calling the Grayson County Jail)? It was obvious to the brother and sister that Ashley was a big part of the escape, and authorities were certain to make the same connection soon.

What's disconcerting about Tim's phone calls to the Grayson County Jail after Bob escaped was the extent of the detailed information that Tim provided to the clerk, and the fact that it came directly from Tim himself.

Only those who were directly involved with planning the escape knew exactly what was going on.

Tim couldn't have possibly known any of this, unless of course Ashley told her dad and Tami everything that was going on beforehand. Therefore, Tim and Tami both knew what Bob was planning all along.

Tim was keeping himself busy by relaying information to law enforcement and claiming he didn't have a clue about Ashley's whereabouts, or so he claimed. He only volunteered that Bob was somehow involved, because according to Tami, Bob had been calling her from Ashley's phone.[10]

Ashley was obviously in the company of a gang of dangerous and desperate men, but for the time being, Tim was able to play it off to the clerk as his being the concerned parent and Tami the worried aunt.

According to the brother and sister duo, Ashley had made calls throughout the night, intermittently to her father and her aunt, supposedly trying to cover up the fact that she had snuck out of the house without letting anybody know where she was going, or so they said.

Meanwhile, the sheriff's personnel were still trying to

secure the scene of the brazen escape. When the officers went to check the pipe chase area, they saw lights burning that should not have been on. In another corner, there was a light that remained burning and on the ground next to the big hole and tunnel that extended underneath the foundation wall and out to the outside of the building, through which the fugitives had crawled out, were seven orange jail uniforms wadded up and thrown in the mud.[11]

On the ground, the deputies noticed the cups, spoons, serving tray lids, and an old pipe, along with pieces of metal, that the convicts had used to dig their way out of the jail. And outside, next to the hole, were their muddy footprints leading down the street towards Elm.

On the wall was the handwritten message by one of the convicts that read, "Fuck Bin Laden, Catch me if you Can," along with the mud sculpture of a hand with an extended middle finger. Under other circumstances, it might have been funny.[12]

Each escapee's arm identification bracelet was found hanging on the piece of exposed metal that was sticking out from the concrete wall. The scene was exactly how they left it before crawling through the hole to freedom.

At 2:20 a.m., the same officer that the employee of Liberty Bail Bonds spoke with before had previously called her back to ask her what time she saw the people running down the street. The bail bond staffer told him that it happened at 10:45. The jailer then told her the astonishing news that they had lost five prisoners. Not only that, but they also had a four-hour head start.[13]

The little town of Sherman was in an uproar as the news began to spread. Nothing like this had ever happened before. Now they were in a desperate race against time to find five desperate escapees and get them back quickly.

Grayson County's finest realized that they now had a big

problem on their hands. They had to move quickly if they were going to get these men and bring them back under lock and key.

Texas Ranger Tony Bennie and Deputy U.S. Marshals Melinda Robison and Matt Charske were all promptly notified of the escape. In short order, they began making tracks to the Grayson County Sheriff's Office.

Meanwhile, Corporal Davidson from the Grayson County Sheriff's office was sent to Christi Gale's house in McKinney to notify her about the escape. There was a real possibility she might also be on Bob's to-do list. The McKinney Police Department helped to move Christi and her kids to a safe place for the night.

The maddeningly elusive man that authorities had spent so much time trying to jail for his cattle rustling rackets had somehow managed to break out of confinement yet again, but this time he took four inmates with him.

BACK ROADS, COUNTY ROADS AND SOMEWHERE IN BETWEEN

Bob had been making calls throughout the night using Ashley's and Gary's cell phones. He and Ashley both continued to make calls to Tami throughout the night.

According to the telephone records provided by the Grayson County Sheriff's Department, Ashley had been in contact with the same individuals Bob happened to be calling in the early morning hours after the escape, including Haley Phillips, and Bob Conaway, as well as Tami.[1]

Bob was angry and more importantly, he was determined to get revenge on others. His main target was Tami, as she well knew. But since she hadn't let him into the house, he was looking to get even with someone else whom he had a few bones to pick.

Ashley's custodial grandparents may not have been involved with the crimes that Bob and Tami instigated, but Bob needed money to stay on the run, and since Tami wasn't giving it up he went to the only place he could think of to get it, Ashley's maternal grandparents, William and Diane Erhardt.

He convinced the other four escapees that he had a

million dollars hidden in the attic of Ashley's grandparents' home, and that they had to go by there to get it. Bob of course didn't have money stashed in the attic like he told them he did, but he was looking for a quick way to get his hands on some cash. He was desperate, especially after Tami had hidden what she and Bob had acquired, leaving Bob destitute. In addition, Bob's cohorts were expecting their promised payoffs for aiding in the escape, and Bob knew they were not patient men.[2]

According to a statement later given by one of the escapees, they were supposed to go to the house to get the money that Bob told them he had in their attic, and if things didn't go according to plan, they were supposed to rob the couple.[3]

Bob had no intention of leaving their home without having some sum of cash in his pocket. Lucky for them, the Erhardts were not at home that night.

Before they arrived, Ashley made a phone call to her grandparents' house to check on their whereabouts.[4]

It's not clear what was said in their conversation, or if Ashley did in fact actually speak to her grandparents. It's not clear why she didn't say anything to the others if she knew her grandparents were not going to be there, unless she thought it was the only place to stop off at to pilfer some quick cash without anyone finding out about it. Ashley possibly forewarning her grandparents before they got there of a planned robbery that could have easily gone wrong? No one really knows.

When they pulled up to the house in the wee early morning hours, to the surprise of everyone except for Ashley, the house was completely empty. Ashley went inside and grabbed a hundred dollars-worth of loose bills and rushed back outside. Then she got back inside the truck and they drove to their next destination. It's not clear what the other four escapees thought when they drove away without the million bucks. Perhaps that's why Ashley walked out of the house with some money in hand. Maybe she and Bob were somehow hoping to convince the other four convicts that there was at least some money in the house, she just couldn't get to it.

Ashley's grandparents wound up safe and sound, and before the event was over, the Erhardts would end up working with Grayson County Sheriff's Department and comply with their requests in providing information on locating Ashley.

Everyone headed in the direction of Ft. Worth bound for the little town of Oak Point. The next stop off along the way was at Conaway's house. According to statements given by the escapees and Ashley, they stopped at the brick and wooden ranch-style house belonging to Conaway to get rifles and guns, because according to Bob, Conaway had plenty to spare. While they were there, they figured a little revenge would be a good way to let off some steam. During an interview with the author, two individuals claimed that Conaway was a lot closer to Tami than Bob had suspected. Bob felt that something about the two just wasn't right and he would be right to assume that, but that's getting a little ahead of ourselves. But, lucky for him, it turned out Conaway was not at home, either. (Interview with confidential source, private communication, June 23, 2014) (Interview with confidential source, private communication, June 26, 2014)[5]

What with Tami not answering the door, the Erhardts not being at home and now Conaway going AWOL, all in the same night Bob had escaped the Grayson County Jail, many were left wondering just where in the hell everybody was gone off to, and on a weeknight at that.

This was beginning to look more like a pattern instead of a coincidence. Their visits to each of these homes were between the hours of 1:00 a.m. and 3:00 a.m., a time when everyone should have been nestled at home in their beds.[6]

Once they discovered Conaway was not there, they got back into the truck, never even making it into the house and headed to Denton.[7]

They needed to change vehicles, because by now law enforcement would surely know the make and model of the vehicle they were fleeing in. Tami would probably be more than happy to tell them.

The big silver pickup stood out on a highway full of sedans and battered ranch trucks, so Bob came up with someone else's home where they could go and switch out vehicles along the way.

He told everyone that they could go to a woman's house that he knew to get another truck. When they got to the house, the neighbors went outside and started milling around, awakened by the late arrival, which disconcerted the five convicts. Instead of taking off with the vehicle that they intended to steal, they turned around and left before being spotted by anyone, driving off in the exact same truck they were trying to ditch. It was turning out to be not Bob's night.

Ashley later told authorities that every time they stopped somewhere, Bob would take the keys to the truck, preventing her from being able to leave. She got the feeling they were using her as a way of protecting themselves from law enforcement.[8]

It was beginning to look like Ashley's fears of being on the run with the escapees were well founded.

There was no plan of where they were going next. Since no one had been home at their previous stops, they had to find somewhere else to go and quickly. As they zigzagged up and down the back roads of north Texas in a desperate search to find their next stop, they realized that the wee hours of the morning would soon turn to daylight, and the reality that time was ticking fast was beginning to set in. It wouldn't be long before law enforcement was on their tail. They had to swap trucks and quickly if they were going to stay ahead of the game.

They drove to the little town of Aubrey to the home of yet another woman that Bob knew. Bryan claimed Bob made the statement that he wanted to kidnap a woman. But neither of the men took it seriously until a couple of hours later.[9]

Meanwhile, Bob's luck was running true to form; the woman in Aubrey was absent as well.

This was getting ridiculous. They drove to yet another house located in Pilot Point to the home of still *another* woman that Bob knew. He told everyone that the woman had all kinds of explosives, guns and plenty of weed. Now that was more like it.

When they pulled up to the house, they saw her white four-door dually sitting outside. Bob instructed everybody to wait in the truck before getting out. He wanted his lady friend's husband to go to work first, so they could have free access to anything they wanted without him getting in their way.

After the woman's husband left, Gantt and Bryan hopped the fence to go inside and see what they could find.

Once inside, they took camping equipment, knives, and as promised five pounds of weed, along with several pairs of tennis shoes and changes of clothes, several bottles of whiskey and a rifle that unfortunately didn't have any bullets. It's not clear if the woman was home when they stopped, but nonetheless, they got what they needed.

They came back to the truck with their loot in tow. Everyone realized that now they had a little cash to spare, weed to smoke, whiskey to drink and a gun that they couldn't shoot with.

Somewhere along the way they ended up on the back

roads of north Texas driving for several hours, drinking whiskey and smoking pot.

Unsure of where to go next, they drove until they ended up at the Travelodge, a 24-hour truck stop located in McKinney. At three in the morning they were all still trying to figure out what their next move was going to be, praying that daylight would stay far enough away before they became easy to identify. They were still driving the big shiny, conspicuous truck. They all knew it was just a matter of time before someone would see them and call it in, but for now, they were hiding out.[10]

After a little while later, Bob decided he wanted to drive back by his house in Pilot Point to see it one last time. When they arrived at the ranch style home located on Peel Road, they saw it had been taped off by federal agents and the gate was clearly locked.

Bob told everyone that he knew of one other place that they could go and swap out vehicles and get cash. It was his old employer, Jolabec Stables. Bob knew his way around the stables, and more importantly he knew their schedule. They remained on the back roads until they got to the stables.

While they began making their way to Jolabec Stables, the Grayson County Sheriff's Department immediately started contacting all of their available officers to come in and help in the search for the fugitives. Every man, woman—and, as well be seen, canine—went above and beyond the call of duty. Every officer in the department was on the job, desperate to bring the criminals back to confinement.

One of the officers who had been contacted and told to come in was Corporal Rickey Wheeler, who traveled with his canine partner, Aks.[11]

Aks was a German shepherd who was well-loved by everyone on the force. He and Wheeler had been partners for six months when the escape occurred, and the two had already proven just how good of a team they made together. It was no surprise that they were among the first ones called on the scene.

Aks' predecessor, Artie, had passed away in October of 2000, six months prior to Aks joining the force. It wasn't until April when Aks was transported from his home in Holland and sent to the Grayson County Sheriff's Department to join the force. Artie had been loved by all his fellow officers, because he was a shining star, a real asset to the department, so Aks had some big paws to fill.

Aks was trained to take commands in Dutch and he responded to gunfire, as most canine officers are trained to do.

After Wheeler and Aks got to the Sheriff's Department, they, along with all the other officers assembled, were briefed about the events surrounding the escape.

It was clear that Aks and his fellow officers had their work cut out for them, but Aks would excel and prove just how professional a job he would do in tracking the bad guys.

The Grayson County Jail sits one block behind the town square in downtown Sherman. The front of the jail faces the east on Crockett Street. The street that runs parallel to Crockett, located on the west side, is Elm Street which passes the back of the jail. South of the jail is Lamar Street, and directly to the north of the jail is Cherry Street. The fugitives dug their tunnel and escaped on the west side of the jail, the side that faces Elm Street.

Aks was taken to the escape site and he immediately picked up the scent from a muddy sock that was left behind by one of the inmates. Because the ground was muddy from rain from the day before, and it was still dark outside, no one could see the sock that was lying on the ground, no one except for Aks, who picked up its scent. That one sock would prove to be a crucial part of helping Aks to track the inmates and determine which direction they went.

Aks started tracking south on Elm Street, heading in the direction of Lamar Street. He began traversing the streets surrounding the jail, seeking out scents.

Aks continued to methodically search the streets around the jail, trying to zero in on the inmates' escape route.

The dog was making a search grid as thorough and deliberate as any human tracker. Finally, he stopped in front of the Monterey apartment building on South Crockett St., less than a quarter-mile from the jail.

He had taken his handler, Officer Wheeler, on the same path that the fugitives had travelled by foot when they escaped the jail, and he led Wheeler right up to the apartment complex that the fugitives had made a beeline for in order to seek shelter with Gary Reynolds, Jeremy Jon Reynolds' father.

Chapter Twenty-Eight

"HEY, GUYS, WHAT'S GOING ON?"

After confirming the address of Jeremy's father, the officers immediately contacted the apartment manager who happened to live on site and requested a key to Reynolds' apartment. If the escapees were in fact still at Gary's apartment, they had to be able to get inside and quickly, without the convicts knowing they were coming. These fugitives were considered dangerous, and there was no telling what they might do when confronted.[1]

Gary's apartment was located on the first floor of his building in the apartment complex. When the officers arrived, they noticed there were faint muddy tracks on the sidewalk outside of Gary's building leading up to his door. It was an indication that the escapees had in fact been to Gary's apartment. And they might still be. The lawmen approached the door with an abundance of caution.

At 4:30 a.m., the officers used the manager's key to ease the door open. Upon entering Gary's apartment, one of the officers saw him lying in bed. When he heard the noise of the officers coming into his apartment, Reynolds sat straight up in bed and looked directly at them.

He didn't act surprised or upset, or even scared that men in black masks were standing in his bedroom pointing guns at him. His demeanor was calm, as if he was expecting them to show up. He said to the officers in a calm voice, "Hey, guys, what's going on?"[2]

One of the officers began to explain why they were there. Gary told them that he had no knowledge about any jail escape, and that he hadn't seen or heard from any of the men in question. He professed to be just as shocked as anybody else was about what was going on. And he claimed it was the first time he'd heard anything about it.

That was when one of the other officers noticed a pair of muddy tennis shoes lying on the floor next to the bed. The officer asked Gary who the shoes belonged to, and he replied that they were his. He told the officer that he worked for Tate Construction and the mud on the shoes was from a job site that he had been on.[3]

Another officer also noticed a cell phone that was sitting on the nightstand next to the bed. He asked Gary the number to the cell phone and Gary gave it to him. Then he repeated to the officers that he had not had any contact with the escapees. That of course was a lie, because his son Jeremy had been in contact with him hours before, via Gary's cell phone.

The officers did a thorough search of the apartment but didn't find anything else incriminating, so they left.

When they got back to the Sheriff's Department, the officer that had obtained the cell phone number to Gary's phone called Cingular Wireless to see if Gary's cell phone service was administered through their company. The operator confirmed that the phone did indeed have a Cingular account, but it was billed through the construction company for which Gary worked. There was only one phone call that had been made from that number and it was made at 6:01 that very morning.

The operator told the officer that there was also another phone registered to the construction company in Gary's name. On that line, it showed there were four calls that were made on the night of October 11, less than twelve hours previously, and to the same number. The calls were made minutes apart from each other, beginning shortly after 11 p.m. to the cell phone number belonging to Ashley.

This was proof that Gary had lied to the officers, and it tied him in directly to the escapees. They had someone go and find him to bring him in for questioning.

While the officer who was assigned to track Gary down went to look for him, others were divided up into teams and sent on assignments to talk to the friends and relatives of the escapees. One relative in particular caught the attention of the officers when they stopped by her house to question her. Jennifer Reynolds, Jeremy's wife began crying and became visibly upset when one of the officers began to question her about Jeremy's whereabouts and what if any details she knew about the escape.[4]

At first, she denied knowing anything about anything, but when they told her if she withheld relevant information, they would arrest her for obstruction. She asked them if she had theoretically received a call from Jeremy and didn't tell them about it, could she get in trouble? Simply put, yes she could.

She admitted to receiving such a call at 2:30 a.m. telling her that he was out. But as soon as was informed of the news, the line went dead and he was gone. She claimed that Reynolds knew their house would be one of the first places the cops would look and he was not about to show up in person.

Before the officers left, they told her to call them if Jeremy contacted her again.

Meanwhile, Tami called back into the Grayson County Sheriff's Office and left several confusing and contradictory messages about Ashley's whereabouts. She claimed to have received a call from Ashley on her voicemail that the girl might be staying with a friend of Bob's named Wade Chapell. Her brother Tim later relayed the same information to the deputy.[5]

Chapell was one of the wranglers that Tami had employed at the Rockin' L, back before everything went south. Tim also informed the deputies that Chapell had family located somewhere in Louisiana, and Tim suggested following up with them to see what they might know.

In the end, it turned out Chapell hadn't heard from her either.

It was Tim, not Tami, who called back to the sheriff's department to fill in an important piece of the puzzle. He let them know that Bob had escaped the Callahan County Jail a couple of years back. The deputies had no idea Bob had done this sort of thing once before, and that changed the whole dynamic of the situation.

Tim also told the deputies that Ashley had acted scared and suspicious on the phone when she started changing her story about where she was going to stay the night of the escape. He told her that if she was not back home in an hour, then he was going to call the police. Before disconnecting the call with the deputies, Tim filled them in on one more pertinent piece of information, while throwing still more people under the bus.[6]

He told the deputies that he had spoken to Ashley's grandparents, Diane and William Erhardt, just minutes before calling the Grayson County Jail and they claimed they knew Ashley had been in contact with Bob since August.[7]

It was beginning to look like no one in the family was concerned about Ashley's wellbeing. They were content to let this young girl consort with a jailed felon. And now that said felon was on the run, they had no idea of Ashley's whereabouts.

The officers now knew that Ashley wasn't staying at a friend's house like she claimed she would be in all her messages to Tim and Tami. Rather she was on the run with the escapees. And this piece of information was somehow relayed to them through Tim and Tami.

One of the officers at the Grayson County Sheriff's Office contacted the neighboring police department to have them send over a picture of Ashley and send out a teletype about the missing teen.[8]

By 9:15 a.m., the Grayson County Sheriff's Office was in the process of getting Probable Cause Warrants for all five escapees. Soon the newspapers and media would be notified to warn the public to be on the lookout for five fugitives that escaped the Grayson County Jail and were on the run with a sixteen-year old girl named Ashley Nicole Holland.[9]

At the same time, the dimwitted pharmacist Christi was calling into the Grayson County Sheriff's Office to see if Bob had been caught yet. Before disconnecting the call, Christi told the deputy that when she and Bob were traveling together he had talked about going to Colorado or Mexico.

Meanwhile, the Erhardts contacted the Grayson County Sheriff's Office to let them know that they were Ashley's maternal grandparents and that they had legal custody of her. They told the deputy that if there was anything they could do to help in trying to find Ashley, they would. They said they paid Ashley's phone bill and that the deputy could contact Verizon to get any information regarding calls that were made to and from her phone. And after disconnecting the call with them, that's just what the deputy did.

Verizon was able to verify three numbers that had indeed been called from Ashley's phone - the first one was her friend

Haley at 10:09 p.m., then Bob Conaway at 1:39 a.m. and Jennifer Reynolds at 2:30 a.m.[10]

While the sheriff's office was busy looking for leads and following up on those that looked promising, the fugitives and their kid accomplice were pulling up in front of Jolabec Stables.

When they arrived, Bob and Ashley dropped Bryan, Gantt, Reynolds and Jerry off on the north side of the stables. Jerry went to a trailer house belonging to one of the hired hands while Reynolds went to the stables, and Gantt and Bryan went inside the office. When they got there, they kicked the door to the office open, and found that nobody was there.

As Bryan and Gantt began looking around, trying to figure out what their next move would be, Joyce Silvus, the stable owner, pulled up in her silver Dodge truck and got out.

She had two full-time employees during the week, and on the weekends when it was busy, she had four or five extra hands helping her. But at the moment, she was alone.

Chapter Twenty-Nine

"HEY! COME BACK HERE!"

When they saw Joyce pull up out of nowhere, it scared the hell out of them, and everyone except for Bryan scattered. Gantt took off running in one direction and Jerry and Reynolds took off in another, all making a break for the woods located behind the stables.[1]

But Bryan was waiting inside the office for Joyce to enter. As she walked up to the door, she noticed that the padlock she always kept on the door was missing, and the door was wide open. It looked like it had been kicked open, like someone had forced their way in. The doorframe was slightly mangled and the door had damage to it also.

Joyce had no idea who would want to do something like this, much less why. She was running a modest horse-riding stable with 25 horses in it. Things like this didn't happen at a stable, and she would know because she'd been here for twenty years. What possible reason could someone have to want to kick in her door? As nothing worth stealing and Joyce didn't have any enemies, at least none that she knew about. She was even more dumbfounded at what she saw when she walked through the damaged door—a stranger was lurking inside her office. And he was someone who certainly didn't belong there.

She had no idea who he was, much less what he was doing on her property and in her office. Joyce had been to the bank to make a deposit and to get change to have on hand for the weekend, like she'd done every Friday morning. The stables were always busy on the weekends, and her business was primarily cash- based, so it wasn't unusual for her to go to the bank prior to the weekend to get cash to make change. That morning, just like any other Friday morning, she had $350 on her.[2]

As soon as Joyce got inside the office, Bryan grabbed her arm and twisted it behind her back, holding her in place and preventing her from being able to move. He had such a tight grip on her arm that it was virtually impossible for her to get away from him. She panicked and was scared beyond belief by what was happening to her.[3]

Bryan had grabbed the Visa Mastercard machines off her desk. He took a cord belonging to one of the machines and used it to tie her hands together behind her back. Once he had her in place and was sure she could not move, he reached into her pockets and took out all the cash that she had just gotten from the bank, along with the keys to her truck. Now he was $350 richer, with his very own ride. Then he made her lie on the floor with her hands tied behind her back while he figured out what his next move was.[4]

The truth was, he hadn't anticipated doing all this by himself. They all had agreed on a plan about how everything would play out, or at least what each one was supposed to do according to Bob, and this was not it. When Gantt hauled ass, running into the woods to get away, Bryan had no other choice but to take control of the situation, and that's exactly what he did. The only thing he had to defend himself with was one of the knives that he took when they stole the camping gear and pot from Bob's lady friend's house.

They all knew that the gun they stole would only take them so far without bullets. They were there to swap out vehicles and to get money and guns, but anything after that was anybody's guess.

After Bryan tied Joyce up and had her sit down on the floor, he went outside and got into her truck to drive around and find Bob. Thirty minutes later, Bryan came back with Bob and when Joyce saw him walk into the office, she looked directly at Bob and said, "Bob, I should have known it was you."[5]

They hadn't parted on the best of terms the last time they saw each other. Far from it. Bob had stolen several thousands of dollars from her over a period of three months, and no matter how well-liked Bob was at the stables by others, he had to go once Joyce discovered the theft. And she hadn't seen or heard from him until now. That had been almost two years ago.

It was beginning to look a lot like Bob was still harboring some bad feelings towards her for firing him. Beyond that, she had no way of knowing that he was running out of options of where he could get money from and he had decided he could get some from her quickly, having exhausted all his other options. Since he was on the run from the law, she might have been his last chance to get what he needed to make a clean break, or so he thought.

After waiting for thirty minutes in the woods behind the stables, Reynolds finally came out of hiding, and eventually so did the other two fugitives. Gantt had been sitting in Ashley's truck when Reynolds emerged. Ashley initially did not want to get out of the truck because she knew Joyce, and she didn't want her to know that she was aiding and abetting five fugitives who were on the run.[6]

The two of them walked into the stables where they saw Joyce tied up and sitting up in a chair in the office where Bryan had moved her to.

As Bob was telling everybody what to do, he made sure he told the other four men not to hurt "mom" or the Mexican worker who worked at the ranch. Bob was referring to Jesus Hernandez, whom everyone called "the Mexican." Hernandez was due to show up at work any minute and Bob did not want them to hurt him.[7]

When he did show up, Gantt and Bryan told him to get on the floor, as one of them tied his hands behind his back with rope and the other one pointed the rifle at him. Once he was on the ground, they managed to get his money out of his pocket. They not only had Joyce's cash, but now they had Hernandez's too. After a haphazard night of driving around aimlessly, things were looking up.

Gantt decided he wanted to tour the property, so he took off in Ashley's truck to see what he could find.

Meanwhile, Joyce asked the others to lock the gate so no one else could come inside. That's all the situation needed was more potential hostages.

She especially wanted the gate locked this morning, because there was supposed to be a troop of thirty Girl Scouts who were scheduled to come to the stables later that afternoon, around 3:00, to get their Horse Lovers' Merit Badge. They were coming in on a school bus, and she didn't want them to enter the property with all this going on. She wanted the gate locked in hopes that they wouldn't be able to get in.[8]

Reynolds and Bryan drove Ashley's truck to lock the gate, per Joyce's insistence. She didn't relay to any of them why she wanted the gate locked, only that she didn't want any of her horses getting out. Thankfully, it was done and there was no fear of the Girl Scout troop coming on the property.[9]

Bob instructed Bryan to untie Joyce, so she was sitting with her hands free and she was able to move around somewhat. She was too scared to do much of anything, but at least her hands were untied.

A short time later, the escapees acquired another hostage when another worker, a man who drove the tractor for childrens' hayride, arrived. Gantt took the unloaded gun that he'd become so fond of, pointed it at the man and told him to get on the ground.

And just as Joyce had feared, her other employees began showing up for work, and Bob and his group of misfits were still here. The hayride driver was followed by the wrangler. He was young, no older than eighteen and he had no idea what he was walking into. He pulled up in his green Dodge truck and saw Bob standing on the porch watching him. Meanwhile, Gantt was standing behind the door holding his gun to his chest.

There's not a man or woman alive that could turn Gantt on the same way that gun he was holding could. There's no telling how he would have reacted if he would have had a bullet in it.

The young wrangler didn't think anything was out of the ordinary when he saw Bob standing on the front porch, so he got out of his truck and walked inside, only to be met by Gantt standing behind the door with a gun pointed at him. Gantt was like a crazed man in combat, ready to fight anybody that wanted to take him on. The young wrangler, to no one's surprise, was terrified.

Gantt grabbed the kid and tied him up. Somewhere on the long ride between Gary's apartment and the stables, Gantt found his inner miscreant's voice, and he began taunting and verbally torturing everybody he could. The little pimple- faced guy with no confidence whatsoever had suddenly become an oversized attack dog. He was barking out demands and screaming at everybody. He was making big talk for a little punk who had initially run off into the woods. Gantt grabbed the young kid and tied him up, then he and Reynolds tied Joyce up again.

Gantt leaned over to Joyce and told her to do what he said, or he was going to slit her throat. If she didn't fear Gantt before all this, she certainly did now. Then Gantt waved his newfound weapon around at everybody, taunting and threatening each of them. It didn't matter that Bob had told him and everyone else less than an hour ago not to hurt "mom" or the Mexican, because Gantt was on his own high, a sick one at that.

According to the statements given by the escapees and the victims, after everybody was tied with their hands behind their backs and placed on the floor in the office, Bryan handed Jerry the rifle. Somehow amid things, Bryan managed to get the rifle away from Gantt and he gave it to Jerry and instructed him to point it at the hayride driver.[10]

Meanwhile, Bryan and Ashley left in Joyce's truck to get food for everybody. As soon as they were out of sight, Jerry stopped pointing the gun at the man. Suddenly, things didn't seem as tense. It was obvious Jerry wanted out of this situation, because at the first chance he had to put the gun down, he did.[11]

It didn't matter that he put the gun down though, because the hostages were always aware of a bowie knife that was lying in arms' reach of at least one escapee at all times. It was a constant reminder that anything could happen at any minute.

They were traumatized at the thought of what would happen next as each one began to wonder if they were going to make it out of this nightmare alive.

After Bryan and Ashley returned with the food, Bryan

popped the lid on several beer cans and rolled a joint which was passed around from one person to the next.

Bryan put the joint in Hernandez's mouth, forcing him to smoke it.

Out of the blue, Bryan decided he wanted to go to a nearby Home Depot to buy some supplies and toilet cleaner to make dope with, because he thought they could sell it somewhere along the way. Like they didn't have enough on their plate. So, he and Ashley got back into Joyce's truck and headed to Home Depot.[12]

Then for no apparent reason, Gantt looked at Joyce and told her that he could hurt her. He wanted to know where she lived, and he wanted her to tell him now. She was terrified of him, mostly because he managed to get the gun back and he kept waving it around.

Gantt wanted to go to her house. God knows why. He was acting as if he wanted Joyce and everybody else in the office to know that he was the Alpha dog in the pack.

Out of pure fear that Gantt would carry through with his threat, Joyce told him what he wanted to know, hoping he would leave her alone. She told them that she would go with them to her house, but she added that there was an old man living at her home that she did not want to get him hurt. She certainly didn't want Gantt anywhere around him.

Gantt untied her hands then barked at her to get in the truck with him and Bob. Bob let Gantt do all the taunting. He didn't want to look like the bad guy, but all the while he was the one actually telling the fugitives what to say and do.

In the middle of all the chaos, Bob grabbed Joyce's 9mm Glock and another pistol that she had hidden in her office. Not only did he and Gantt have the rifle that they stole from the previous house, but now they had two more guns to use.

From previous visits to her house while still her employee, Bob knew Joyce had plenty more guns at her house, and he relayed that to Gantt. He wanted the kid to scare her into giving them the guns.

Bob wanted access to her guns, but he wasn't going to get them without her cooperation. There was no way he was going to risk going inside her house with some old man inside. Plus, Bob couldn't risk the chance of her getting away and calling the authorities to notify them of where he was, just in case the other four fugitives weren't able to keep everybody at bay. He was the one calling all the shots so far, and he wasn't about to let anybody else take the lead and risk one of the hostages getting loose.

Bob told Joyce, "We're going to your house to get the guns, now get in the truck." Then he motioned for Gantt to put her in the cab of the green Dodge, the same one that belonged to the young wrangler who was forced at gunpoint into the office.[13]

While Bob and Gantt were putting Joyce in the cab of the truck, another man who boarded his horse at Joyce's stables happened to be pulling into the driveway. And that's when he recognized Bob.

Everything from that point on played out so fast, that the man barely had time to think. He saw Gantt raise his gun into the air and point it directly at his windshield. That's when the man's adrenaline began to set in. He turned his truck around as fast as he could in the driveway and he sped off, heading back in the same direction that he just came from. He was driving like a bat out of hell trying to put as much distance as possible between him and the fugitives. The same men forcing Joyce into the truck were the same escaped criminals whose faces were now plastered all over the newspapers and television.

The reports that came across the airwaves said the men were armed and dangerous, and armed and dangerous was right.

As the man took off towards the gate to get off the property, Bob told Gantt to get Joyce in the truck, because they had to go. Their initial plan to go to her house and get her guns had just changed to chasing down a witness who was about to inform the law that Bob and the boys had been spotted. Bob didn't want that, because whatever plans he had didn't involve a whistle-blowing witness coming forward now. Getting to him before he got to that gate and onto Hwy 380 was their first order of business. And they were taking Joyce with them.

The man was fast, but the fugitives were just as fast, because within a matter of seconds they had Joyce loaded up into the truck, seated between them, with Bob driving and Gantt on her right side.

The ride was bumpy and hard, and Joyce was sitting there hoping the whole thing would come to an end, but it was just beginning.

Bob was going so fast that he didn't have time to stop, and when he did, he hit his brakes so fast that he lost control of the truck, sending it directly into his quarry's truck parked at the closed gate.

Bob's quarry managed to get out of the truck just in time to try to unfasten the lock to get out into the road, away from Bob and the speeding automotive bullet coming directly at him. The terrified driver was trying to enter a combination on the lock to get the gate open, and frankly that took a lot more time than he had. Because when he looked back up, he saw the same green Dodge pickup truck coming right at him, going like a bat out of hell.[14]

As much as he fiddled with the lock and tried to punch in the code to get it to open, he couldn't get it entered fast enough. His fingers were shaking. The man looked at the lock, looked at the green Dodge truck speeding right for him, and barely had enough time to jump over the fence beside the gate. He barely managed it. Had he waited a few more seconds, he would have been crushed.

Justifiably panicked, he ran into oncoming highway traffic to stop a motorist.

He looked back and saw Gantt get into his abandoned truck. Bob hung his head out of the driver's side window and hollered at the man who had just jumped the gate to escape him. "Hey!" hollered Bob, "Come back here!" Understandably, the stranger declined Bob's invitation.[15]

After Gantt got into the man's truck, he backed it up from in front of the gate, and then rammed the green Dodge truck through the gate. Bob and Gantt and the captive Joyce took off down the highway heading in the opposite direction of the man Bob just hollered at.

It was clear that Bob and Gantt were determined to hurt anyone that got in their way, no matter their age or who they were.

Reynolds and Jerry remained at the stables. Perhaps they were tired of running and realized there was nowhere else to go. Ashley and Bryan had not returned from their fools' errand to Home Depot. If they weren't spotted by the law, it would be a miracle.

While all this was playing out at the stables, calls continued to come in to the Grayson County Sheriff's Office about possible sightings of the fugitives. The deputies were quick to respond to every lead, but they all turned up nothing, putting the officers right back at square one. But they dared not ignore any tip from the public.

While investigators continued to track leads and follow up with friends and family of the escapees, Corporal Ricky Wheeler and Officer Rusty May went to Tate Construction, where Gary worked, to bring him in for further questioning.

Gary told the officers that the five men did in fact show up at his apartment on the night of the escape. He stated that he gave them cigarettes, he let each one take a shower, provided them with clothes to wear, and he gave them an extra cell phone that he had. He drove them to McKinney in his extended cab truck. He heard the men say the name "Ashley" several times and he surmised that was who would pick them up once they got into McKinney.[16]

After Gary gave his statement to the officers, they issued a warrant for his arrest for harboring fugitives, and then he was carted off to the Grayson County Jail. The irony was not lost on him.

The deputy that contacted the Verizon Telephone Company about Ashley's cell phone received a call that Ashley's phone was hitting one of their towers located in the Van Alstyne and McKinney area. This was the first solid lead that law enforcement had received since they discovered the escapees were dropped off by Gary in McKinney just hours earlier.[17]

Ten minutes after the deputy from Grayson County Sheriff's Department received the call from Verizon, another call came in to the Collin County Sheriff's Department about a robbery on Hwy 380 at the Jolabec Stables. The boarder who ran into oncoming traffic to get away from Bob and Gantt called the authorities to let them know that two of the escapees they were looking for had just sped away from the stables and they took Joyce, the owner, with them.[18]

While Bryan and Ashley were on their way back from Home Depot, they saw several police cars speeding by in the same direction, flashers blazing.

They decided to keep going toward the stables to see what was going on. As if they couldn't guess.

As they got closer, they saw all the police cars parked in front of the barn and office, so they turned Joyce's truck around and went in the other direction, hauling ass. For the time being, they were just trying to get away. According to

Ashley, Bryan told her that he had family in Bonham, over in East Texas, and that was going to be their next stop.

Meanwhile, the deputies from Grayson County Sheriff's Department were on their way to neighboring Collin County.

When officers from Grayson County Sheriff's Office got to Jolabec Stables, Collin County authorities had already been there interviewing witnesses. They'd also already taken two of the escapees into custody. Jeremy Reynolds and Jerry Riley were in the process of being carted off to the Collin County Jail.[19]

After the Collin County Sheriff's Department got statements from both Jerry and Reynolds, law enforcement from the Grayson County Sheriff's Department arrested them and took them back to Sherman. Jerry was arrested for an outstanding warrant for escape from custody of a penal institution and Reynolds was arrested for escape while arrested. By nightfall, they were both back in the same jail they so desperately dug their way out of just the night before.

Chapter Thirty

LET'S GET THE HELL OUT OF HERE

When authorities questioned Riley and Reynolds, they learned that Bryan had talked about going to Oklahoma. This expanded their search not only throughout Texas but now also Oklahoma, and even though they didn't know where in Oklahoma Bryan might go to or if he in fact even did, they knew the general direction of where he and Ashley might be heading.

Now, instead of looking for five fugitives in one vehicle on the run, law enforcement was looking for two fugitives with a hostage in one truck and one fugitive with a teenager in another, and they were all headed in opposite directions.

Authorities got a tip that Bob and Gantt had been seen traveling along Hwy US 76 and going into a beer barn store called Harlow's, located close to the tiny town of Melissa. Shortly after that tip came in, another one followed it stating Bob was at a residence in Melissa. But by the time personnel from the Grayson County Sheriff's Office and the Collin County Sheriff's Office responded to that call, Bob and company had already left.[1]

It was the biggest cat and mouse chase in the history of Northeast Texas, and Bob was running it.

The authorities discovered that Bob was using two other phones besides Gary's to make calls. One of the phones belonged to Joyce and the other one was wired into the green Dodge truck that Bob and Gantt were driving. This gave law enforcement more options to track them when a call was made.

At 10:15 p.m., Tami called the Grayson County Sheriff's Office to let them know that Bob had just called her, only this time he was calling her from a number she didn't recognize. When the agent from the United States Marshals Service verified the number that Bob called Tami on, they discovered that he was using Joyce's cell phone.[2]

Tami told the deputy that she asked Bob where Ashley and her truck were and he told her he did not know. Before the call ended, he told her he had been in contact with his attorney, Linda Risinger, but Tami didn't seem to care. As far as she was concerned, she was covering her own ass by helping the authorities to bring Bob down. This was a different side of the law that Tami was walking on now, and it was one she'd never been on before.[3]

While Bob was talking on the phone to Tami, the cell phone he was calling from was hitting the tower in Euless. There were several more calls that were made to other individuals. These calls were hitting the towers in the Denison and Oklahoma City area.

As they drove through towns and cities making random calls along the way, the towers continued to pick up the general area of where Bob and Gantt were located. But, by the time law enforcement arrived Bob and Gantt were nowhere to be seen.

According to Joyce, they drove a winding route through Sherman, Denison and Durant, Oklahoma. Then they took off for Bochita, Hugo, Paris, Bonham and somehow ended up back in Sherman along Hwy 56. When they got to Hwy 82, they turned and went to Trenton, Greenville and Emory, where they stopped again for more gas, then they continued on to Canton. When they got to Wolf City they stopped again to gas up and then they drove toward Bonham. If there was a logic to Bob's survey of two-bit Texas towns, it was a secret to everyone but him. The object seemed to just keep moving.[4]

And the calls kept coming, and the authorities were quick, but not quick enough to locate them.

While the authorities were busy following up with calls that were hitting various towers, Bryan and Ashley made their way to Bryan's mother-in-law's house located just outside of Bonham.

On Oct. 13 at 2:30 a.m., the Keller Police Department notified the Grayson County Sheriff's Office that they had found Ashley asleep in Joyce's truck on the side of the road in Roanoke, north of Ft. Worth. She had gotten lost trying to find her way out of Fannin County.[5]

Ashley had taken off with Bryan from Jolabec Stables, headed for McKinney. Ashley ended up leaving on her own after telling Bryan she wanted to go her own way and when the authorities found her, she told them what had happened.

After the officers took Ashley's statement they released her to the care of her grandparents, William and Diane Erhardt. As a juvenile, she was exempt from the serious charges the adult escapees faced.

At 9:42 a.m., while the media were reporting the fugitives were still on the loose, a woman named Arlene Seifert called into the Grayson County Sheriff's Office, and told an officer that she wanted to speak to him about Bob. Arlene said that she knew Bob, and that she visited him twice while he was in prison. She was concerned because she had given Bob her telephone number and address, and with all the reports on the news with everything going on, she wanted to make sure that she wasn't going to be one of his victims. Apparently, she did not know him as well as she thought she did, or she wouldn't have given him all of her information.[6]

She informed the officer that Bob had called her at approximately 2:00 a.m. on Friday morning, and he told her that he was going to Costa Rica, of all places.

He was trying to get out of town, and that was the only place he could think of where he believed he wouldn't get caught. Then he told her to take care of herself and then he hung up the phone.

Arlene said that Bob called her back about twenty minutes later, and twice more after that, but she didn't pick up. She'd decided to heed her inner voice advising caution and the warnings that were blanketing the media. Suddenly, she was beginning to regret giving her personal information to a convict. It just didn't seem to settle too well with Ms. Seifert.

Law enforcement, in the person of Texas Ranger Tony Bennie, was looking for the house in Fannin County that Ashley described to authorities where she left Bryan. In the process of his search, Ranger Bennie came across a person who was of interest to him at the time—a frequent jailhouse visitor of Bob's, Robert Conaway.

Ranger Bennie started following Conaway when he realized that a silver Volkswagen with Texas plates was also tailing Conaway. The Volkswagen was registered to Arlene Seifert, the same gal who called into Grayson County Sheriff's Office to report that she, too, was a frequent visitor to the jail, specifically there to see Bob.[7]

Ranger Bennie continued to follow Conaway and Seifert until they left Fannin County and went into Collin County, which is where he pulled them over.

According to the Ranger, Conaway and Seifert stated that they had been to the Red River Horse Sale, located in Ector, not far from the Oklahoma line, with some other people.[8]

It seemed too coincidental to the authorities that one of the escapees who was with Bob, namely Bryan Riley, was in the same area as two other individuals who were also on his visiting lists. This was beginning to raise official eyebrows.

According to Ranger Bennie's statement, it appeared that it was just a coincidence that they happened to be in Fannin County at the exact same time that Bryan Riley was also spotted in Fannin County. After questioning Conaway and Seifert, Ranger Bennie let them go. He had nothing to hold them on.[9]

Just as they had checked the fugitives' visiting lists after the escape, law enforcement also had a list of people that were being watched simply because they had been associated in one way or another with the men.

Bob pulled the truck over in a little grove of trees just outside of Anna, located south of Sherman, not too far from Hwy 75. He got out of the truck to make a phone call to his attorney, leaving Gantt and Joyce in the truck by themselves. Gantt, taking it upon himself to share his feelings with Joyce, told her that he would not go back into the prison system.

"I'll take a lot of people with me before that even happens," he told her. "And I'll take them all down. Somebody like me won't make it in prison. I can't do it and I won't."[10]

Despite having just met her, and under dire circumstances at that, Gantt seemed to want to share what he was feeling with her, what his deepest thoughts contained. In fact, he insisted on telling her things that she didn't want to hear, but she had no other choice but to sit and listen to him ramble on, because she believed he would shoot her if she tried to run. He was telling her things he hadn't shared with anyone.

The more Joyce heard, the more she decided he was a sick little fuck.

Joyce later told authorities that she was more scared of their driving than anything else in terms of bodily harm. She said oftentimes they would be driving down a road and Bob would see a dirt road and, without any notice, he would sharply turn the truck at top speed. She often wondered if they got into a chase if they would survive.[11]

Chapter Thirty-One

"HAVE YOU GOT A PAIR OF JUMPER CABLES?"

After Bob and Gantt left Jolabec Stables, with "mom" in the front seat between them, they ended up in Golden, a rural area located in Wood County in the Sabine River bottoms. It was about as far off the grid as you could get.[1]

The only way to get to the area, which is threaded with creeks and bayous, is by turning off a farm-to-market road onto a blacktop road that eventually turns into a smaller dirt road, that dead ends just before a creek bed. The area is heavily wooded and makes an ideal spot for an avid hunter looking for deer or turkeys. And, as fate would have it, the fugitives encountered two young hunters in their late teens, who happened to be out hunting for bobcats.

They turned off onto a dead-end road, where Bob heard the young men driving in their truck. Bob and Gantt knew the description of their own truck had been broadcast by the authorities. It was time for a new ride. So, Bob quickly turned the Dodge truck that he was driving in the center of the road to block the men from being able to drive out. Then he stepped out of the truck and lifted the hood, to make it look like he was having car trouble.

As for the young pair of hunters, they had bagged their bobcat and were on their way out of the wooded river bottom. As they began to head out they soon came upon a green Dodge pickup truck with its hood sticking straight up in the air.[2]

Little did they know that they were fixing to encounter two of the Grayson County Five escapees—wanted fugitives, and dangerous ones at that. These young men had no idea what was about to unfold.

The green Dodge appeared to be stalled and the driver was evidently having some kind of car trouble, because it was parked in the middle of the primitive road blocking any oncoming traffic from either direction. The two men had no other choice but to stop their vehicle to see what was going on, and maybe offer some kind of assistance.

As they sat in their truck waiting to see what was going on, and not thinking anything out of the ordinary was about to happen, they saw Bob approach their truck.

"Hi there, you boys got some jumper cables on ya?" asked Bob. He came across in a friendly manner, but that only lasted for a short minute, because he had every intention of taking their truck anyway he saw fit.[3]

The young men got out of their truck and walked to the back to look and see if they had any cables. Bob followed them to the back of the truck. When they discovered that they didn't have any jumper cables, the driver of the truck looked at Bob and said, "No."

Bob nodded his head and replied in a southern drawl, "Alright, then," and that's when Gantt walked around the front of the Dodge truck holding the 12-gauge shotgun that he had stolen.[4]

One of the young men later described in court seeing an elderly woman sitting in the front seat of the truck. That woman, of course, was Joyce.

The young hunters were terrified out of their minds, not sure of what they should do next. They were trapped in an isolated area and there was no way out. Nothing like this that they were aware of had ever happened around here, certainly nothing like this. They were trapped.

The hunters were forced out of their truck at gunpoint, and that's when the real horror began. Gantt held the shotgun within a foot of each man's head, pointing it directly at them, while yelling at them to get on the ground and stay down. Gantt was apparently taking orders from Bob, because according to testimony given by one of the young men in court, Bob was telling Gantt that if they moved, to shoot them.[5]

Gantt was just itching to pull the trigger, looking for his chance to cause more terror for the new-found young victims. He appeared to get satisfaction out of tormenting the men, and he dared either of them to move for his chance to shoot one of them.

Bob and Gantt pulled the shoelaces out of each man's boots and they began to hogtie them with their own shoelaces.

This was beginning to look a lot like something from a slasher film—remote woods, helpless victims, armed gunmen with evil intent...

Bob carried each man individually to the Dodge truck and placed them in the bed. He searched their pockets, taking $40 cash and a driver's license from one of them, and a pocket knife that was clipped in the pocket of the other man's jeans. Bob searched each man's pockets thoroughly, or so he thought, but somehow the other man's pocket knife was overlooked.[6]

Then the fugitives drove the men approximately 200 yards, taking them into a well-hidden brushy and wooded area that was barely visible.

The men did not know exactly what to think, but neither one believed they were going to make it out alive from this harrowing ordeal.

Somehow, Joyce laid a newspaper with the picture of the Grayson County escapees on it beside the men while they lay on the floor of the bed of the truck while neither Bob nor Gantt was looking. Joyce whispered to the young men, "When the Wood County police get here you tell them that the Grayson County escapees are in your area."[7]

As the men lay trussed up in the back of the Dodge truck, terrified that at any minute the fugitives would kill them, they heard the men and Joyce flee in their newly-acquired Nissan truck. As Bob drove their new getaway car, Joyce was once again sitting in the middle between the two fugitives, and Gantt was literally riding shotgun. At the moment, Joyce seemed to be his only target.

It wasn't until Bob, Gantt and Joyce drove off that the men allowed themselves to believe they would be okay. The two men began trying to loosen the laces that had been tightly tied around them, trying desperately to wriggle them free.

It was difficult to do, but the man who had had his pocket knife well hidden, was able to loosen the binding laces just enough where he could get to the blade. Then, he was able to flip the blade of the knife open and he tossed the knife to the other man who was able to free himself.

Once they were able to cut themselves free, they looked at the paper that the woman had left. There was an article explaining in full detail about the fugitives and their escape from Grayson County Jail. It said that they had abducted an elderly woman from Jolabec Stables, and authorities were searching for them. The men realized that the elderly woman that had been abducted was the same woman who left the newspaper for them to read when the fugitives were not looking.

A short time later, after the men were able to cut themselves free and were getting ready to leave to find help, they heard the truck in which the fugitives fled speeding back down the road towards them.

When they discovered that the criminals were turning around, the men lay back down in the bed of the truck and acted as if they were still bound.

They began to fear that they might be coming back to kill them, or worse, possibly try to abduct them. They feared the worst was yet to come.

But in the end, all that happened was one of the men (they couldn't see which) walked up to the Dodge and fetched something out of the cab without checking on their two victims. The stolen Nissan truck drove off again and did not return.[8]

After the fugitives left for a second time, and the hunters convinced themselves that they were gone for good, the men were finally able to escape. They eventually made their way to a friend's house located a mile up the road, where they were able to call the Wood County Sheriff's Department to report the incident.

When the investigator from the Criminal Investigations Division of Wood County arrived at the residence to speak to the two men, they were still so shaken by what happened, that the investigator had to drive them twenty miles to the Sheriff's Office to get a statement from each of them. Even then, the men wouldn't speak about the events until sometime later. The hunters were so shaken by what had happened to them that it took them a good long while to calm down before they were able to relay an account of the actual events of any kind.

Chapter Thirty-Two

THE CALM BEFORE THE SNEEZE

After they took off in their new vehicle, Bob, Gantt and Joyce traveled down Highway 69 towards Greenville. And they eventually ended up on Route 2 running between Paris and Bonham. They were deep into East Texas now. The Nissan truck that they had stolen from the hunters had plenty of guns and ammo behind the seat of the truck. And they had the two cell phones, the one belonging to Gary that he gave them after he dropped them off in Plano and the one that belonged to Joyce.[1]

Besides their weapons and ammo, they also had a hostage that they intended on using to shield themselves from being apprehended by law enforcement.

They were five steps ahead, but not for long, because while Bob and Gantt weren't as easy to spot as before, they knew it would only be a matter of time before the law was after them again, armed with a description of the hunters' vehicle.

Joyce later claimed in one of her statements that she was so naïve when she was riding around with the fugitives after they'd left Wood County that she actually thought they would let her go. She asked Bob if he would let her go and he responded to her, "We can't let you go, because the law won't shoot at us if we have you as a hostage."[2]

She claimed that's when she realized just how much danger she was actually in. It was also the moment that Bob realized how dimwitted she was at thinking he was going to let her go. She stated that she never thought they were holding her as a hostage, and when she heard that term, she knew they weren't planning on releasing her anytime soon. She just figured they would open the door out in the middle of nowhere and let her run on her own. The thought of her being a pawn in the middle of a gunfight terrified her.[3]

She began to re-examine the severity of the situation in which she found herself. She was only 55 years old, but she thought of herself as elderly and meek. She later told the court, when she was asked why she didn't try to leave when her hands were not tied together and she had the opportunity to do so, that she wouldn't have been able to get very far, because in her mind she was feeble and old. She rationalized that they were bigger than she was, and she feared that if she did get away from Bob or Gantt, that Gantt would come after her and shoot her.

Joyce came up with a plan. The truck that they had just stolen from the hunters was dirty from all the mud in the Sabine River Bottom.

She told Bob that when those hunters got loose, they would give their statement to the cops and when they did, they would tell them that their truck was covered in mud. And that's just what law enforcement would be looking for, a mud-spattered Nissan pickup. She told him it would be better to wash it so they were less obvious to everyone else.[4]

They pulled over at the first self-serve car wash they saw, located in Emory, approximately forty miles from Greenville. Bob got out of the truck and washed it while Gantt remained in the truck with "mom." As always, Joyce never left Gantt's sight. Everywhere she went, he was there watching her every move like a hawk stalking his prey.

A phone call came into the Grayson County Sheriff's Department from an officer named Miller at the Rusk Police Department. He was calling to tell one of the officers at Grayson County that one of the gals who worked in the front office at the Rusk Police Department was friends with Bob from back in his cattle scam days.[5]

The woman told Officer Miller that Bob had called her and told her that he wanted to meet her in Frankston, about 35 miles northwest of Rusk. She gave the phone number that Bob called her from to Officer Miller, and he in turn relayed it to the Grayson County Sheriff's Department.

The phone that Bob used was the same phone that was in the green Dodge truck that they just left behind in the river bottom.

Twelve hours after receiving the phone call from Officer Miller, the officer from Grayson County directly contacted the woman who claimed that Bob wanted to meet her in Frankston.

According to her statement, she met Bob sometime in February 2001. She kept referring to him as "Bobby," and she said that he had come down to move some cattle in Frankston. She said that he called her once last night and then again in the morning.[6]

Bob told the woman that he was in Greenville, and that he wanted to go to her house, but that he was seven hours away from where she was at. Bob could have called her from anywhere.[7]

The woman had heard about the jail escape on the news, just as everyone had. And she'd also heard that they had kidnapped a woman. She asked him, "What the hell is the most-wanted man in Texas doing calling me?" But she never got a straight answer from him.

The fact that Bob and his buddy Gantt kidnapped Joyce terrified the woman beyond belief. And she didn't know why Bob would be calling her, because what little contact that they'd had in the past was minimal. So, what possible reason could he have now to contact her? They'd been friendly a time or two, but that was it. She had no idea why he would be calling, especially since he was on the run with a female hostage. This wasn't the "Bobby" she thought she knew.

She was determined to find out anything she could that might help the authorities trying to track him down. If she could just find out where he was or where he was planning on going, maybe she could relay the information to the local authorities.

She asked Bob if anybody was with him. He told her no, that he was by himself. In the middle of their conversation, the woman heard a loud sneeze in the background, as if someone was with Bob and it startled her. It did confirm that the Bobby she knew was lying to her. She knew after she heard that sneeze that there was somebody with him, she just didn't know who or how many people.[8]

She asked Bob who it was that sneezed and followed that question up with a demand that he explain why he told her that he was by himself when he clearly wasn't. He admitted that he was not alone, that there was someone with him, but he didn't tell her who.

Then he changed the subject, trying to deflect her question, but she had watched the news like everyone had, and she knew the old woman who had been kidnapped had to be with him, along with the other escapee.

That sneeze may have been what saved that woman's life, because she abruptly realized that Bob had just lied to her on the phone and that he was not alone.

Bob continued talking to her as if nothing had happened, passing his deception off as if it were no big deal. He told her that he wanted to meet her in Frankston at one of their friend's ranches, someone who happened to be a mutual acquaintance of theirs. The woman realized she might become a hostage herself.

She stated that Bob called her eight more times after that phone call, but she would not answer the phone.[9]

The officer from Grayson County called the person at whose ranch Bob wanted to make his rendezvous and told the man he needed to make himself scarce until the fugitives were caught. From the sound of it, Bob was on his way to see them.

It's not clear what would have transpired at the ranch, if anything, but the owner took heed and quickly moved himself and his loved ones to safety.

Chapter Thirty-Three

RILEY IS FOUND IN FANNIN COUNTY

Law enforcement was exhausted. They had been running nonstop for three days straight without any rest, and so far, only two of the escapees had been captured. Meanwhile, Christi continued to call and pester the Grayson County Sheriff's Department to see if they had gotten Bob yet. The gal was like a dog with a bone.[1]

She was relentless, constantly wanting to be updated, but the authorities could only tell her or anyone else merely what they knew at the time: They were still looking for him.

The law was still after Ashley to pinpoint the house that she left Bryan at. The only information she could give them was that it was a small two-bedroom white frame house with a swing in the front yard. She told them that the house sat on the curve and there was a dark blue Explorer parked in the driveway.

After hours of trying to locate the house to no avail, they had Ashley lead them to the exact house she last left Bryan Rile at in Fannin County. When the officers knocked on the front door of the little white frame house, Bryan's mother-in-law, Karen Woolsey, came to the door, but she did not open it. They told her that they were there for Riley and then they heard a loud banging noise coming from inside the house. Bryan's mother-in-law was hesitant about opening the door and the authorities told her that if she did not open it, they would kick it in.[2]

After hesitating, she finally opened the door and the officers moved her to the couch. As they raided the house, they smelled a strong odor of burned marijuana and they saw a large stash sitting out on the kitchen counter. Bryan was discovered in the back of the house hidden in one of the bedrooms.[3]

The officers noticed a newspaper with an article about Bryan and the rest of the escapees on the couch next to where Woolsey sat. The officers told her they wanted to know what she knew about the escape.

On October 13 at 8:45 p.m., Woolsey was read her rights while the authorities continued to question her in her home. But she told them she did not know anything about the escape other than what she had read about in the newspaper. The only crime that she was guilty of was smoking a joint on the couch when the officers knocked on her front door. Because of that, they charged her for the marijuana that they found in her house.[4]

While Woolsey was taken into custody by the Fannin County Sheriff's Office, Bryan was arrested for Escape while Arrested/Confined and he was taken into custody. After he was arraigned, he was then taken back to the Grayson County Sheriff's Office where investigators and Sheriff Gary questioned him extensively.[5]

Chapter Thirty-Four

THE BACK ROADS OF TEXAS

Bob, Joyce and Gantt were driving up and down a lot of country roads, looking for a place to stop and lay low, when Bob spotted a mobile home that was sitting on a piece of land all by itself. The three had been driving around for hours when they ended up in Fannin County, which is where Bob saw the trailer and decided he wanted to stop.

There weren't any lights around for miles, and, in Bob's mind it was an ideal spot in which to hide out. It was too dark to see anything, and well hidden, so when Bob spotted the place, he pulled on into the driveway and decided he would make himself at home.[1]

As they edged their way closer onto the property, they saw not one mobile home, but two. And it looked like there was no one at home either, which was even better for them.

Bob parked the truck in front of one of the mobile homes and he and Gantt got out of the vehicle to look around, leaving Joyce in the truck all by herself. She was not tied or bound, her hands were completely free, but she stated she was terrified to leave or run for fear that Gantt would shoot her, even though this represented another missed opportunity she had to get away. Not that she knew where she was or had anyplace to run to.

Gantt had remarked that one of the guns that he had found in the back seat of the truck had a night vision scope on it, and she didn't want him to test its accuracy on her. She thought it would just be easier to be a victim and do whatever they wanted, so she stayed in the truck.[2]

Instead of picking up the gun that Gantt was telling everyone about, like any sensible hostage with freedom of movement would do, Joyce decided to sit in the truck and wait. She wouldn't have known what to do next if she'd taken off on her own.

When they came back to the truck, they took her inside where they made her sit in a chair and then tied her up again. So once again, Joyce was confined to a chair where she couldn't do a thing but sit and wait to see what her captors would demand next.

The first mobile home was evidently somebody's home office, with computers and electronic devices all over the place.

While Joyce sat tied up, Bob and Gantt went to the second mobile home, which was the actual residence of the owners.

When they broke into the house, they came upon the family's pets, two beautiful dogs, a German shepherd and a black lab shepherd mix.

The canines knew that the perpetrators didn't belong on the property and their instincts to protect their home kicked in. They lunged forward. Then Gantt did something most people would have thought unimaginable. He pointed the same gun that he had threatened Joyce with; put it into the mouth of the pup known as Tango, and then the sick son of a bitch pulled the trigger. (Interview with Sheriff J.K. Gary, private communication, April 15, 2014) (Interview with Lt. Mark Hudson, private communication, April 15, 2014)

They tore through the house, ransacking it, looking for guns, ammo, money, anything of value that they could get their hands on. At one point, Gantt dragged the dog that he shot from the living room and threw him in the kitchen.

After Bob and Gantt tore the house apart, they went back to the other mobile home where Joyce was still bound. They untied her hands and feet and then took her next door to the other mobile home. They took her to a bedroom in the back of the home and tied her up again.

On Friday, October 13, at approximately 11:30 p.m., Mike and Lindsay LaRue, the couple that lived on the property that Bob and Gantt had invaded, came home to something they couldn't have imagined. When the wife went into the home to let their German shepherds out, she let out a blood-curdling scream. Instead of two dogs coming to the door to be let out, only one of them ran out. The other one was laying on the floor shot to death, leaving a trail of blood from the living room to the kitchen.[3]

When the husband heard his wife scream, he jumped out of their truck as fast as he could to get to her, but he didn't get far. Before he could take off running to check on his wife, one of the fugitives pulled down on him with a rifle from behind his truck, forcing him onto the ground. While one man forced the husband to the ground, the other was inside the house telling the wife to do likewise.[4]

Inside the house, she was forced to lie on the floor face down, in the living room, in front of the television while the husband was defenseless outside. Everything had happened so quickly.

After a few minutes of being forced to lie on the ground

at gunpoint, the man was lifted off the ground and taken inside where his wife was being held at gunpoint.[5]

One of the invaders tried to place a pair of handcuffs on the man's hands, forcing his hands behind his back, but the man's arms were so big that the cuffs would not fit around his hands. So they used rope to tie the man's hands behind his back instead in order to restrain him. They both knew that if they hadn't, then he would have whooped both their asses, and he could have done it too. Bob was big, but the man that he and Gantt were trying to subdue was much bigger and stronger than the two of them put together. If the man had had a chance to get a hold of one of his pistols, Bob and Gantt would have ended up dead.

While all this was going on, Joyce remained in the back bedroom where Bob and Gantt had left her. She was able to hear bits and pieces of what was transpiring in the front part of the mobile home. She heard loud threatening voices and then for a while it was silent.[6]

In the living room, Gantt placed a thin pillowcase over the man's head and went into the bedroom where they were keeping Joyce tied up. Gantt reached over and turned on the radio that was sitting on the nightstand to drown out any noises that were about to come from the front of the house. And then Gantt looked at Joyce and he left the room, closing the door behind him.[7]

As the night wore on, the couple was continually harassed and assaulted as if it was a scene in a horror movie. They were hoping and praying that the intruders would leave.

Sometime during the evening, Bob and Gantt revealed that there was another person tied up in their master bedroom. The couple had no idea who Joyce was, and she didn't know them either. Just at that point, Joyce managed to struggle out of her bonds and walked out of the bedroom into the living room to ask if she could use the bathroom. It was a surreal moment.[8]

At one point, the couple was told that if they did not cooperate, then they would be shot and killed. These kinds of threats went on throughout the night reminding the couple that their lives hung in the balance.

Sometime later in the night, Joyce claimed that she was able to untie her feet from the rope once more. She walked out of the bedroom and went into the living room to look around. Bob and Gantt remained awake the whole time.[9]

It's not clear what she was doing in there, or what she saw, or more importantly, why she didn't try to help the couple. She could never explain herself properly to the authorities. Perhaps she was in shock or denial.

At any rate, it seemed that she had free rein to walk around the mobile home, and then at some point in the evening she walked back into the bedroom and tied her feet back together and then lay back on the bed, as if awaiting further instruction. It's not clear why she did this, but it was obvious she was not willing to risk the chance of escaping out the window to try to help the couple who were forced to remain in the living room.

That Sunday morning, after daylight rose, the fugitives began to load the couple's Lincoln Navigator SUV up with food, and various items from the house, along with clothes and beer and other alcohol. Once they were done, Gantt told the husband that if he called the cops, then rest assured they would use his wife as a human shield, and they took off with her, leaving him tied, bound and angry. They also left Joyce behind.

Ten minutes after Bob and Gantt took off, the husband managed to untie himself and call 911.

Then he made his way into the master bedroom where

Joyce remained on the bed, and he untied her. Bob and Gantt had abandoned her like a sack of dirty laundry.

After being forced to spend two and a half days with her captors, Joyce was finally free.

That's when she stated that she really began to panic; she said later that she thought they would come back and set the house on fire or take the husband and herself as additional hostages after all.[10]

Chapter Thirty-Five

A TEXAS SIZE SHOOTOUT

Bob and Gantt sped out of the couple's driveway at 9:30 a.m. in their red 2000 Lincoln Navigator taking their loot with them and leaving Joyce behind. They had a new hostage, a new vehicle, three additional guns and a lot more whiskey than they did before they arrived.

As the husband relayed information to the Fannin County dispatch operator about his wife being abducted by the two escapees from the Grayson County Jail, the deputies from Grayson County contacted the Texas Department of Public Safety to see if they could assist in getting a helicopter to help look for the red Lincoln Navigator.[1]

Texas Department of Public Safety's helicopter wouldn't be ready to go up for at least another twenty minutes, but the Oklahoma Department of Public Safety had already sent their own airplane up thirty minutes prior to TX DPS even being notified.

By 11:00 a.m. the Oklahoma aircraft was in the air trying to locate the Lincoln Navigator, and roadblocks were set up on highways around the area. While law enforcement continued scouting the area for the Lincoln Navigator, Bob made several calls to his attorney Risinger who kept telling him to turn himself in, but he wouldn't do it.[2]

By 2:00 p.m., the Grayson County Sheriff's Office was briefing their Special Response Team about what was going on. Now, instead of looking for three fugitives, they were searching for two. And the two they were looking for had more weapons, were in a different vehicle and now they had a new hostage. The ante had been raised, clearly. The law began stopping every red Lincoln SUV they could find on the road. (Interviews with confidential sources, private communication, May 9, 2015)[3]

While officers continued to sweep the area for the red Navigator, Bob and Gantt pulled over on the side of the road somewhere between Montague and Cooke counties because they believed somebody was watching them. They left the woman sitting in the backseat with handcuffs on her wrists while they got out to scope the area. When they were far enough out of sight, she threw the backdoor open and took off running towards a pasture filled with burrs and stickers in a desperate attempt to get away from them. She ended up banging on the door of a home located in Montague County, begging for someone to help her. (Interviews with confidential sources, private communication, May 9, 2015)[4]

When Bob and Gantt got back to the Navigator and saw that their hostage was gone, they took off in the direction of Montague County, where they were soon spotted by local authorities south of the town of Muenster.[5]

As recounted in a newspaper article that appeared on October 18 in *The Nocona News* by Tracy R. Mesler, Montague County Constable Herman Conway was headed to the little town of Lindsay to get a bite to eat at the local barbeque joint when he got a call from his son Willie, who was an animal control officer in Bowie. Willie told his dad that he had answered a call from Tom Gordon, a local resident in the tiny town of Hardy, located in Montague County telling Willie that the woman, Lindsay LaRue who had been abducted by the Grayson County Jail escapees had fled her captors and was at his home.[6]

Constable Conway asked Willie to call the Muenster Police Department to let them know about the call that he just received, while he himself contacted the Cooke County Sheriff's Office to let them know what was going on. Because Gordon lived so close to the Cooke County line, it made sense that the Cooke County Sheriff's Office be notified about the escapees being in the area.[7]

Before hanging up with his dad, Willie told him that he was going to the Gordon's house to recover the woman, and he was taking his 30-30 with him.[8]

Willie called the Muenster Police Department and spoke with Officer Gary Whitaker letting him know about the call, and that the Grayson County escapees had been seen in the area. Officer Whitaker had only been on the job for four days when the call came in, though he'd had years of experience working in law enforcement before.[9]

When Willie showed up to the Gordon residence, the woman was still wearing a pair of handcuffs. He cut them off and she wrapped her arms around his neck and thanked him. She also told him that her abductors hadn't let her have anything to eat for two days.[10]

The owners of the home also called the Montague County Sheriff's Department to report what had happened, and they in turn relayed the news to Grayson County. Grayson deputies made plans to pick her up and reunite her with her husband.[11]

Everyone in the area remained on high alert.

Constable Conway had no other choice but to put his barbecue dinner plans on hold, because there were more pertinent matters at hand. He made arrangements to meet with Officer Whitaker in Muenster to see if they could locate the Lincoln Navigator. By the wildest stroke of luck, while they were heading south out of Muenster, they spied a red Lincoln Navigator. It had to be their men. [12&13]

According to an interview that Constable Conway gave to *The Nocona News*, he said that they were not sure if the escapees had any more hostages with them or not, because they could not tell if there were two or three individuals in the vehicle. Both patrol cars and the Lincoln Navigator met at a T-intersection in the middle of the road, where everyone was forced to come to a complete stop. As they began approaching the vehicle, Gantt had hopped in the backseat while Bob was driving, which made it hard for the officers to know exactly how many people were in the vehicle. [14]

Before the officers had a chance to do anything, Gantt grabbed a rifle and pointed it directly at the officers. Instantly, Bob hit the gas pedal and tore off down the road heading southbound onto FM 677 at top speed, searching for an escape route. [15]

Both officers followed the Navigator in pursuit, and radioed in to the Muenster Sheriff's Department that they were tracking the vehicle with the escapees and, more importantly, they needed backup and quick. And the chase ensued. [16]

As Bob tried to get away, he suddenly came upon a dirt road that led into a driveway, where he turned in and drove around to the backside of a house located a hundred yards from the main road.

As the Navigator came to a complete stop in the driveway, Bob and Gantt rushed out of the vehicle. Bob grabbed the 30-06 deer rifle with the night scope and started shooting in the direction of the officers while Gantt took off running inside the house.

As the officers got closer, they were forced to come to an abrupt stop.

Both officers took shelter behind their vehicles, trying their damndest to escape the fusillade. Each kept asking the other if they were hit. They had no means of protection beyond their service revolvers and a shotgun, both of which were useless against Bob at that range.[17]

Within a matter of minutes, DPS Trooper Robert Fuller and Deputy Billy Poynor of the Montague Sheriff's Department arrived on the scene, and they, just like the other two officers, were forced to pull over on the side of the road for fear of being hit by the flying bullets.[18]

Meanwhile, Gantt ran up the steps at the back of the house, and entered. He immediately encountered the homeowner, Irma Forrester. Irma had no idea there was a shootout going on outside her house. She simply could not hear the shots of gunfire between Bob and law enforcement. She was sitting at her table doing the crossword puzzle. (I. Forrester, personal communication, April 13, 2011)

Irma and her husband Vincent Forrester had been married for many years and they were well loved by everyone that knew them. She was a young 63 and he was 65.

Vincent was a former long-haul trucker who wound up driving a school bus for the local school district. (I. Forrester, personal communication, April 13, 2011), (V. Forrester, personal communication, April 13, 2011)

Irma worked as a jailer at the Montague County Jail and later the jail in Denton County, north of Dallas. (I. Forrester, personal communication, April 13, 2011)

Vincent and Irma had spent most of the day at the Forestburg Rodeo Arena where they were having a Play Day for the kids. It was a chance for family and friends to get together and they looked forward to seeing their grandkids. (Interviews with confidential sources, private communication, May 9, 2015)

They got home from the rodeo arena sometime that afternoon and Irma made lunch like she always did. (Interviews with confidential sources, private communication, May 9, 2015)

But then Gantt entered the house. He walked around the kitchen counter and pointed a gun at her.

His hand was shaking the whole time he held the gun to Irma. She said later she could tell he was scared. He asked her if anyone else was in the house with her and she told him that her husband was in the shower. Gantt grabbed Irma and quickly put his arm around her neck and told her to take him to her husband. (I. Forrester, personal communication, April 13, 2011)

Irma had to think fast. She relied on her training from her years of experience of working in the jail. She wasn't scared by any means, she was mad and she had every right to be.

As they stood outside the bathroom door waiting for what seemed like an eternity, Irma asked Gantt what was going on and why he was in her home, but he wouldn't speak. He just stood behind her the whole time with his arm around her neck, and his gun pointed at her. She told him to take her car, take her money - anything that he wanted he could have, she just wanted him to leave, and leave now. But he kept standing there waiting for Vincent to open the door. (I. Forrester, personal communication, April 13, 2011)

When Vincent finally opened the bathroom door and stepped out, he was shocked beyond belief to behold an intruder with his arm around his wife, and holding a gun. (V. Forrester, personal communication, April 13, 2011)

Irma asked Gantt if he would let Vincent get some clothes to put on, but Gantt kept saying no. Irma told him that Vincent was cold-natured and he needed to put some clothes on and Gantt finally relented. All three of them went into the bedroom so Vincent could get some clothes and Gantt continued to hover over Irma the whole time, keeping an eye on both of them. (I. Forrester, personal communication, April 13, 2011)

As they walked back into the living room, the phone rang. It was one of their sons calling to see if she had a bottle of Wesson oil that he could borrow. Irma replied, "Yes, I've got some, but don't come, don't come!" and then she hung up. He was confused by her response and wondered what was up. Irma later said that her son told his wife that something's going on up there and momma said not to come. Irma later said that her daughter-in-law said, "You know how they are. They're probably just fussing about something." (I. Forrester, personal communication, April 13, 2011)

After Irma hung up the phone, Gantt tied her hands together. Then he tied Vincent's hands together as well, wrapping the cord so tightly that it would be three months before Vincent regained feeling in that hand again. Gantt also tied Vincent's feet together with another cord and then he turned off all the lights in the house to make it look like no one was at home.

Gantt asked if they had any guns in the house and Vincent and Irma both said no. They, being Texans, of course did have firearms on hand, but Gantt completely overlooked the gun rack above his head that displayed a .30-.30, a couple of shotguns and an old military rifle. (Interviews with confidential sources, private communication, May 9, 2015)

While Gantt was inside the house tormenting Vincent and Irma, Bob remained outside the whole time keeping law enforcement at bay, firing rounds at the officers. A sudden gun battle seemed to be turning into a protracted stand-off.

One of the ladies at Grandpa's Corner Store located in nearby Forestburg was wearing a pager from the fire department. Suddenly it went off, alerting everyone that the road in front of Vincent and Irma's house was being shut down because of a shoot-out. (Interviews with confidential sources, private communication, May 9, 2015)

One of the neighbors, who happened to be a close friend of one of Vincent and Irma's other sons, had heard the same thing, so he called the couple's house to see if they were okay.

When the phone rang, Vincent was allowed to answer it, but he acted as if he didn't know who the person was on the other end of the line and then he hung up. He and Irma both were scared that one of their kids or grandkids or someone else would pop over to check on them and they didn't want this guy hurting them. (Interviews with confidential sources, private communication, May 9, 2015)

The friend called their son to let him know that there was a shoot-out at the end of Forrester Road and he was worried about Vincent and Irma. Vincent hadn't mentioned anything unusual, but something about that phone call wasn't right.

Their son then called the house and this time Gantt answered the phone. Not recognizing who the unfamiliar voice was on the other end of the line and wondering why a stranger would be answering his parents' phone, he asked, "Who's this?" and Gantt in turn replied, "Who's this?" before hanging up the phone. Their son called back to find out what was going on and Gantt answered the phone and he hung it up again.—(Interviews with confidential sources, private communication, May 9, 2015)

That was enough to send their son running to their house to find out what was going on and who the stranger in his parents' house was. But when he pulled up, he was halted by the officers already on the scene. A shoot-out at his parents' house? His mom and dad taken hostage? Their son couldn't get his head around it, but he took shelter nonetheless.

In the middle of all the chaos, Gantt chose to call his

mother. Perhaps he was afraid or had some sort of premonition. Gantt told her that he was tired of running and he was going to end it all tonight. He asked his mother to take care of his little brother and sister as he cried to her over the phone. (I. Forrester, personal communication, April 13, 2011)

Irma later said that she thought, "Well, that's great, here he is worried about his little brother and sister and he has a gun pointed on us." (I. Forrester, personal communication, April 13, 2011)

Meanwhile outside, Bob had stopped shooting, but only for a little while. The police were keeping their distance and he wanted to conserve ammunition. (Interviews with confidential sources, private communication, May 9, 2015)

However, when Vincent and Irma's son pulled up, Bob resumed popping off rounds. Nobody knew what to do from one minute to the next, because of all the excitement that was going on. (Interviews with confidential sources, private communication, May 9, 2015)

Bob paused long enough to yell out, "We've got five hostages inside!" and the shooting continued. Of course, there were only two hostages, Vincent and Irma, but the officers didn't know that and at the time neither did Bob. He had yet to go inside. (Interviews with confidential sources, private communication, May 9, 2015)

Vincent and Irma's son managed to get past the officer and scurried to Constable Conway's car.

He found Conway wedged under his vehicle, taking shelter from the flying bullets. Conaway told him to get away and find safety himself. The younger man, desperate to know what was going on inside his parents' house, exclaimed, "He's not shooting at us! The bullets aren't even coming over here!"

Bob was in fact only firing warning shots, not shooting at law enforcement, rather he was shooting around them. But to be fair, when a fugitive has a gun and he's firing it, everybody's going to be on edge. But Bob was an excellent marksman, and every shot landed exactly where he intended. (Interviews with confidential sources, private communication, May 9, 2015)

As additional law enforcement from surrounding counties arrived on the scene, they set up roadblocks to discourage passers-by and sightseers. It was turning into quite the standoff.

It seemed like everyone wanted a piece of the action: DPS, Montague, Cooke, Wise and Grayson Counties along with the Grayson County Swat Team, the Saint Jo Police Department, the Texas Rangers, agents from the FBI, game wardens, the U.S. Marshal's Service and seemingly countless others. Every law enforcement entity that was within a hundred-mile radius that could show up did.[19]

A command post was set up to try to coordinate all of the disparate personnel.

Agents from the FBI and the Marshal's Service went to the south side of the house, near where Bob was firing. The fugitives were cornered, and everyone was waiting to see what would happen next.[20]

Irma didn't realize there was another man outside until Bob started firing at law enforcement a second time. For the longest time, neither she nor Vincent knew about Bob. (I. Forrester, personal communication, April 13, 2011)

What happened next was Bob making a strategic retreat. When Bob walked into the house, he entered through the garage door. He laid his gun on the washing machine located in the entryway before going inside the kitchen. Vincent and Irma later said that Bob never brought his gun inside with him. (I. Forrester, personal communication, April 13, 2011), (V. Forrester, personal communication, April 13, 2011)

When Irma saw Bob she asked him, "What did you do,

shoot my dog?" and Bob said, "No, I was shooting at the cops."

Irma wanted to make sure that her loveable Dalmatian dog Dot was not in the line of fire. Irma got Dot from one of her sons as a Christmas gift and she loved that dog.

Irma later said, "It was like a flood of relief to know that there was law enforcement already out there." (I. Forrester, personal communication, April 13, 2011)

Bob said, "You don't know who we are?" and Irma said, "No," and Bob said, "We're the Grayson County escapees."

Irma had read in the paper about them tying up Joyce and she told Bob about it. Then she said, "She was seventy years old?" and Bob said, "That seventy year old woman was fifty seven." Irma said, "Oh good, they'll probably make me out to be eighty then." (I. Forrester, personal communication, April 13, 2011),

Vincent asked him, "Why didn't you stop down the road?" (V. Forrester, personal communication, April 13, 2011)

Neither Bob nor Gantt either one said anything. They just looked at them and couldn't believe they were being questioned. These fugitives were the same type of individuals that Irma had been trained to deal with while working in the jail. It was her training and years of experience that was helping get through this. (Interviews with confidential sources, private communication, May 9, 2015); (I. Forrester, personal communication, April 13, 2011)

Bob pulled all the curtains closed so no one could see inside and then he untied Vincent's feet. He asked Vincent if he had a jacket that he could wear, because the only thing Bob had on were the sweatpants he got from Gary Reynolds when they first broke out of Grayson County. Vincent told him yes and he gave him a jacket to wear. (V. Forrester, personal communication, April 13, 2011)[21]

Gantt walked outside through the garage door and fired

off several shots at the officers. They needed to find a way to surround the house without being shot at, and the only way to do that was by going through the pasture located on the west side of the house.[22]

The reality was, the longer they were out there, the later and darker it got making it almost impossible to see. They needed to find someone who knew the exact layout of the property, and was familiar with it.

It just so happened that Vincent and Irma's son-in-law was at Grandpa's Corner Store when several of the patrolmen walked in. One of the patrolmen asked him if he could draw a map of the property, so they could use it to help guide them in. He promptly did so. He also agreed to guide officers, along with a team of snipers, through the pasture on the western side of the property.[23]

He warned them that walking through the pasture was not going to be easy. There was a big sinkhole that Vincent had covered, but it was still there, and they had to be careful not to step in it. And, oh yeah, the emus. Vincent raised the exotic birds, and they were not the friendliest animals.

While law enforcement was making their way through the pasture, Gantt kept popping off rounds. But Gantt's shots were so random, that the bullets were hitting tree limbs above officers' heads. Gantt stalked the property, firing randomly from various vantage points. He was totally unpredictable. At certain points, he would retreat inside the house to taunt and torment Vincent and Irma.

The negotiators at the command post managed to get Bob on the phone to see how they could bring this whole thing to an end. Bob would talk to the negotiators and then after a while, he would leave the phone dangling off the hook. This continued throughout the night. Everyone at the command post could hear what was going on inside the house because the call was still connected.[24]

At one point, Gantt got on the phone with the negotiators, but the only thing he asked for was to talk to his mom once again. It's not clear what he thought she could do, but he kept asking for her anyway. Gantt later told the negotiators that he was ready to end it all and die right there.[25]

At last, worn out from tension, and probably owing to all the alcohol he had consumed, Gantt succumbed to exhaustion and fell asleep. But not for long. Bob woke Gantt up to let him know he, Bob, was going outside for a little while. Irma later said that when Bob went outside, it seemed like he was gone for an hour and a half. (I. Forrester, personal communication, April 13, 2011)

Law enforcement had a few of their snipers sitting in the trees around Vincent and Irma's house, so they were able to see what was going on inside.

They said that they could see through the kitchen window that Gantt was threatening Vincent with his gun.

According to a witness who overheard what was being said at the command post, one of the members of the SWAT team said about Gantt, "He has a cigarette. Do you want me to tell you what kind it is?" and then one of the officers in the room told the negotiator to tell the sniper to "Shoot that son of a bitch so we can go home!" (Interviews with confidential sources, private communication, May 9, 2015)

Vincent later said after Bob left to go outside, there was one time when he thought Gantt was going to shoot him for certain. Vincent turned to look at him and when he did, Gantt saw him. Vincent said Gantt gave him the meanest go-to- hell look that you ever did see. He thought that Gantt was going to kill him right then, but he didn't. Instead, he went back to lie down and fell asleep once more in a chair in the living room across from Irma. She was still tied up, but once Gantt dozed off, and Bob was outside, she was able to free herself. (V. Forrester, private communication, Nov. 17, 2018)

Irma later said she was tempted to take that cord and choke Gantt with it, but Vincent was sitting right beside him and she didn't want to endanger him if Gantt struggled. (I. Forrester, personal communication, April 13, 2011)

Gantt abruptly woke up when Bob came back inside, and just like before, Gantt started in on Vincent. The tension between Gantt and Vincent was so bad, that Bob got on the phone with the negotiators and told them that he was afraid that Gantt was fixing to kill the old man. Of course, no one knew, except for Vincent, that Irma's hands had been untied the whole time. She kept the cord around her wrists so that Bob or Gantt, neither one would know. (V. Forrester, private communication, Nov. 17, 2018)

Everyone at the command post could hear what was going on inside the house, because the call that the negotiators made to talk to Bob and Gantt hours before was still connected. In addition, the snipers outside could relay what they were seeing. Like Bob, the combined law enforcement outside was afraid Gantt was about to snap. (Interviews with confidential sources, private communication, May 9, 2015)

The cops wanted to get a clearer view of the house, so they asked Texas DPS to send their helicopter in to fly overhead. As the helicopter flew over the property, Gantt raised his gun and started firing rounds into the air, hitting the aircraft. The pilot had no other choice but to land at a school on the road behind the house. (Interviews with confidential sources, private communication, May 9, 2015) (I. Forrester, personal communication, April 13, 2011)[26]

Irma later said that when they heard the helicopter flying overhead, it made them feel so good to know there was a helicopter outside, but when they heard the gunshots and it began to fly off, they wondered where it went. (I. Forrester, personal communication, April 13, 2011)

When things settled down a bit, Irma and Vincent began

talking to Bob and they discovered that they knew the same individuals in the cattle business. Bob began calling Vincent "Pop" and Irma "Mom."As they talked, everyone at the command post, from law enforcement to family, could overhear what they were saying, because the phone was still off the hook. As one family member put it, "It sounded like they were old friends sitting around a table having a cup of coffee instead of being held up by two fugitives on the run." (I. Forrester, personal communication, April 13, 2011) (V. Forrester, personal communication, April 13, 2011)

Bob wanted to get Vincent and Irma out of the house, because this situation had gone too far. Bob had already had some whiskey before he got to Vincent and Irma's house, and he started drinking again. Irma later said she was worried that Bob was going to get too drunk and wind up shooting his own toe off. (I. Forrester, personal communication, April 13, 2011)

As the evening wore on, Gantt, by contrast, got even more antagonistic and abusive towards the couple. He tied them up in the chairs in which they were sitting, making it impossible for either one to move. Then he grabbed a 10 mm semi-automatic and began waving it around. (I. Forrester, personal communication, April 13, 2011) (V. Forrester, personal communication, April 13, 2011)

As the night wore on, Bob was trying to figure out how to get Vincent and Irma safely out of the house.

He saw his chance when Gantt started to doze off in the chair once again while holding the semi-automatic close to him, rather than training on the couple. Whispering over the phone line, the negotiators told him over the phone that he needed to move them into the bathroom where they could climb out of the window to escape.

As Gantt lay sleeping in the chair, Bob directed Vincent and Irma into the bathroom where he removed the cord from

Irma's hands and stepped out to close the door behind him. Bob didn't have to work very hard to take the cord off of Irma, because she showed him it had been loose the whole time. Irma, in turn, untied Vince's hands. (I. Forrester, personal communication, April 13, 2011)[27]

The lights in the bathroom remained out while she and Vincent got into the bathtub and waited. They were not supposed to turn the light on until they were ready to crawl through the window, signaling to law enforcement that they were coming out. This would also help the authorities to know which room of the house they were in.[28]

As Vincent and Irma waited in the bathroom for a signal to turn the light on so they could crawl out the window, the negotiators were back on the phone with Bob.

According to Corporal Wheeler, he told the negotiators to tell Bob that he had permission to use whatever action he deemed necessary, including deadly force, to protect Vincent and Irma from Gantt. (Interview with Sheriff J.K. Gary, private communication, April 15, 2016)[29]

Irma told Vincent that they were going to crawl through the window when the SWAT team was ready for them. While they stood in the tub waiting for the signal, Vincent told Irma that he didn't know what was taking so long. Irma replied, "This isn't television. It's not going to get done in an hour. They've got to get everything just right where we can out." (I. Forrester, personal communication, April 13, 2011)

Forty minutes later, Bob came back into the bathroom and told Vincent and Irma that the SWAT team was ready to receive them. He turned to leave and closed the door behind him.

Irma turned on the bathroom light, opened the window and then waved so the agents could see her. She told Vincent to go first. As he was crawling out of the window, Irma shoved him. And within a matter of seconds, Irma crawled through the same window, landing on her feet too. (V. Forrester, private communication, Nov. 17, 2018)

They ran through the chicken yard out to the other gate underneath the carport. One of the members of the SWAT team handed each of them a jacket to put on and they made their way to the other side of the well house where another SWAT team member was waiting for them. He told them to go to where the school bus was parked by the house and there would be someone there to direct them where to go. When they got to the school bus, another member of the SWAT team told them to go to the other side of where the hay bales were at and wait until it was safe for the deputies to come get them.[30]

According to Corporal Wheeler's report, Vincent and Irma were out of the house by 3:08 a.m.

As they sat behind the hay bales waiting for law enforcement to come and get them, Bob and Gantt remained in the house. Shortly after Vincent and Irma crawled out of the window, Gantt woke up again and wanted to know where the couple had gotten to. His specific words were, "Where's the bitch at?" referring to Irma. (V. Forrester, private communication, Nov. 17, 2018) (Interviews with confidential sources, private communication, May 9, 2015)

Bob told him it was over, and they needed to walk out. Gantt never let go of the semi-automatic and when he spoke, he stated clearly that he was ready to die and that everybody was going down with him. More words were exchanged and the conversation became more heated. In the end it was a matter of who would live and who would die, because Bob and Gantt were both holding a gun. It's not clear when Bob grabbed his gun, but by the time he approached Gantt he was holding it. Of the two, Bob was the one who drew his the quickest and then everyone outside the house heard a gunshot. Bob came out of the house through the garage door, but not before dropping his gun and he surrendered, while Gantt, still inside, suddenly had a different perspective on dying and taking everybody with him.

As law enforcement converged on the house, they asked for assistance from the paramedics to help Gantt with his injury. He was only shot in the gut, a painful but non-fatal wound, but the way he was carrying on, it sounded like he was on death's doorstep. As the paramedics began working on him, twelve officers stood behind the paramedics pointing their guns at him. And the whole time they were working on him, he was crying and repeatedly saying over and over again, "Oh God, please don't let me die! Oh God, please don't let me die!" (Interviews with confidential sources, private communication, May 9, 2015)

A Ranger who happened to be in the room while the paramedics were working on him said, "Son, God can't hear you. You got a tattoo of the devil on your arm. He doesn't give a shit about you!" It was obvious that everyone in the room felt the same, because one of the paramedics said, "I really don't care either. Shut up and quit whining." (Interviews with confidential sources, private communication, May 9, 2015)

Bob was taken into custody and placed underneath an old pecan tree to wait. As law enforcement made their way inside the house to deal with Gantt, the deputies directed Vincent and Irma away from the hay bales to where the school bus was parked. Once there, Vincent went to where Bob was sitting underneath the pecan tree while Irma found her son-in-law and pulled him aside to tell him there was one last thing she wanted to do before they took Gantt off. (Interviews with confidential sources, private communication, May 9, 2015)[31]

Irma grabbed her son-in-law by the arm and told him, "You're coming with me."

He said, "Where are we going?"

And Irma responded, "I'm fixing to slap the shit out of that son-of-a-bitch!"

Not sure he wanted to do this, he said, "You're gonna slap him?"

And Irma answered, "Yeah. They don't give a shit."

After contemplating what to say next and worried that they might get into trouble for what Irma was thinking, he said, "I don't know. We're not going to get in trouble, are we? Are you sure you want to slap him?"

And the only answer Irma had was, "You're damn right I want to slap him."

When the paramedics finished patching Gantt up and they brought him out on a stretcher, Irma walked over to where he was lying and they stopped him. The same Texas Ranger who spoke up inside the house, asked Irma if she had something to say to which she replied, "I damn sure do," and without a second's hesitation, she spit right in Gantt's face. Irma had the final word and she deserved it.

When Vincent got to the pecan tree, Vincent asked one of the officers if he could see Bob, who was still seated hand-cuffed under the pecan tree. They told him that he couldn't touch him, and Vincent said, "Well, I don't want to touch him. I want to thank him." As Vincent walked up to where Bob was sitting, he thanked him for getting them out. And Bob said, "You're welcome." (V. Forrester, private communication, Nov. 17, 2018)

Gantt was transported by Care Flite to John Peter Smith Hospital in Ft. Worth and Bob was taken to the Montague County Jail where he was charged with a parole violation and escaping the Grayson County Jail.[32]

Before it was all over with, Bob and Gantt were charged with four counts of aggravated assault on a public servant, two counts of aggravated kidnapping and one count of burglary of habitation, all first-degree felonies.[33]

Chapter Thirty-Six

WILL THE CIRCLE, BE UNBROKEN

"But do not be afraid of those who threaten you. For the time is coming when everything that is covered will be revealed, and all that is secret will be made to all." Matt10:26 New Living Translation[1]

Over the years, others have had interest in telling the story of Bob's life. Others didn't want to be any part of such a project. One individual in particular did not want to be mentioned, nor did he want his buddies mentioned in the story. It was Richard Calvin Lee, the crony who refused to leave Bob alone through the years. Lee's words were very specific, right up to the point when he said if he or they are mentioned in the story then he could very easily make a car wreck look like an accident. (Interviews with confidential sources, private communication, Aug. 13, 2011) (Interviews with confidential sources, private communication, April 23, 2016)

As it turned out, Bob's dad Marvin reached out to one of Lee's old running buddies for help when Bob was facing hefty charges in multiple counties including Comanche County against Trooper Kubiak. The thugs that Lee runs with ended up paying for Bob's bonds totaling $70,000 while at the same time offering the services of their attorney, Doyle Wayne Neighbors. While Lee is not the main one who has caused troubles over the years, he is one of the key players in a group of thugs who refused to back down.[2]

Tami faced charges stemming from theft by fraud in Louisiana. The charges were theft of 65 head of cattle from Miller Livestock. She turned herself into a Denton County Texas Ranger on the fugitive warrant who booked her immediately. Denton County granted extradition to Louisiana; however, Tami appealed and filed writs claiming she was not in Louisiana on the dates listed on the warrant. Her attorneys also found other discrepancies listed on the warrant and filed for dismissal. On March 4, 2004 the appeal was dismissed, but it is not clear why because the author was unable to access all the case records.[3]

Since Tami's days of working at EDS, she now uses the alias Kimberly Burkett and sometimes she goes by the name of Tami Burkett. Most recently, she uses her birth name, Tami Holland. During the research of this book, it was discovered that she has moved onto working in Christian based organizations and like Lee, she herself enjoys working with children. Over the last decade, she has moved from one church affiliated position to another, praying for others along the way. Her most recent stint includes her service at the ABBA Fund Adoption Assistance Resource where she is a Managing Director of ABBA Fund. She helps childless couples who are looking to someday adopt find a way to become financially stable so that they can someday adopt a child, all while praying for them in the process.[4]

Before any work ever began on this book, Robert Conaway contacted the author and made a proposition that he wanted to be known as a silent partner in telling Bob's story, working side by side as an anonymous co-author. He did not want his name associated with Bob in any way or want others to know his ties to Bob, nor did he know or claim to know how to write a book. According to him, he wanted to do his business dealings tied to the book without Bob having any knowledge whatsoever about it. And he only wanted to be known to Bob as a friend in the background, not as someone potentially turning a profit off of Bob's misdeeds.[5]

Conaway's offer was quickly declined and the meeting ended, but not before he admitted to firmly believing that Tami was guilty for her part in the crimes and he believed that she got away with her part in all of it.

He also claimed that he had no knowledge of Bob or Tami hustling cattle at the time. To hear him tell it, he too was completely naive to their con. What's more disconcerting is the fact that Conaway was and still is on Bob's visiting list, and he still keeps in constant contact with him, for reasons unbeknownst to family.

In addition to his in-person visits, he wrote numerous letters. His disturbing correspondence to Bob still remains a mystery to this day, leaving many to wonder what his real intentions towards Bob really are.[6]

What's even more bizarre is that Conaway claims he has had no contact with Tami or anyone else in her family, yet he stays in constant contact with them through social media.

Based on this alone, Conaway's intentions are misleading in more than one way.

While there were many more people who were involved in the crimes that Bob committed, they will not be mentioned here as many of the cases are ongoing. During the writing of this book, the Leach family has decided to pursue legal actions against others' involvement, therefore reopening several of the cases. That being so, it's evident the entire tale of Bob Leach has yet to be told.

For legal to have any meaning, whatsoever, there has to be a
level playing field, and only then will the word stand true to
the meaning of correctness.
-Bob Davis

INDEX

It's Fannin County Time, Boys

1. Grayson County Sheriff's Office, *Detective Detail,* (Case No. 148153, 2001)

2. Grayson County Sheriff's Office, *Detective Detail,* (Case No. 148153, 2001)

3. Tracy Mesler, Cornered, Escapees Gun Fire Pins Down Pursuers, (2001), 'One Helps Hostages Escape', *The Nocona News, Vol. 96 Issue 18, Oct. 18;* Grayson County Sheriff's Office, *Detective Detail,* (Case No. 148153, 2001)

4. Janet Felderhoff, Muenster Police Officer, Gary Whitaker, in on Fugitive Chase, (2001), *Muenster Enterprise Inc.;* Tracy Mesler, Cornered, Escapees Gun Fire Pins Down Pursuers, (2001), 'One Helps Hostages Escape', *The Nocona News, Vol. 96 Issue 18, Oct. 18.*

5. Janet Felderhoff, Muenster Police Officer, Gary Whitaker, in on Fugitive Chase, (2001), *Muenster Enterprise Inc.*

Southern Roots

1. Heart Attack Takes A.D. Leach, Sr., Sunday Morn, (1955), *Williamson County Sun,* Thursday, Aug. 4, Pg. 3

2. A.D. Leach Gets Honors Two Years In Succession, (1938), 'First Bale Of 1938 Season Comes to Geo'town Thurs.', *Williamson County Sun,* No. 13, Friday, Aug. 5.

3. Pfc. Leach Goes 2 Days In Okinawa Campaign Wearing But One Shoe, (1946), *Williamson County Sun,* No. 43, Friday, Mar. 8.

4. More Local Men Found Who Signed Up For Both Wars, (1942), *Williamson County Sun,* No. 43, Friday, Feb, 27.

5. Contributions to Red Cross Are Received by Roll Call Chairman, (1940), 'Membership Drives Near 250 Mark', *Williamson County Sun*, No. 32, Friday, Dec. 13.

6. Jonah News, (1946), *Taylor Daily Press*, Thursday, Jan. 31, Pg 7.

Hello There, Comanche County

1. Theft Ring Said Initiated Here, (1976), *Brownwood Bulletin*, Vol. 76 No. 291, Tuesday, Sept. 28, Pg. 1

2. www.texasmonthly.com/articles/candy

3. *The State of Texas vs. Hal Dean Windham*, 1978, Theft over $10,000.00.

4. *The State of Texas vs. Roy Kubiak*, 1986, Tampering With a Witness.

The Lawman Wants a Few Head of Cattle

1. [Leach] Aff. [¶1]

2. [Leach] Aff. [¶1]

3. [Leach] Aff. [¶1]

4. [Leach] Aff. [¶2]

5. [Leach] Aff. [¶2]

6. [Leach] Aff. [¶6]

7. [Leach] Aff. [¶5]

8. [Leach] Aff. [¶6]

9. [Leach] Aff. [¶7]

10. [Leach] Aff. [¶7]

11. [Leach] Aff. [¶7]

The Cattle Contract

1. [Joy] Aff. [¶2]

2. [Joy] Aff. [¶3]

3. [Joy] Aff. [¶3]

4. [Joy] Aff. [¶4]

5. [Joy] Aff. [¶8]

6. [Joy] Aff. [¶10]

7. *The State of Texas vs. Bob Harold Leach*, 1986, Theft of the Value of $20,000.00 or More; *The State of Texas vs. Bob Harold Leach*, 1986, Theft of the Value of $750.00 or More But Less Than $20,000.00; *The State of Texas vs. Bob Harold Leach*, 1986, Theft of the Value of $20,000.00 or More.

8. [Joy] Aff. [¶11]

Things Come to a Head

1. Tom McWhorter, TM, *Supplementary Investigation Report*, (8274, 8275, 8276), Erath County Sheriff's Department.

That's One Dandy of a Conversation, Your Honor

1. "What are you doing? I didn't call collect. I'm at the office." (M. Leach, Recorded phone conversation)

2. In The State of Texas vs. Roy Kubiak, No. 978, 220th Judicial District Court of Comanche County, Texas, 1986.

Yer' Mingling With the Wrong Crowd There, Son

1. *The State of Texas vs. Harvey Glenn Edwards*, 1986, Burglary of a Habitation, [1986] Cause No. 2188-86-2, Nacogdoches County; *The State of Texas vs. Harvey Glenn Edwards*, 1986, Theft of Cattle, [1986] Cause No. 6876, Jasper County; *The State of Texas vs. Harvey Glenn Edwards*, 1988, Theft, [1988] Cause No. 18,700, Brazoria County.

2. The State of Texas vs. Bob Harold Leach, Vol. 2, B.K.Castloo, Pg. 143, 402nd Judicial District Court of Wood County, 2003.

3. The State of Texas vs. Bob Harold Leach, Vol. 2, B.K.Castloo, Pg. 144, 402nd Judicial District Court of Wood County, 2003.

4. [Beach] Aff. [Page 1]

5. The State of Texas vs. Bob Harold Leach, Vol. 2, B.K.Castloo, Pg. 145, 402nd Judicial District Court of Wood County, 2003.

6. [Beach] Aff. [Page 3]

7. [Beach] Aff. [Page 3-4]

8. [Beach] Aff. [Page 4]

9. [Beach] Aff. [Page 4-5]

10. [Beach] Aff. [Page 8]

11. [Beach] Aff. [Page 8]

12. [Beach] Aff. [Page 12]

13. [Beach] Aff. [Page 14]

14. [Beach] Aff. [Page 13]

15. *Cross Plains Review* (1990), 'Courthouse News', Thursday, Apr. 26, Pg. 2; (The State of Texas vs. *Bob Harold Leach*), 1990, Cause No. 5446 in the 42nd District Court of Callahan County, TX, Aggravated Kidnapping and Aggravated Robbery, Motion to Dismiss

Escaped! The Callahan County Jailbreak

1. *The State of Texas vs. Richard Calvin Lee* (Note)

2. *The State of Texas vs. Richard Calvin Lee* (Note)

3. United States. National Weather Service. United States, 1990, https://www.weather.gov/abr/ This_Day_in_Weather_History_Apr_25

4. Bob Harold Leach, Warrant No. 2-45, Escaped Callahan County Jail 4/25/1990; Richard Calvin Lee, Warrant No. 2-46, Facilitating Escape.

5. *The State of Texas vs. Bob Harold Leach*, 1990, Cause No. 12,072, Form No. 1-3; *The State of Texas vs. Bob Harold Leach*, 1990, Cause No. 12,071, Form No. 1-3; *The State of Texas vs. Bob Harold Leach*, 1991, Cause No. 5461, Vol. K. Pg. 881-883.

Bob Meets Tami

1. Leach, B. (1990c, 21 Oct.)

2. Leach, B. (1990f, 30 Dec.)

3. Leach, B. (1990f, 30 Dec.)

4. Leach, B. (1991h, 5 Feb.)

5. Leach, B. (1990f, 30 Dec.)

6. Leach, B. (1990f, 30 Dec.); Holland, T. (1990, 26 Dec.) The original letter was destroyed, but a copy of it was scanned into TDC was regenerated where the author could view it, then it was destroyed again.

7. Leach, B. (1990f, 30 Dec.)

8. Leach, B. (1990f, 30 Dec.)

9. Leach, B. (1990f, 30 Dec.)

10. Leach, B. (1991h, 5 Feb.)

11. Leach, B. (1991g, 30 Jan.); Leach, B. (1991h, 5 Feb.)

12. Leach, B. (1991g, 30 Jan.); Leach, B. (1991h, 5 Feb.)

How It All Started

1. The State of Texas vs. Bob Harold Leach, Vol. 2, B.K.Castloo, Pg. 49, 402nd Judicial District Court of Wood County, 2003.

2. FBI (2001) USA: Routine, FD-302(Rev. 10-6-95). Name of Field Inspector deleted, Released under FOIA; FBI (2001) USA: Routine, FD-302(08-28-2000). Name of Field Inspector deleted, Released under FOIA.

3. FBI (2001) USA: Routine, FD-302(Rev. 10-6-95). Name of Field Inspector deleted, Released under FOIA; FBI (2001) USA: Routine, FD-302(08-28-2000). Name of Field Inspector deleted, Released under FOIA.

Settling Into Married Life

1. FBI (2001) USA: Routine, FD-302(Rev. 10-6-95). Name of Field Inspector deleted, Released under FOIA; The State of Texas vs.

Bob Harold Leach, Vol. 2, B.K.Castloo, Pg. 104-108, 402nd Judicial District Court of Wood County, 2003.

2. The State of Texas vs. Bob Harold Leach, Vol. 2, B.K.Castloo, Pg. 104, 402nd Judicial District Court of Wood County, 2003.

3. The State of Texas vs. Bob Harold Leach, Vol. 2, B.K.Castloo, Pg. 104-109, 402nd Judicial District Court of Wood County, 2003.

4. The State of Texas vs. Bob Harold Leach, Vol. 2, B.K.Castloo, Pg. 105, 402nd Judicial District Court of Wood County, 2003.

5. The State of Texas vs. Bob Harold Leach, Vol. 2, B.K.Castloo, Pg. 133, 402nd Judicial District Court of Wood County, 2003.

6. FBI (2001) USA: Routine, FD-302(Rev. 10-6-95). Name of Field Inspector deleted, Released under FOIA.

7. FBI (2001) USA: Routine, FD-302(Rev. 10-6-95). Name of Field Inspector deleted, Released under FOIA.

Rolling the Dice

1. The State of Texas vs. Bob Harold Leach, Vol. 2, B.K.Castloo, Pg. 53, 402nd Judicial District Court of Wood County, 2003.

2. The State of Texas vs. Bob Harold Leach, Vol. 2, B.K.Castloo, Pg. 50-51, 402nd Judicial District Court of Wood County, 2003.

3. FBI (2001) USA: Routine, FD-302(Rev. 10-6-95). Name of Field Inspector deleted, Released under FOIA; FBI (2001) USA: Routine, FD-302(08-28-2000). Name of Field Inspector deleted, Released under FOIA.

4. FBI (2001) USA: Routine, FD-302(Rev. 10-6-95). Name of Field Inspector deleted, Released under FOIA; FBI (2001) USA: Routine, FD-302(08-28-2000). Name of Field Inspector deleted, Released under FOIA.

5. FBI (2001) USA: Routine, FD-302(Rev. 10-6-95). Name of Field Inspector deleted, Released under FOIA; FBI (2001) USA: Routine, FD-302(08-28-2000). Name of Field Inspector deleted, Released under FOIA.

6. FBI (2001) USA: Routine, FD-302(Rev. 10-6-95). Name of Field Inspector deleted, Released under FOIA; FBI (2001) USA: Routine, FD-302(08-28-2000). Name of Field Inspector deleted, Released under FOIA.

7. FBI (2001) USA: Routine, FD-302(Rev. 10-6-95). Name of Field Inspector deleted, Released under FOIA; FBI (2001) USA: Routine, FD-302(08-28-2000). Name of Field Inspector deleted, Released under FOIA.

8. FBI (2001) USA: Routine, FD-302(Rev. 10-6-95). Name of Field Inspector deleted, Released under FOIA; FBI (2001) USA: Routine, FD-302(08-28-2000). Name of Field Inspector deleted, Released under FOIA.

9. FBI (2001) USA: Routine, FD-302(Rev. 10-6-95). Name of Field Inspector deleted, Released under FOIA; FBI (2001) USA: Routine, FD-302(08-28-2000). Name of Field Inspector deleted, Released under FOIA.

10. FBI (2001) USA: Routine, FD-302(Rev. 10-6-95). Name of Field Inspector deleted, Released under FOIA; FBI (2001) USA: Routine, FD-302(08-28-2000). Name of Field Inspector deleted, Released under FOIA.

11. FBI (2001) USA; Routine, FD-302(Rev. 10-6-95). Name of Field Inspector deleted, Released under FOIA; FBI (2001) USA; Routine, FD-302(08-28-2000). Name of Field Inspector deleted, Released under FOIA.

12. FBI (2001) USA; Routine, FD-302(Rev. 10-6-95). Name of Field Inspector deleted, Released under FOIA; FBI (2001) USA; Routine, FD-302(08-28-2000). Name of Field Inspector deleted, Released under FOIA.

13. FBI (2001) USA; Routine, FD-302(Rev. 10-6-95). Name of Field Inspector deleted, Released under FOIA; FBI (2001) USA; Routine, FD-302(08-28-2000). Name of Field Inspector deleted, Released under FOIA.

Welcome to the Party Ranch

1. Tanya Brazil, "Rockin Ranch Rustic Area Provides Retreat", (*Denton Record-Chronicle/Stacey Cooper*), Date unavailable to author, Pg. 1E-2E.

2. The State of Texas vs. Bob Harold Leach, Vol. 2, B.K.Castloo, Pg. 109-110, 402nd Judicial District Court of Wood County, 2003.

Somebody Call the Banker, We Need More Money

1. FBI (2001) USA: Routine, FD-302(Rev. 10-6-95). Name of Field Inspector deleted, Released under FOIA; FBI (2001) USA: Routine, FD-302(08-28-2000). Name of Field Inspector deleted, Released under FOIA.

2. FBI (2001) USA: Routine, FD-302(Rev. 10-6-95). Name of Field Inspector deleted, Released under FOIA; FBI (2001) USA: Routine, FD-302(08-28-2000). Name of Field Inspector deleted, Released under FOIA.

3. FBI (2001) USA: Routine, FD-302(Rev. 10-6-95). Name of Field Inspector deleted, Released under FOIA; FBI (2001) USA: Routine, FD-302(08-28-2000). Name of Field Inspector deleted, Released under FOIA.

4. FBI (2001) USA: Routine, FD-302(Rev. 10-6-95). Name of Field Inspector deleted, Released under FOIA; FBI (2001) USA: Routine, FD-302(08-28-2000). Name of Field Inspector deleted, Released under FOIA.

5. FBI (2001) USA: Routine, FD-302(Rev. 10-6-95). Name of Field Inspector deleted, Released under FOIA; FBI (2001) USA: Routine, FD-302(08-28-2000). Name of Field Inspector deleted, Released under FOIA.

It's Time to Come Clean

1. FBI (2001) USA: Routine, FD-302(Rev. 10-6-95). Name of Field Inspector deleted, Released under FOIA; FBI (2001) USA:

Routine, FD-302(08-28-2000). Name of Field Inspector deleted, Released under FOIA.

2. FBI (2001) USA: Routine, FD-302(Rev. 10-6-95). Name of Field Inspector deleted, Released under FOIA; FBI (2001) USA: Routine, FD-302(08-28-2000). Name of Field Inspector deleted, Released under FOIA.

3. FBI (2001) USA: Routine, FD-302(Rev. 10-6-95). Name of Field Inspector deleted, Released under FOIA; FBI (2001) USA: Routine, FD-302(08-28-2000). Name of Field Inspector deleted, Released under FOIA.

4. The State of Texas vs. Bob Harold Leach, Vol. 2, B.K.Castloo, Pg. 135, 402nd Judicial District Court of Wood County, 2003.

5. The State of Texas vs. Bob Harold Leach, Vol. 2, B.K.Castloo, Pg. 111-112, 402nd Judicial District Court of Wood County, 2003.

6. Jay Kirk, "High Plains Grifter", *GQ*, Aug. 2005.

7. The State of Texas vs. Bob Harold Leach, Vol. 2, B.K.Castloo, Pg. 111-113, 402nd Judicial District Court of Wood County, 2003.

8. FBI (2001) USA: Routine, FD-302(Rev. 10-6-95). Name of Field Inspector deleted, Released under FOIA; FBI (2001) USA: Routine, FD-302(08-28-2000). Name of Field Inspector deleted, Released under FOIA.

9. FBI (2001) USA: Routine, FD-302(Rev. 10-6-95). Name of Field Inspector deleted, Released under FOIA; FBI (2001) USA: Routine, FD-302(08-28-2000). Name of Field Inspector deleted, Released under FOIA.

10. FBI (2001) USA: Routine, FD-302(Rev. 10-6-95). Name of Field Inspector deleted, Released under FOIA; FBI (2001) USA: Routine, FD-302(08-28-2000). Name of Field Inspector deleted, Released under FOIA.

11. FBI (2001) USA: Routine, FD-302(Rev. 10-6-95). Name of Field Inspector deleted, Released under FOIA; FBI (2001) USA: Routine, FD-302(08-28-2000). Name of Field Inspector deleted, Released under FOIA.

12. FBI (2001) USA: Routine, FD-302(Rev. 10-6-95). Name of Field Inspector deleted, Released under FOIA; FBI (2001) USA: Routine, FD-302(08-28-2000). Name of Field Inspector deleted, Released under FOIA.

13. FBI (2001) USA: Routine, FD-302(Rev. 10-6-95). Name of Field Inspector deleted, Released under FOIA; FBI (2001) USA: Routine, FD-302(08-28-2000). Name of Field Inspector deleted, Released under FOIA.

14. FBI (2001) USA: Routine, FD-302(Rev. 10-6-95). Name of Field Inspector deleted, Released under FOIA; FBI (2001) USA: Routine, FD-302(08-28-2000). Name of Field Inspector deleted, Released under FOIA.

15. FBI (2001) USA: Routine, FD-302(Rev. 10-6-95). Name of Field Inspector deleted, Released under FOIA; FBI (2001) USA: Routine, FD-302(08-28-2000). Name of Field Inspector deleted, Released under FOIA.

16. Jay Kirk, "High Plains Grifter", *GQ*, Aug. 2005.

She Got Booked and Charged, and He's on the Run

1. Federal Bureau of Investigation, *Denton County Jail*.
2. Federal Bureau of Investigation, *Denton County Jail*.

Hiding Out in Motel Rooms

1. The State of Texas vs. Bob Harold Leach, Vol. 2, B.K.Castloo, Pg. 112-115, 402nd Judicial District Court of Wood County, 2003.
2. The State of Texas vs. Bob Harold Leach, Vol. 2, B.K.Castloo, Pg. 112-114, 402nd Judicial District Court of Wood County, 2003.
3. The State of Texas vs. Bob Harold Leach, Vol. 2, B.K.Castloo, Pg. 118, 402nd Judicial District Court of Wood County, 2003.

4. The State of Texas vs. Bob Harold Leach, Vol. 2, B.K.Castloo, Pg. 114-115, 402nd Judicial District Court of Wood County, 2003.

5. The State of Texas vs. Bob Harold Leach, Vol. 2, B.K.Castloo, Pg. 139, 402nd Judicial District Court of Wood County, 2003.

6. The State of Texas vs. Bob Harold Leach, Vol. 2, B.K.Castloo, Pg. 114-115, 402nd Judicial District Court of Wood County, 2003.

7. The State of Texas vs. Bob Harold Leach, Vol. 2, B.K.Castloo, Pg. 138, 402nd Judicial District Court of Wood County, 2003.

8. The State of Texas vs. Bob Harold Leach, Vol. 2, B.K.Castloo, Pg. 114-119, 402nd Judicial District Court of Wood County, 2003.

9. The State of Texas vs. Bob Harold Leach, Vol. 2, B.K.Castloo, Pg. 112-118, 402nd Judicial District Court of Wood County, 2003.

10. The State of Texas vs. Bob Harold Leach, Vol. 2, B.K.Castloo, Pg. 121, 402nd Judicial District Court of Wood County, 2003.

High-Speed Car Chase

1. Lt. Robison, Gary. Incident Report, Grayson County Sheriff's Office, July 26, 2001; Cpl. M.D. Stephens, Mike. Supplementary Report, Grayson County Sheriff's Office, July 27, 2001.

2. Lt. Robison, Gary. Incident Report, Grayson County Sheriff's Office, July 26, 2001; Cpl. M.D. Stephens, Mike. Supplementary Report, Grayson County Sheriff's Office, July 27, 2001; FBI (2001) USA: Routine, FD-302(Rev. 10-6-95). Name of Field Inspector deleted, Released under FOIA; FBI (2001) USA: Routine, FD-302(08-28-2000). Name of Field Inspector deleted, Released under FOIA.

3. Lt. Robison, Gary. Incident Report, Grayson County Sheriff's Office, July 26, 2001; Cpl. M.D. Stephens, Mike, Supplementary Report, Grayson County Sheriff's Office, July 27, 2001.

Escaped! The Grayson County Jailbreak

1. Cpl. Stephens, Mike, 2001, Investigative Detail Report, Case No. 10-10-2955, Grayson County Sheriff's Office.

2. Cpl. Stephens, Mike, 2001, Investigative Detail Report, Case No. 10-10-2955, Grayson County Sheriff's Office.

3. Cpl. Stephens, Mike, 2001, Suspect Voluntary Statement, Case No. 10-10-2955, Grayson County Sheriff's Office.

4. Cpl. Stephens, Mike, 2001, Investigative Detail Report, Case No. 10-10-2955, Grayson County Sheriff's Office.

Fuck Bin Laden, Catch Me if You Can

1. Cpl. Stephens, Mike, 2001, Investigative Detail Report, Case No. 10-10-2955, Grayson County Sheriff's Office.

2. Cpl. Stephens, Mike, 2001, Investigative Detail Report, Case No. 10-10-2955, Grayson County Sheriff's Office.

3. Cpl. Stephens, Mike, 2001, Investigative Detail Report, Case No. 10-10-2955, Grayson County Sheriff's Office.

4. Cpl. Stephens, Mike, 2001, Investigative Detail Report, Case No. 10-10-2955, Grayson County Sheriff's Office.

5. Cpl. Stephens, Mike, 2001, Investigative Detail Report, Case No. 10-10-2955, Grayson County Sheriff's Office.

6. Reserve Deputy Cranford, Jerry, 2001, Information Report, Case No. 10-10-2955, Grayson County Sheriff's Office.

7. Cpl. Stephens, Mike, 2001, Investigative Detail Report, Case No. 10-10-2955, Grayson County Sheriff's Office.

8. Reserve Deputy Cranford, Jerry, 2001, Information Report, Case No. 10-10-2955, Grayson County Sheriff's Office.

9. Cpl. Stephens, Mike, 2001, Investigative Detail Report, Case No. 10-10-2955, Grayson County Sheriff's Office.

"Did You Just See That?"

1. Cpl. Stephens, Mike, 2001, Investigative Detail Report, Case No. 10-10-2955, Grayson County Sheriff's Office.
2. Officer Harris, Jonathan, 2001, Supplementary Report, Case No. 10-10-2955, Grayson County Sheriff's Office.
3. Officer Harris, Jonathan, 2001, Supplementary Report, Case No. 10-10-2955, Grayson County Sheriff's Office; Cpl. Stephens, Mike, 2001, Investigative Detail Report, Case No. 10-10-2955, Grayson County Sheriff's Office.
4. Cpl. Stephens, Mike, 2001, Investigative Detail Report, Case No. 10-10-2955, Grayson County Sheriff's Office.
5. Cpl. Stephens, Mike, 2001, Investigative Detail Report, Case No. 10-10-2955, Grayson County Sheriff's Office.
6. Cpl. Stephens, Mike, 2001, Investigative Detail Report, Case No. 10-10-2955, Based on interviews with Bryan Riley and Jerry Riley, Grayson County Sheriff's Office.

Cell Block D is in Disarray

1. Cpl. Stephens, Mike, 2001, Investigative Detail Report, Case No. 10-10-2955, Based on interviews with Bryan Riley and Jerry Riley, Grayson County Sheriff's Office.
2. Cpl. Stephens, Mike, 2001, Investigative Detail Report, Case No. 10-10-2955, Grayson County Sheriff's Office.
3. Cpl. Stephens, Mike, 2001, Investigative Detail Report, Case No. 10-10-2955, Grayson County Sheriff's Office; Cpl. Cummins, Michelle and Officer Robison, Gary, 2001, Voluntary Statement, Case No. 10-10-2955, Grayson County Sheriff's Office.
4. Cpl. Stephens, Mike, 2001, Investigative Detail Report, Case No. 10-10-2955, Grayson County Sheriff's Office.
5. Cpl. Stephens, Mike, 2001, Investigative Detail Report, Case No. 10-10-2955, Grayson County Sheriff's Office.

Back Roads, County Roads and Somewhere In Between

6. Cpl. Stephens, Mike, 2001, Investigative Detail Report, Case No. 10-10-2955, Grayson County Sheriff's Office.

7. Cpl. Stephens, Mike, 2001, Investigative Detail Report, Case No. 10-10-2955, Grayson County Sheriff's Office.

8. Cpl. Stephens, Mike, 2001, Investigative Detail Report, Case No. 10-10-2955, Grayson County Sheriff's Office.

9. Cpl. Stephens, Mike, 2001, Investigative Detail Report, Case No. 10-10-2955, Grayson County Sheriff's Office.

10. Cpl. Stephens, Mike, 2001, Investigative Detail Report, Case No. 10-10-2955, Grayson County Sheriff's Office.

11. Cpl. Wheeler, Rickey, 2001, Supplementary Report, Case No. 10-10-2955, Grayson County Sheriff's Office.

"Hey, Guys, What's Going On?"

1. Cpl. Stephens, Mike, 2001, Investigative Detail Report, Case No. 10-10-2955, Grayson County Sheriff's Office.

2. Cpl. May, Rusty, 2001, Supplementary Report, Case No. 10-10-2955, Grayson County Sheriff's Office.

3. Cpl. Stephens, Mike, 2001, Investigative Detail Report, Case No. 10-10-2955, Grayson County Sheriff's Office.

4. Officer Harris, Jonathan, 2001, Supplementary Report, Case No. 10-10-2955, Grayson County Sheriff's Office.

5. Cpl. Stephens, Mike, 2001, Investigative Detail Report, Case No. 10-10-2955, Grayson County Sheriff's Office.

6. Cpl. Stephens, Mike, 2001, Investigative Detail Report, Case No. 10-10-2955, Grayson County Sheriff's Office.

7. Cpl. Stephens, Mike, 2001, Investigative Detail Report, Case No. 10-10-2955, Grayson County Sheriff's Office.

8. Cpl. Stephens, Mike, 2001, Investigative Detail Report, Case No. 10-10-2955, Grayson County Sheriff's Office.

9. Cpl. Stephens, Mike, 2001, Investigative Detail Report, Case No. 10-10-2955, Grayson County Sheriff's Office.

10. Cpl. Stephens, Mike, 2001, Investigative Detail Report, Case No. 10-10-2955, Grayson County Sheriff's Office.

"Hey! Come Back Here!"

1. Cpl. Stephens, Mike, 2001, Investigative Detail Report, Case No. 10-10-2955, Grayson County Sheriff's Office.

2. The State of Texas vs. Bob Harold Leach, Vol. 2, B.K.Castloo, Pg. 51, 402nd Judicial District Court of Wood County, 2003.

3. The State of Texas vs. Bob Harold Leach, Vol. 2, B.K.Castloo, Pg. 53, 402nd Judicial District Court of Wood County, 2003.

4. The State of Texas vs. Bob Harold Leach, Vol. 2, B.K.Castloo, Pg. 54, 402nd Judicial District Court of Wood County, 2003.

5. Cpl. Stephens, Mike, 2001, Investigative Detail Report, Case No. 10-10-2955, Grayson County Sheriff's Office.

6. Cpl. Stephens, Mike, 2001, Investigative Detail Report, Case No. 10-10-2955, Grayson County Sheriff's Office.

7. Cpl. Stephens, Mike, 2001, Investigative Detail Report, Case No. 10-10-2955, Grayson County Sheriff's Office.

8. The State of Texas vs. Bob Harold Leach, Vol. 2, B.K.Castloo, Pg. 57, 402nd Judicial District Court of Wood County, 2003.

9. Cpl. Stephens, Mike, 2001, Investigative Detail Report, Case No. 10-10-2955, Grayson County Sheriff's Office.

10. Cpl. Stephens, Mike, 2001, Investigative Detail Report, Case No. 10-10-2955, Grayson County Sheriff's Office.

11. Cpl. Stephens, Mike, 2001, Investigative Detail Report, Case No. 10-10-2955, Grayson County Sheriff's Office.

12. Cpl. Stephens, Mike, 2001, Investigative Detail Report, Case No. 10-10-2955, Grayson County Sheriff's Office.

13. The State of Texas vs. Bob Harold Leach, Vol. 2, B.K.Castloo, Pg. 54-55, 402nd Judicial District Court of Wood County, 2003.

14. The State of Texas vs. Bob Harold Leach, Vol. 2, B.K.Castloo, Pg. 57, 402nd Judicial District Court of Wood County, 2003.

15. Cpl. Stephens, Mike, 2001, Investigative Detail Report, Case No. 10-10-2955, Grayson County Sheriff's Office.

16. Cpl. Stephens, Mike, 2001, Investigative Detail Report, Case No. 10-10-2955, Grayson County Sheriff's Office.

17. Cpl. Stephens, Mike, 2001, Investigative Detail Report, Case No. 10-10-2955, Grayson County Sheriff's Office.

18. Cpl. Stephens, Mike, 2001, Investigative Detail Report, Case No. 10-10-2955, Grayson County Sheriff's Office.

19. Cpl. Stephens, Mike, 2001, Investigative Detail Report, Case No. 10-10-2955, Grayson County Sheriff's Office.

Let's Get the Hell Out of Here

1. Cpl. Stephens, Mike, 2001, Investigative Detail Report, Case No. 10-10-2955, Grayson County Sheriff's Office.

2. Cpl. Stephens, Mike, 2001, Investigative Detail Report, Case No. 10-10-2955, Grayson County Sheriff's Office.

3. Cpl. Stephens, Mike, 2001, Investigative Detail Report, Case No. 10-10-2955, Grayson County Sheriff's Office.

4. Cpl. Stephens, Mike, 2001, Investigative Detail Report, Case No. 10-10-2955, Grayson County Sheriff's Office.

5. Cpl. Stephens, Mike, 2001, Investigative Detail Report, Case No. 10-10-2955, Grayson County Sheriff's Office.

6. Cpl. Stephens, Mike, 2001, Investigative Detail Report, Case No. 10-10-2955, Grayson County Sheriff's Office.

7. Cpl. Stephens, Mike, 2001, Investigative Detail Report, Case No. 10-10-2955, Grayson County Sheriff's Office.

8. Cpl. Stephens, Mike, 2001, Investigative Detail Report, Case No. 10-10-2955, Grayson County Sheriff's Office.

9. The State of Texas vs. Bob Harold Leach, Vol. 2, B.K.Castloo, Pg. 70, 402nd Judicial District Court of Wood County, 2003.

10. Cpl. Stephens, Mike, 2001, Investigative Detail Report, Case No. 10-10-2955, Grayson County Sheriff's Office.

11. Cpl. Stephens, Mike, 2001, Investigative Detail Report, Case No. 10-10-2955, Grayson County Sheriff's Office.

"Have You Got A Pair of Jumper Cables?"

1. The State of Texas vs. Bob Harold Leach, Vol. 2, B.K.Castloo, Pg. 15, 402nd Judicial District Court of Wood County, 2003.

2. The State of Texas vs. Bob Harold Leach, Vol. 2, B.K.Castloo, Pg. 15-17, 402nd Judicial District Court of Wood County, 2003.

3. The State of Texas vs. Bob Harold Leach, Vol. 2, B.K.Castloo, Pg. 17, 402nd Judicial District Court of Wood County, 2003.

4. The State of Texas vs. Bob Harold Leach, Vol. 2, B.K.Castloo, Pg. 17, 402nd Judicial District Court of Wood County, 2003.

5. The State of Texas vs. Bob Harold Leach, Vol. 2, B.K.Castloo, Pg. 18, 402nd Judicial District Court of Wood County, 2003.

6. The State of Texas vs. Bob Harold Leach, Vol. 2, B.K.Castloo, Pg. 20-21 & 24, 402nd Judicial District Court of Wood County, 2003.

7. The State of Texas vs. Bob Harold Leach, Vol. 2, B.K.Castloo, Pg. 27 & 60, 402nd Judicial District Court of Wood County, 2003.

8. The State of Texas vs. Bob Harold Leach, Vol. 2, B.K.Castloo, Pg. 21-22, 402nd Judicial District Court of Wood County, 2003.

The Calm Before The Sneeze

1. The State of Texas vs. Bob Harold Leach, Vol. 2, B.K.Castloo, Pg. 61, 402nd Judicial District Court of Wood County, 2003.

2. The State of Texas vs. Bob Harold Leach, Vol. 2, B.K.Castloo, Pg. 59, 402nd Judicial District Court of Wood County, 2003.

3. The State of Texas vs. Bob Harold Leach, Vol. 2, B.K.Castloo, Pg. 59, 402nd Judicial District Court of Wood County, 2003.

4. The State of Texas vs. Bob Harold Leach, Vol. 2, B.K.Castloo, Pg. 62, 402nd Judicial District Court of Wood County, 2003.

5. Cpl. Stephens, Mike, 2001, Investigative Detail Report, Case No. 10-10-2955, Grayson County Sheriff's Office.

6. Cpl. Stephens, Mike, 2001, Investigative Detail Report, Case No. 10-10-2955, Grayson County Sheriff's Office.

7. Cpl. Stephens, Mike, 2001, Investigative Detail Report, Case No. 10-10-2955, Grayson County Sheriff's Office.

8. Cpl. Stephens, Mike, 2001, Investigative Detail Report, Case No. 10-10-2955, Grayson County Sheriff's Office.

9. Cpl. Stephens, Mike, 2001, Investigative Detail Report, Case No. 10-10-2955, Grayson County Sheriff's Office.

Riley Is Found in Fannin County

1. Cpl. Stephens, Mike, 2001, Investigative Detail Report, Case No. 10-10-2955, Grayson County Sheriff's Office.

2. Cpl. Stephens, Mike, 2001, Investigative Detail Report, Case No. 10-10-2955, Grayson County Sheriff's Office.

3. Lt. Hudson, Mark, 2001, Supplementary Report, Case No. 10-10-2955, Grayson County Sheriff's Office.

4. Cpl. Stephens, Mike, 2001, Investigative Detail Report, Case No. 10-10-2955, Grayson County Sheriff's Office.

5. Lt. Hudson, Mark, 2001, Supplementary Report, Case No. 10-10-2995, Grayson County Sheriff's Office.

The Back Roads of Texas

1. The State of Texas vs. Bob Harold Leach, Vol. 2, B.K.Castloo, Pg. 62-63, 402nd Judicial District Court of Wood County, 2003.

2. The State of Texas vs. Bob Harold Leach, Vol. 2, B.K.Castloo, Pg. 63, 402nd Judicial District Court of Wood County, 2003.

3. The State of Texas vs. Bob Harold Leach, Vol. 2, B.K.Castloo, Pg. 79-80, 402nd Judicial District Court of Wood County, 2003.

4. The State of Texas vs. Bob Harold Leach, Vol. 2, B.K.Castloo, Pg. 65, 402nd Judicial District Court of Wood County, 2003.

5. The State of Texas vs. Bob Harold Leach, Vol. 2, B.K.Castloo, Pg. 81, 402nd Judicial District Court of Wood County, 2003.

6. The State of Texas vs. Bob Harold Leach, Vol. 2, B.K.Castloo, Pg. 65, 402nd Judicial District Court of Wood County, 2003.

7. The State of Texas vs. Bob Harold Leach, Vol. 2, B.K.Castloo, Pg. 91, 402nd Judicial District Court of Wood County, 2003.

8. The State of Texas vs. Bob Harold Leach, Vol. 2, B.K.Castloo, Pg. 66, 402nd Judicial District Court of Wood County, 2003.

9. The State of Texas vs. Bob Harold Leach, Vol. 2, B.K.Castloo, Pg. 66, 402nd Judicial District Court of Wood County, 2003.

10. The State of Texas vs. Bob Harold Leach, Vol. 2, B.K.Castloo, Pg. 75-76, 402nd Judicial District Court of Wood County, 2003.

A Texas Size Shootout

1. Cpl. Stephens, Mike, 2001, Investigative Detail Report, Case No. 10-10-2955, Grayson County Sheriff's Office.

2. Cpl. Stephens, Mike, 2001, Investigative Detail Report, Case No. 10-10-2955, Grayson County Sheriff's Office.

3. Cpl. Stephens, Mike, 2001, Investigative Detail Report, Case No. 10-10-2955, Grayson County Sheriff's Office.

4. Tracy Mesler, Cornered, Escapees Gun Fire Pins Down Pursuers, (2001), 'One Helps Hostages Escape', *The Nocona News, Vol. 96 Issue 18, Oct. 18;* Grayson County Sheriff's Office, *Detective Detail,* (Case No. 148153, 2001); Janet Felderhoff, Muenster Police Officer, Gary Whitaker, in on fugitive chase, (2001), *Muenster Enterprise, Vol. 65 No. 47, Oct. 19.*

5. Janet Felderhoff, Muenster Police Officer, Gary Whitaker, in on fugitive chase, (2001), *Muenster Enterprise, Vol. 65 No. 47, Oct. 19.*

6. Tracy Mesler, Cornered, Escapees Gun Fire Pins Down Pursuers, (2001), 'One Helps Hostages Escape', *The Nocona News, Vol. 96 Issue 18, Oct. 18.*

7. Tracy Mesler, Cornered, Escapees Gun Fire Pins Down Pursuers, (2001), 'One Helps Hostages Escape', *The Nocona News, Vol. 96 Issue 18, Oct. 18.*

8. Tracy Mesler, Cornered, Escapees Gun Fire Pins Down Pursuers, (2001), 'One Helps Hostages Escape', *The Nocona News, Vol. 96 Issue 18, Oct. 18.*

9. Tracy Mesler, Cornered, Escapees Gun Fire Pins Down Pursuers, (2001), 'One Helps Hostages Escape', *The Nocona News, Vol. 96 Issue 18, Oct. 18.*

10. Tracy Mesler, Cornered, Escapees Gun Fire Pins Down Pursuers, (2001), 'One Helps Hostages Escape', *The Nocona News, Vol. 96 Issue 18, Oct. 18.*

11. Tracy Mesler, Cornered, Escapees Gun Fire Pins Down Pursuers, (2001), 'One Helps Hostages Escape', *The Nocona News, Vol. 96 Issue 18, Oct. 18.*

12. Tracy Mesler, Cornered, Escapees Gun Fire Pins Down Pursuers, (2001), 'One Helps Hostages Escape', *The Nocona News, Vol. 96 Issue 18, Oct. 18.*

13. Janet Felderhoff, Muenster Police Officer, Gary Whitaker, in on fugitive chase, (2001), *Muenster Enterprise, Vol. 65 No. 47, Oct. 19.*

14. Tracy Mesler, Cornered, Escapees Gun Fire Pins Down Pursuers, (2001), 'One Helps Hostages Escape', *The Nocona News, Vol. 96 Issue 18, Oct. 18.*

15. Tracy Mesler, Cornered, Escapees Gun Fire Pins Down Pursuers, (2001), 'One Helps Hostages Escape', *The Nocona News, Vol. 96 Issue 18, Oct. 18;* Janet Felderhoff, Muenster Police Officer, Gary Whitaker, in on fugitive chase, (2001), *Muenster Enterprise, Vol. 65 No. 47, Oct. 19.*

16. Tracy Mesler, Cornered, Escapees Gun Fire Pins Down Pursuers, (2001), 'One Helps Hostages Escape', *The Nocona News, Vol. 96 Issue 18, Oct. 18.*

17. Tracy Mesler, Cornered, Escapees Gun Fire Pins Down Pursuers, (2001), 'One Helps Hostages Escape', *The Nocona News, Vol. 96 Issue 18, Oct. 18.*

18. Tracy Mesler, Cornered, Escapees Gun Fire Pins Down Pursuers, (2001), 'One Helps Hostages Escape', *The Nocona News, Vol. 96 Issue 18, Oct. 18.*

19. Cpl. Stephens, Mike, 2001, Investigative Detail Report, Case No. 10-10-2955, Grayson County Sheriff's Office; Officer Harris, Jonathan, 2001, Supplementary Report, Case No. 10-10-2955, Grayson County Sheriff's Office; Cpl. May, Rusty, 2001, Supplementary Report, Case No. 10-10-2955, Grayson County Sheriff's Office; Officer Douglas, Bob, 2001, Supplementary Report, Case No. 10-10-2955, Grayson County Sheriff's Office; Deputy Householder, Jeremy, 2001, Supplementary Report, Case No. 10-10-2955, Grayson County Sheriff's Office; Officer Price, Josh and Sgt. Brown, David, 2001, Supplementary Report, Case No. 10-10-2955, Grayson County Sheriff's Office; Cpl. Wheeler, Rickey, 2001, Supplementary Report, Case No. 10-10-2955, Grayson County Sheriff's Office; Lt. Hudson, Mark, 2001, Supplemental Report, Case No. 10-10-2955, Grayson County Sheriff's Office; FBI (2001) USA: Routine, FD-302(Rev. 10-6-95). Name of Field Inspector deleted, Released under FOIA; FBI (2001) USA: Routine, FD-302(08-28-2000). Name of Field Inspector deleted, Released under FOIA.

20. FBI (2001) USA: Routine, FD-302(Rev. 10-6-95). Name of Field Inspector deleted, Released under FOIA; FBI (2001) USA: Routine, FD-302(08-28-2000). Name of Field Inspector deleted, Released under FOIA.

21. Cpl. Stephens, Mike, 2001, Investigative Detail Report, Case No. 10-10-2955, Grayson County Sheriff's Office.

22. Lt. Hudson, Mark, 2001, Supplementary Report, Case No. 10-10-2955, Grayson County Sheriff's Office; Cpl. Wheeler, Rickey, 2001, Supplementary Report, Case No. 10-10-2955, Grayson County Sheriff's Office.

23. Lt. Hudson, Mark, 2001, Supplementary Report, Case No. 10-10-2955, Grayson County Sheriff's Office.

24. Cpl. Stephens, Mike, 2001, Investigative Detail Report, Case No. 10-10-2955, Grayson County Sheriff's Office.

Will the Circle, Be Unbroken

1. Matthew, 10:26, Holy Bible, New Living Translation Touch Point Bible

2. The State of Texas vs. Bob Harold Leach, Bail Bond, 1986, Cause No. 928, Theft over $750 but less than $20,000, 220th District Court of Comanche County, Feb. 14; The State of Texas vs. Bob Harold Leach, Bail Bond, 1986, Cause No. 3510-2, Theft by deception over $20,000, 266th District Court of Erath County, Jan. 9; The State of Texas vs. Bob Harold Leach, Bail Bond, 1986, Cause No. 35069, Theft over $750 under $20,000, Precinct 1 Justice Court of Comanche, Jan. 9.

3. EX PARTE vs. Tami Holland Leach, Application for Writ of Habeas Corpus, 16th Judicial District of Denton County, No. 2002-10061-16, 2003; Executive Order, In 2003, Governor Rick Perry issued Executive Order – Oct. 1, 2003; Executive Order, In 2003, Governor M.J. Mike Foster, Jr. issued Executive Order – Sept. 23, 2003.

4. ABBA Fund Website: https://business.facebook.com/pg/abbafund/posts/

5. [31744252] R.P.C. Robert P. Conaway, Email, Mar. 26, 2012; [116024465] R.P.C. Robert P. Conaway, Email, Dec. 7, 2014.

6. [46756523] R.P.C. Robert P. Conaway, Email, Jan. 4, 2013; [48562849] R.P.C. Robert P. Conaway, Email, Feb. 4, 2013; [167074352] R.P.C. Robert P. Conaway, Email, Oct. 19, 2015.

ACKNOWLEDGMENTS

I owe many thanks to a lot of people who took time out of their busy schedules to meet and speak with me, so that I could learn about, and share, the story of Bob with others. If it had not been for all of you, this book would not have seen the light of day. Thank you for allowing me to step into your world so that I could hear your stories and share them with others.

To my editor John T. Davis, who helped me pull out the real story and make it more exciting than I ever thought possible. I am forever indebted to the Forrester family; you are all part of my family and I am forever grateful to have met each and every one of you.

To both the Late Captain Mark Hudson of the Grayson County Sheriff's Office and the Late Sheriff Keith Gary for being so compassionate and kind with me. These two gentlemen, along with the staff and other law enforcement officials at the Grayson County Jail exemplify what law enforcement should be; their passion and driven dedication to fight for justice is what the rest of us imagine law enforcement to be. To District Attorney Joe Brown of Grayson County, thank you for being patient with me while I was learning the ropes of how to conduct an interview, you were my first interview and it was obvious, and I appreciate your patience! A many thanks to District Attorney Richard Glaser of Fannin County for speaking with me and allowing me the chance to hear your side of the story. Both you and your Assistant Butch

Henderson were very kind to me and I greatly appreciate you making time to speak with me.

Special thanks to the Stephenville District Clerk's Office, Comanche County District Clerk's Office, Callahan County District Clerk's Office, Callahan County Jail, Brown County Sheriff's Office, Brown County District Clerk's Office, Erath County Sheriff's Department, the FBI agents for providing me the FOIA records so that I could put the real story out there for others to read. A special thanks to all the corrections officers at TDC for your kindness and professionalism during my many visits to the various prisons to see Bob. I am so grateful to all of the Board Members (2013) who took the time to meet and speak with me at the Open Public Board Meeting when I requested for a hardship transfer to have Bob moved closer to me and to Director Bill Stephens for approving the hardship transfer.

To Mike and Gwen, thank you for keeping an eye out to make sure I was safe and for double checking to make sure I dotted every I and crossed every T. Bob Davis, thank you for everything. You were able to help me see the real story about Bob and for that I'm grateful. A special thanks to Tim Walker for all your hard work, The Muenster Enterprise, The Nocona News and The Saint Jo Tribune and Darrel Johnson.

And a very special thank you to my PA, Laura Martinez, for all the last minute prepping and hard work that you've put into this project, to make sure it's published in a timely manner. You did a fantastic job, thank you!

ABOUT THE AUTHOR

Pepper Anne grew up in the Central Texas area. She is a proud seventh-generation Texan and has always called Texas her home. Pepper Anne is a passionate author who is seeking to bring light to the injustice that was committed by a well-known individual. She has performed private investigative work over the years on her own terms and has unveiled corrupt information that needs to be brought to light. She was driven to uncover what many have paid large amounts of money to cover up as this has impacted her and her family over the years. Her mission is to bring justice to this corrupt group of individuals that are falsely idolized by so many.

Pepper Anne is personally committed to unveiling the truth behind the real story of Bob Harold Leach as it has remained a falsehood to protect the guilty even to this day.

For updates and more:
https://www.pepperanneauthor.com

www.ingramcontent.com/pod-product-compliance
Lightning Source LLC
Chambersburg PA
CBHW071359150726
48000CB00001B/90